First Names First

First Names First

Leslie Alan Dunkling

J. M. Dent & Sons Ltd

LONDON TORONTO MELBOURNE

First published 1977
Reprinted September 1977
© Leslie Dunkling 1977
All rights reserved. No part of this publication may be reproduced, stored in a retrieval
system, or transmitted, in any form or by any means, electronic, mechanical,
photocopying, recording or otherwise, without the prior permission of
J. M. Dent & Sons Ltd

Made in Great Britain by
William Clowes & Sons Ltd
London, Beccles and Colchester
for
J. M. Dent & Sons Ltd
Aldine House, Albemarle Street, London

This book is set in 11/13pt Monophoto Ehrhardt

ISBN 0 460 12025 5

Dunkling, Leslie
　First names first.
　Bibl.–Index.
　ISBN 0–460–12025–5
　I. Title
　9929.4'0942　　　CS2367
　Names, Personal–History

Contents

List of featured pages

Acknowledgements

A great many people have contributed to this book in one way or another and I acknowledge their help most gratefully. I would especially like to thank the following: C. V. Appleton, William Gosling, Jodi Cassell, George Hubbard, Darryl Francis, Cleveland Kent Evans, Barbara Dyroff, Terrence Keough, Kathleen Sinclair, Cecily Dynes, Phyllis du Sautoy (who kindly provided the photographs of the Victorian and Edwardian name brooches), G. M. du Sautoy, G. P. V. Akrigg, Adrian Room, David Aitken, Kelsie and Louise Harder, Elsdon C. Smith, Margaret Brown, Jenny Shove, Patricia Pilling, Anne Godfrey, Jean Trend, Roberta Symes, Catherine Riding, Frederick Payne, Keith Washington and Julian Fox.

Correspondents in the U.S.A., Canada, Britain, Australia and New Zealand, too numerous to mention individually, have also helped me a great deal by writing to me during the last few years about various aspects of names and naming. There are also the many friends who have discussed names with me at different times or have patiently answered my questions. I am most grateful to them all.

A great deal of this book is based on name counts, the results of which are published for the first time. These counts would not have been possible but for the cooperation of university administrators in several countries. My request for graduate student lists for 1975, together with those for 1950, 1925 and 1900 where possible, received a very generous response, and I would like to thank the Registrars of the following academic institutions for their invaluable help:

(U.S.A.) Alabama State University, Alcorn State University, Alma White College, Arkansas State University, Augustana College, Belhaven College, Black Hills State College, Brandeis University, Brigham Young University, Brown University, California Baptist College, California Lutheran College, California Polytechnic State University, The Colorado College, College of Idaho, College of Notre Dame, Dr Martin Luther College, Drexel University, Duke University, Duquesne University, Florida State University, Fordham University, Georgia Institute of Technology, Georgia State University, Graceland College, Grinnell College, Hawaii Loa College, Hebrew College, Hebrew Union College, Howard University, Idaho State University, Indiana Central College, Indiana State University, The Institute of Paper Chemistry, The Jewish Theological Seminary of America, Louisiana College, Louisiana Technical University, Millsaps College, Minnesota Bible College, Nathaniel Hawthorne College, Nebraska Wesleyan University, New Mexico State University, New York University, North Carolina State University at Raleigh, North Dakota State University, Northern Illinois University, Northwestern University, The Ohio State University, Oklahoma City University, Pacific Union College, Rice University, Stanford University, State University of New York at Albany, Syracuse University, Temple University, Texas A & M University, University of Alabama in Birmingham, University of Alabama in Huntsville, University of Alaska, University of Arizona, University of Arkansas at Monticello, University of California, San Diego, University of Cincinnati, University of Connecticut, University of Delaware, University of Iowa, University of Kansas, University of Kentucky, University of Maine at Farmington, University of Maine at Fort Kent, University of Maine at Portland-Gorham, University of Maine, Presque Isle, University of Maryland, University of Massachusetts, University of Miami, University of Minnesota, University of Missouri-Columbia, University of Nevada, Las Vegas, University of North Carolina at Chapel Hill, University of Notre Dame, University of Oregon, University of Rochester, University of South Carolina, University of Southern Mississippi, University of Tennessee, University of Texas at Austin, University of the Pacific, The University of Utah, University of Vermont, University of Wisconsin, University of Wyoming, Villanova University, Virginia Commonwealth University, Virginia Polytechnic Institute and State University, Virginia State College, Virginia State University, Virginia Union University, Virginia Wesleyan College, Washington State University, Wayne State University, West Liberty State College, West Virginia State College, West Virginia Wesleyan College, Western Reserve College, Whitworth College.

(Canada) University of Prince Edward Island, St Mary's University, Nova Scotia; Mount Allison University, New Brunswick; McGill University, Quebec; Queen's University, Ontario; Carleton University, Ontario; University of Winnipeg, University of Saskatchewan, University of British Columbia.

(Australia) The Australian National University, The University of Sydney, The University of Adelaide, The University of New South Wales, The University of Western Australia.

It is said that a woman should be allowed the last word, and I gladly give it in this instance to my wife, Nicole. In her own way she has made it possible for this book to be written, thus increasing my debt to her.

Preface

This book offers a completely new approach to a subject that concerns us all—our own first names. There have been many previous books on the subject, but invariably they have concentrated on name origins, or upon absurdities such as a name's 'vibrations'. The origins of names do have a certain fascination, but the meaning a name had a thousand years ago is obviously not the meaning it has for us today. We instinctively classify names as being fashionable or unfashionable, having a youthful image or an old one, being pleasant or ridiculous. **Gladys,** for instance, arouses one kind of response in us, while **Susan** evokes a different image entirely.

Such reactions depend not upon the origins of those names, but on the way those names have been used in the past and are being used now. That is where this book offers so much that is new. It presents the results of a great deal of original research into name-usage in the U.S.A., Britain, Canada and Australia. There is much here that has never before appeared in print, including the up-to-date information needed by young parents who are currently choosing names.

Just as we react to the names of other people, so they react to our names. One purpose of this book is to enable the reader to stand back from his or her own name and assess it objectively. That name is creating an image whether one likes it or not. It is worth asking oneself whether it is creating the right kind of image. If it isn't, what should be done about it?

Apart from such personal considerations, the first names in use around us have many tales to tell. Most of them have been in existence for centuries and have had a few adventures along the way. Some are like fading movie-stars whose day is past; others suddenly find the spotlight upon them for the first time. As you will see, their stories are sometimes surprising, sometimes amusing, always interesting.

Here then is a feast of first names. I dedicate it to all those who bear the names, in the hope that they will enjoy it.

Twelfth Night, 1977   Leslie Alan Dunkling

1 Introduction

The significance of first names

'A name is a kind of face', wrote Thomas Fuller in the seventeenth century, with brilliant perception. In those few words he summed up the way most of us think not only about our own names, but about those of other people. My name—spoken aloud or written down—is a reflection of me, like my face in a photograph. The name of a friend, or his photograph, serves equally well to bring all my memories of him into my mind. More importantly perhaps, say a name to me that I have never heard before and I will begin to 'see' the person whose name it is. It will be as if I have been shown a photograph of a stranger and decide that this unknown person 'looks' intelligent, or trustworthy.

Fuller's statement, then, that a name is a kind of face has three separate aspects to it. We feel as intimately bound up with our own names as we do with our reflections in a mirror. Next, our names, as much as our faces, are intensely meaningful to our friends. Finally, and in a different way, our names can have meaning for those who have never met us. Our names are interpreted in the way that a face is interpreted.

When I say that our names can have 'meaning' for strangers I do *not* mean the kind of 'meaning' a name is given in a traditional book on the subject. You have probably seen one or two publications of the type I have in mind, dealing with the historical explanations of names. This is the sort of book which says that **Harold**, say, means 'army power', and **Margaret** means 'a pearl'. Such books often add biographical notes to the names. For Harold there would no doubt have been a reminder of King Harold and Harold Lloyd, the comedian. Margaret would have been associated with Margaret Mitchell, perhaps, the author of *Gone With The Wind*, or with the actresses Margaret Leighton and Margaret Lockwood.

The real meaning of a name

Such comments are not entirely without interest, but they do not begin to touch upon the really important facts about those names. Names carry all kinds of associations along with them which together constitute a 'meaning' far more realistic than 'army power' or 'pearl'. Imagine, for example, that tomorrow you will be meeting two people who bear the names Margaret and Harold. You have no other information about them at all. On the basis of their names alone you will begin to have certain ideas about them. Think about it for a moment. How old will they be, for example? Will Margaret be easy to get on with? Will Harold be the kind of person who sits quietly in a corner?

In theory it seems absurd to ask such questions about people on the basis of their names alone. In practice there would be a surprising amount of agreement amongst a group of Americans, Englishmen or other English-speaking people as to the answers. Most would expect Harold to be at least forty years old, for instance, and Englishmen especially would tend to think of him as being considerably older. Margaret would fare a little better, though Americans, in her case, would expect her to be older. A group of Scotsmen, on the other hand, would say that Margaret could be any age from twenty to eighty. The name has remained constantly in fashion in Scotland in a way that is not paralleled elsewhere in the English-speaking world.

There are actually sound reasons, in view of fluctuating name fashions, for making judgements about age on the basis of a name. But as Nathan Schoenfeld discovered in 1942, when he investigated the reactions of Americans to names that were popular at the time, his informants were willing to go much further. There was considerable agreement amongst them that a **Mary** would be 'quiet', an **Edward** 'friendly', a **Richard** 'good-looking', a **Joan** 'young and good-looking', a **Barbara** 'charming' and an **Adrian** 'artistic'.

Roger Price and Leonard Stern were later to make use of this willingness to associate complete personalities with names in their *What Not To Name The Baby*. They adopted a humorous approach to their subject, declaring that a **Bettina**, for example, would have a big bust, and that a **Maureen** would have freckles on her chest. Similar comments are made in their book about 400 other names, and the whole exercise is good for a laugh.

But this joking approach should not make us dismiss entirely the idea of linking names with personalities. We tend to make such links partly because a name often makes us recall, perhaps subconsciously, individuals who have borne that name. The personalities of those individuals seem to be right for that name so we form a stereotyped image of it and its associated personality.

Naming the Face

Many people believe that names 'fit' faces. Can you match the right names to the faces below? In each case I have included the person's real name amongst three others. The answers are on page 18.

Photo 1

Joan
Anne
Betty
Dorothy

Photo 2

Jean
Margaret
Kathleen
Barbara

Photo 3

Rosalind
Joanna
Roberta
Andrea

Photo 4

William
Frederick
Thomas
James

Photo 5

Anthony
Luke
Russell
Julian

Photo 6

Reginald
Terrence
Brian
Donald

Michael Nellis has suggested how these ideas about stereotypes can be reinforced. 'Because of the selective nature of perception a stranger's name encourages us to take note, firstly, of the features we associate with his name, and possibly to amplify them to the extent that they become, in our eyes, his main characteristics. Thus it may be that we always come to regard bearers of the same name as possessing similar characteristics to each other.'

Beyond this, we also tend to make personality assessments because we extend our judgement about a name's age. Let us suppose that we are told that Harold is twenty years old, not over forty as we supposed. Because of the clash in our minds between the age of the name and the age of the person bearing it, we will instinctively begin to think of him as somehow out of step with fashion and current trends. For a young man, the name has a great deal acting against it. Try asking an attractive young girl which blind date she would choose if one were a Harold, the other a **David**, say, or a **Paul, Stephen** or **Robert**. You will soon see whether Harold has a good image.

Name preferences amongst American students

Harold was not one of the names included in a 'semantic differential analysis' made by E. D. Lawson in 1973, but his studies showed that men and women largely agreed about stereotyped images associated with names. Lawson tested reactions to three forms of certain names—**Daniel, Dan, Danny**; **David, Dave, Davey**, etc., and appeared to prove that the forms used were highly significant. A David who was regularly known as Dave, for instance, scored very well in terms of 'strength', 'activity' and 'goodness'. Davey was uniformly disliked, however, as being 'weak', 'passive' and 'bad'. This may well have had to do with the fact that the -y ending on a name, also spelt as -ie, -i, -ee, etc., is now associated strongly with girls' names, as we shall see in a later chapter.

There was a general preference amongst the informants—university students—for the short forms of names. **Dave, Jim** and **Tom** were much preferred to **David, James** and **Thomas**. Exceptions to this rule were **Dan** and **Ed**, where **Daniel** and **Edward** were felt to be better. Other popular names were **Robert, John** and **Joseph**. **Frederick**, in any of its forms, was disliked, while **Joey** and **Eddy** also fared badly.

In a later study Lawson asked for similar reactions to women's names. Surprisingly, in view of the significant results he had obtained with different forms of men's names, he seems to have presented the women's names in their full form only. Male students showed a distinct preference for **Karen, Nancy** and **Mary**. Women students preferred **Susan, Joan** and **Jean**. **Cynthia** was disliked by both men and women, and the men also disliked **Patricia** and **Linda**. Women added **Diane** and **Sharon** to their list of unpopular names.

The most surprising feature of Lawson's survey, perhaps, was the men's dislike of Linda. In terms of frequency it must have been one of the most usual names amongst the female students at that time. It was thus well-established as a youthful name in the minds of the men, but something else made them dislike it. Incidentally, it is a pity that Lawson did not ask his informants to 'date' the names in his survey.

Names and sex appeal

The results of the Lawson studies were published in *Names*, the journal of The American Name Society, in 1973 and 1974. At the beginning of 1976 I conducted my own informal survey, assisted by Mandi Fishburn, into the name preferences of young men and women living in London rather than New York. This time Linda did rather better.

In the London survey the men were asked for their views on women's names, and vice-versa, and instead of having terms like strength or weakness, goodness or badness suggested to them, the informants were asked to say which names they considered to have most sex appeal. The results of this survey were obviously unscientific, but I offer them for you to compare with your own views:

Men's preferences	Women's preferences
1. Susan	1. David
2. Samantha	2. Stephen
3. Carol	3. Paul
4. Linda	4. Mark
5. Jennifer	5. Adam
6. Catherine	6. Robert
7. Amanda	7. Richard
8. Kerry	8. Michael
9. Claire	9. Christopher
10. Natalie	10. Philip

These were preferences shown by men and women in their twenties. Older informants would obviously have chosen differently, as would groups of any age from other parts of the English-speaking world. Neither Harold nor Margaret, by the way, was mentioned at all by the Londoners, but Lawson included Margaret in his New York survey. Men disliked it rather more than the women.

It is in these kind of ways, then, that our names can be meaningful to others, just as their names may be meaningful to us. Let us return now to the question of a name's importance to the person who bears it. Normally we care about the judgements other people make about us. We are concerned that our physical appearance, the clothes we wear, the objects we have about us should reflect the personality we wish to project. Our name, whether we like it or not, will be considered to be an important part of that personality, and we must consider objectively what effect it is producing.

There is nothing new in this idea. We readily accept that those who are trying for professional reasons to create a public image, such as actors and actresses, should dispose if they wish of the names their parents chose for them and adopt new ones. Often the name change is a complete one—surname as well as first name disappears. Sometimes a new first name does the trick; **Frank** Cooper becomes **Gary** Cooper, **Leslie** Hope becomes **Bob** Hope. In such cases the new name is usually chosen by instinct, by saying it aloud many times and listening to its echoes. The new name has to 'feel' right.

In this book I begin with the premise that these feelings about names exist, then show how our instinctive reactions are largely based on facts about name usage. For it is primarily the *use* of first names at different times and in different places that eventually leads to the images the names invoke. This usage is constantly changing, and has certainly changed a great deal in our lifetime. It also varies in different parts of the English-speaking world. The basic facts about the use of first names in English-speaking countries are presented for the first time in this book. They will enable you to check what your instincts have been telling you about names and their associations, and to make an objective assessment of your own name.

The establishment of the facts about first name usage is a major step forward in this process. In such matters as clothes and hair styles, for example, it may be impossible to say *why* fashions change but at least we know what the fashion is now and what went before. With names this has not been the case. Some name counts have been made in the past, but almost always they were based on city or telephone directories. The people listed in such directories spanned two or three generations, so that it was impossible to pin-point which names were being used in particular years, or even by a particular generation.

The counts which form the basis of this book have been made with that point very much in mind. The object has been to establish with great accuracy which names were being used in different parts of the English-speaking world at specific times. When a name was being much used by one generation, but was virtually ignored by the next—leaving the name

Marilyn Novak's studio ran a competition to find her a new name. As we all know, she became Kim Novak, but suggestions that were made and discarded included Kavon Novak, Iris Green and Windy City.

A great deal of importance is attached, in this book, to the 'Top 50' names used in a particular year. This is because of the regular pattern of name usage that is found throughout the English-speaking world. Although all parents could in theory give their children unique names (perhaps having invented them), less than 2% seem to want to do so. Most parents are content to use the established names, even though they know that many other parents will also be choosing those names.

Every year certain names are fashionable and are more used than others. The most popular girl's name in a particular year will probably be given to one girl in every twenty-five: the boy's name which heads the list will be given to one boy in fifteen. One girl in two will receive one of the top 50 names: the boys' top 50 will supply names for three boys in every five.

The distribution of names varies amongst national, racial and religious groups. In the figures given below:

Column 1 relates to white Americans, Canadians, Australians, Englishmen; *Column 2* relates to black Americans and West Indians; *Column 3* relates to Scotland, and to religious groups such as Roman Catholics whose naming habits are more conservative than those of the general public.

These figures show how many boys or girls born in a particular year will receive one of the most popular names.

Girls

	1.	*2.*	*3.*
One of top 10 names	20%	16%	29%
top 20	30%	25%	43%
top 30	38%	33%	53%
top 40	45%	39%	60%
top 50	50%	44%	66%

Boys

	1.	*2.*	*3.*
One of top 10 names	36%	32%	46%
top 20	46%	42%	63%
top 30	53%	48%	73%
top 40	57%	52%	79%
top 50	61%	56%	84%

In any one year 125 different girls' names and 100 boys' names would easily account for 80% of the children named in any of the English-speaking countries.

stranded, as it were, with an age-label attached to it—this will become apparent. Later in the book you will find suggestions as to several courses of action that are open to you if your name falls into that category.

Name surgery

Whether one should do anything about a name that can be shown to be a hindrance is a decision that must be made by each individual. For my part I have often been surprised to see a woman who has clearly exercised great dietary control, made use of considerable cosmetic skill and displayed excellent dress-sense, all in an effort to make herself look ten years younger, sabotage those efforts in a moment simply by announcing her name. Often all that would be needed would be a little re-shaping of the name to rejuvenate it. Only occasionally is drastic surgery needed—the complete removal of the name and its replacement by another—and even then the process is remarkably painless compared to a face-lift or other cosmetic surgery. It has the other great advantage of being free.

One of the aims of this book, then, is to enable you to hold up a mirror to your name, or any other name that interests you, and see something like a true reflection of its 'face'. I shall be disappointed, however, if the interest of the book ends there. Names in themselves are fascinating, and I will hope to make you far more aware of the names that surround you in your daily life.

Beyond the names themselves we go back to the people who chose them, and who reflect in their choice what is important to them. There are those who respect the traditional, and those who demand novelty; there are those whose choice of a name for a child is a defiant challenge to the world, and others who seem to wish for obscurity. These different attitudes are all reflected in the names of the people we meet every day.

The names of the past, like the names of today, also accurately reflect the complexities and absurdities of human behaviour, 'the more extraordinary convulsions', as one writer called them, 'which sometimes seize the body corporate of society'. To put it another way, the game of names has been played for a long time, and as you will see, it has always been worthy of being a spectator sport.

The answers to the 'Naming the Face' quiz on p. 13 are 1: Anne. 2: Jean. 3: Roberta. 4: Frederick. 5: Julian. 6: Terrence.

One more test—more difficult than the one on p. 13. This time can you decide what names these faces ought to have? The answers are on p. 272.

2 Full Names

Surnames, titles and middle names

Most of this book is concerned with first names, but let us look for a moment at the whole range of personal names that surround them. We all have a surname, for instance, which can be used to identify us along with some kind of social or professional title. The man who is **Harold** to his friends may be Mr or Dr Johnson to others. **Margaret** Smith may insist on being Ms Smith these days, and her sex as well as marital status can disappear behind a title such as Professor. In modern times these more formal titles are what Thoreau called 'names you take off with your jacket'.

If Harold and Margaret are normal, in a statistical sense, they will also have middle names. Harold, as a male, is likely to have one or more nick-names. By some curious kind of discrimination, Margaret is less likely to have such a name, leaving aside for the moment pet forms of her first name. If she has a husband or boy-friend he may well address her by various substitute names, but these are hardly nicknames as we generally under-stand the term. They are more like the role names by which all of us are addressed in different situations. I shall be discussing them later in some detail.

Finally, as citizens of a complex society, both Harold and Margaret will have several number names by which various computers identify them. There is little to be said about such names other than that they are necessary, but it is worth commenting more fully on the other personal names. They all form part of an individual's identity, and they provide a backcloth for the first names which occupy the centre of the stage in this book.

Surnames

Let us leave aside for the moment the question of how and why surnames came into being and think about their use as terms of address. In the present century there has been a very great change in the way people address one another, as older people will recall. Until the 1920s, for example, men who might have known each other for fifty years and who were on the friendliest of terms still addressed each other by their surnames. One can imagine how shocked Sherlock Holmes would have been had Dr Watson called him anything but Holmes. As for Watson, the author of the stories seems to have been uncertain himself whether he was **John** or **James**. It really did not matter at that time.

This apparent formality was the custom in polite society, both in America and Britain, for at least two hundred years. First names might be bandied about by the lower orders, but anybody who was anybody was hardly ever so addressed. Passionate young lovers in the eighteenth century, for instance, such as Tom Jones and Sophia Western, remained Mr Jones and Miss Western (or 'Madam') to each other no matter how strong their feelings became. When Jane Austen's Emma at last admitted her love for George Knightley she would accept to call him by his first name on one occasion only—during the wedding ceremony itself. As for Dickensian husbands and wives, even when producing large families they normally avoided the intimacy of first name usage. If Dickens was reflecting the actual habits of nineteenth century middle-class society, it is clear that husbands and wives usually remained Mr and Mrs to each other even when alone.

For a long time the use of a first name by a lady or gentleman implied great condescension rather than intimacy. Village labourers were addressed as Tom, Dick or Harry, but the lower middle-class shopkeepers would be honoured by Mr or Mrs and their surnames. Servant girls, being on a par with young children and animals, were addressed by first names, though not necessarily their own. If their own names were considered by their superiors to be too fanciful they were quickly replaced with something more 'suitable'.

Shaw makes an interesting comment on British name usage in the early part of this century in *Pygmalion*, the fore-runner of *My Fair Lady*. Pickering addresses Eliza as Miss Doolittle, showing a politeness that astonishes and delights her. She later tells him that it was this act which 'began my real education'. She then invites Pickering to call her Eliza in future but adds that she would like Professor Higgins 'to call me Miss Doolittle'. 'I'll see you damned first', is the professor's ungentlemanly reply.

Shaw would have been unable to write such a scene twenty years later. The use of names had changed in Britain by the 1930s, and in America somewhat earlier. The reasons for the change were many, and it clearly had something to do with the gradual breakdown of a rigid class system. These days the existence of a social or professional hierarchy may still be indicated by the way we address one another, but there are no longer such sharp divisions. Traces of condescension are still present, perhaps, when bosses refer to employees by their first names but expect to be addressed more formally in return, but it is doubtful whether those whose first names are used feel inferior because of it.

The first name trend is likely to continue among English-speakers, though people from other countries remain far more formal with each other. Our surnames may well recede still further into the background, remaining useful for identification purposes but playing a decidedly minor role as terms of address. Their rise to prominence in that role was a temporary phase, a feature of the artificial manners of the eighteenth and nineteenth centuries. It would seem ridiculous now to hear young men and women addressing one another formally, as ridiculous as it would have been in the seventeenth century to hear Romeo and Juliet, say, declaring their love for Miss Capulet and Mr Montague.

Titles

Any surname sounds rather different, of course, if the title that precedes it is something more exotic than Mr or Mrs. It is therefore understandable in a way that many parents decide to help their offspring along by giving them a 'title' as a first name. **Earl**, or **Earle**, is probably the commonest such title-name, more common in the U.S.A. than Britain, but others I have noted in use include **Baron, Duke, Count, Lord, Princess, Queen** and **King**. **Leroy** and **Elroy** are also slightly disguised forms of 'king', and **Basil**, amongst older-established names, is from a Greek word meaning 'kingly'. We should also note the Latin **Regina**, 'queen', and Hebrew **Sarah**, 'princess'. **Deborah**, 'bee', was also symbolic of a female ruler. Many Old English names contained an element such as **Ethel-**, 'noble'. The bestowal of rank in first names is certainly not a new idea.

Some of the modern names mentioned above are not necessarily quite what they seem. Baron, Lord and King occur as surnames, and may have been used as first names originally for that reason. Duke is frequently a pet form of **Marmaduke**, a name especially popular in former times in the North of England. Nevertheless, parents who give their children such names can hardly be unaware of the fact that they are also social titles. In this connection, I was interested to note the comment of a British politician, opposed to the system of bestowing titles as a reward for political or other services to the country, when the subject was being publicly debated in 1976. If enough parents named their children **Lord** or **Lady**, he claimed, the House of Lords would collapse overnight.

*At the turn of the century, when the South African town of Ladysmith was in the news, an English Smith family named their daughter **Lady**, thus giving her an unusual titled place name as her own name. The town had been named in honour of Lady Smith, wife of Sir Harry Smith, governor of the Cape Colony.*

Certain professional titles also have great status value, and many people will subject themselves to long drawn-out rites in order to earn the right to use them. The academic doctorate is a case in point. There are plenty of men and women who are willing to sacrifice years of their lives in order to see that magical Dr in front of their name.

Not surprisingly, then, it has occurred to many parents to save their children a great deal of tedious work by using **Doctor** as a first name. The Mormons, reportedly, reserve this name for the seventh son of a seventh son, and a similar custom prevails in parts of Ireland, but instances occur too regularly for these to be the only uses. Some are occasioned by gratitude to the doctor who assisted at the birth, but there must also be at the back of parents' minds the thought of reflected glory. When someone in the family is a doctor the whole tone of the family is raised.

Other equally distinguished names have been given by fond parents. I have come across an **Admiral**, a **Captain**, a **Colonel**, a **Commodore** and many **Majors**. Religious titles are far more rare as first names, presumably because a clergyman would draw the line at baptising a child **Reverend**, but **Rabbi** has been noted, both in America and Britain.

Such names can only be considered as curiosities, and they will not come into general use. They testify to the value of the titles they imitate, but it is precisely because they are imitations that they make, as far as most parents are concerned, rather unsatisfactory first names. Of them all, the most unusual I recall is a boy named Smith, born in 1848, whose parents decided to call him **Mister**. One wonders how many bets he won in his lifetime by claiming to be the only Mister Smith in town.

Junior

As well as having a variety of titles in front of them, surnames can be modified by adding something after them, such as a number, or words like *Junior*. Both habits are American rather than British, though an English public school might list brothers as Jones *Major* and Jones *Minor*.

In Britain, because of the Royal Family, numbers after a name are looked upon as the prerogative of kings and queens. In such cases the number becomes a kind of sequential surname. George V is distinguished from George VI, as it were, just as George Brown is distinguished from George Smith. A British George Brown who happens to be the son of a George Brown, however, is unlikely to become George Brown II.

In a sample of 500 male American university students who graduated in 1975, one had II after his name, 22 had III, and two had IV. I would expect a similar sample in twenty-five years time to show far fewer examples. There is overwhelming evidence on all sides, as we shall see later, that the custom of naming sons after fathers, grandfathers or uncles is rapidly dying out.

One would expect the habit of numbering the generations to die out with it.

Fifty of the 500 students had Junior after their names, and this again is a habit that will presumably disappear. Many of the students so listed were probably addressed as *Junior* within the family circle, and indeed **Junior** has occasionally been given as a first name. The mood of the times, however, is now totally against linking a son to his father in a subordinate way. There is also the point that, with name fashions now changing so rapidly, the passing on of a father's name is likely to mean the bestowal of a name that is old-fashioned. If a father does insist on this practice, he should at least have the fairness to sign himself George Brown *Senior*, publicizing his own age.

Middle names

Historically speaking, middle names came after surnames, which them-selves came after first names. They are a comparatively modern pheno-menon, but are now well-established. Ninety-five per cent of American men, and ninety-two per cent of American women, judging by a count based on university students, have one middle name. Four per cent of the men have no middle name and one per cent have two or more such names. Four per cent of the women likewise have no middle name, but another four per cent have two or more names. These figures would probably be applicable in the other English-speaking countries.

Parents frequently say to themselves when they name a child that if the first name is not liked, the middle name can be used by their child instead. A count of students who listed themselves by their first initial, followed by middle name in full—presumably indicating that they normally used their middle names—showed that only three per cent of the men and one per cent of the women actually made use of this option. One reason for this may lie in the nature of middle names, which differs somewhat from that of first names. When parents choose a first name, expecting that name to be the one that will be used, they take care to select a name which will cause as little embarrassment as possible, while retaining a certain degree of individuality. They usually try to avoid a name that is clearly out-dated or has any other negative qualities.

Middle names are chosen in a different way. Family names are often 'preserved' as middle names: roughly twenty-five per cent of such names are surnames rather than traditional christian names. When the latter are used as middle names it is often because of their sound in relation to the names that precede them. This accounts for the great popularity of girls' names like **Ann(e)**, **Jean**, **Jane**, **Lee**, **Lynn**, **Sue**, **Gail**, **Kay**, **Jo**, **Ruth** and **Fay** as middle names, for the first names that go with them are frequently polysyllabic. Men's middle names, by contrast, are more likely to be **Alan**, **Stephen**, **Michael**, **David**, **Edward**, **Joseph**, **Thomas**, **Anthony**—

A person's full name—first name, middle name or names and surname—can sometimes have a very sonorous ring to it. The examples quoted below are mostly taken from the collection of that ardent name-collector, George F. Hubbard, of New York. All are, or were, borne by real people.

Susan Eatwell Burpitt
Mary Cutter Bottorff
Sherlock Bronson Gass
Birdie Fawncella Feltis
Coma Lee Tippit
Albion Moonlight Butters
Elizabeth Turner Down-
ward
Abraham Lincoln Death
Cornelius Dan Dam
Missy Ann Harris
Thanks Giving Carraker
Iris Gay Flowers
Sweet Clover Goodrich
Margery Ready First
Martin Independence
Gump
Ouida Watkins Wright
Mary Hatt Box
Truth Delight Becquette
Larry Harry Barry
Julius Caesar Sherard
King Solomon Jones
Nellie Hawk Eagle
Singular Onions Gally-
hawks
Bertha Big Foot
Zita Ann Apathy
Saint Leon Mizell
Albina Terrasina Rosina
Beak
Juliet Seashell Moonbeam
Gamba
John Will Fail
Carl Barrazzealousce
Whyte
Diana Brown Beard
Mary Ada Berry
Barbara Womble Groat
Armenia Funk Goff
Forty Three Ford
Dong Jim D'Ambrosia
Hooker Earl Pepper

Lil Lovey Dove
Icie Snow Furr
Themistocles Hamilcar
Faraone
Cora Ora Akridge
Strange Odor Andrews
Early Caraway Smith
Temple Hicks Hill
Della Fearer Fike
Evie Ott Gott
Longhorne Bullitt Dick
Anna Dumpling Cheese-
cake
Friend Herbert Jenkins
Lockington St. Lawrence
Bunn
Bobby Joe Gothard
Dorothy May Grow
Renee Bass Fisherman
Almond Dwight Price
Marcia Shaw Caress
Precious Darling Dare
Minor Elizabeth Kyger
Ann Trout Blinks
Memory Lane Brown
Hazel May Call
Gay Richard Hyre
Amy Waters Cleverley
Welcome Baby Darling
Dominick Dominick
Dominick
Adeline Horsey de Horsey
Serene Watchell Parish
Ruth Pinches Finch
Nancy Pigg Bacon
Fredna Jewel Parker
Little John Trott
Henry Will Burst
Herbert Youle Gotobed
Last Gale First
Twinkle Starr Gibbs
Patsy Jack Smith
Coqui Jeanne Kades

Heidi Yum-Yum Gluck
John Burns Brown
Henry Ford Carr
Victoria Regina Zarubin
William Thrower Fitts
Count Forty Lee
Janet Isadore Bell
Margaret Wears Black
Della Short Speed
Be Careful McGee
Shirley Foote Eye
Wava White Flagg
Queen Elizabeth Green-
spoon
Luke Tea Orange
Money May Rumph
Nancy Hertz Good
Ima June Bugg
Claudia Snowball
Biddulph
Franklin Delano Roosevelt
Herbert Hoover Gibson
Elsie Leer Cutlip
Silence Buck Bellows
Margaret Scattergood
Bacon
Anna Kittleburger Funi-
corn
Pearl Lively Wiley
Appleyard
Evan Evan Evans
Corrinna Fattman Conkle
Mary Rhoda Duck
Virginia Burns Feine
William Otto Grow
Daisy Etta Cock
Earl Burns Combs
Elizabeth Sloppy Gug
Penelope Palm Tree
Groves

contrasting with single-syllable first names such as **John, Paul, George** and **Mark**.

But even when the middle name is suitable for use as a first name, the way one feels about it may prevent the change being made. When you have always been addressed by your first name it is easy to believe that you *are* that name; that you and the name are inextricably entwined. The middle name has always been there, but it has been a long way in the background. Young children, for example, often find it difficult to remember what their middle names are because they hear them so rarely. In such circumstances the middle name is almost just another name, carrying associations with other people rather than the million and one personal associations that are linked to your own first name. For many, then, a switch from first name to middle name may be as dramatic a wrench as the adoption of a totally new name. The only consolation in the case of the middle name will be some vague thought that it is, after all, *your* name. You were given it at birth and have every right to use it.

Letter names

When the middle name remains permanently in that position its main use will be as an initial. It then becomes, to all intents and purposes, a letter name. David Wagner, let us say, has the middle name Jeffrey, but he will usually style himself David J. Wagner. When his name is said aloud it is as if his middle name is **Jay**.

Jay and Kay exist as names, of course, and attract no undue attention, but others less common have been used. The best-known by far is the S middle name of Harry S Truman, where S, or **Ess**, was the complete name. The President's parents hit on the idea of a compromise between Solomon and Shippe, the names of the grandfathers, and realized that it would not look or sound odd because it would be mistaken for an initial. In his discussion of *Proper Names in America*, H. L. Mencken says that letter-names of this type became relatively common between the two World Wars, usually as middle names but occasionally used as first names.

In another presidential family initials were significant in a different way. L.B.J. stood not only for Lyndon Baines Johnson, but also for Lady Bird Johnson and the two daughters, Lynda Bird and Lucy Baines.

Some parents have made use of letter-names in a genuine attempt to allow a child to choose names for itself later in life. D R Scott, of the University of Missouri, received those letters—the initials of his father's first and middle names—as his own names. He did not bother to fill them out later in life, presumably because **Dee** would in any case be perfectly acceptable as a first name. With the initials D R one would also imagine that a nickname such as Doc or Doctor would be bestowed quite quickly.

> *'Magnus is my name. It's rather a good name, I think, sir.'*
>
> *'A very good name, indeed,' said Mr Pickwick, wholly unable to suppress a smile.*
>
> *'Yes, I think it is,' resumed Mr Magnus. 'There's a good name before it, too, you will observe . . . There—Peter Magnus—sounds well, I think sir.'*
>
> *'Very,' said Mr Pickwick.*
>
> *'Curious circumstance about those initials, sir,' said Mr Magnus.*
>
> *'You will observe—P.M.—post meridian. In hasty notes to intimate acquaintance, I sometimes sign myself 'Afternoon.' It amuses my friends very much, Mr Pickwick.'*
>
> *'It is calculated to offer them the highest gratification, I should conceive,' said Mr Pickwick, rather envying the ease with which Mr Magnus's friends were entertained.*
>
> Charles Dickens, The Pickwick Papers

Another man who owed his first name to the initials of his father's name was **Arjay** Miller, former President of the Ford Motor Company. He was naturally quite accustomed to receiving letters addressed to R. J. Miller. Incidentally, it is merely a coincidence that **Elsie** sounds as if it was inspired by the letters L and C. It owes its origin, ultimately, to **Elizabeth**.

A tendency to convert normal names into compound letter-names was once fashionable in business circles, though in recent times it has become something of a joke. Senior executives were referred to by their initials rather than their names, the practice probably originating in the initialling of memos and other documents. Because of the status value attached to such letter names their use spread rapidly and inevitably made them suspect.

One other aspect of middle names should not be forgotten. They play an important part in converting sets of initials into meaningful words. Elsdon C. Smith, in *Naming Your Baby*, remarks that black Americans consider it a lucky omen if one's initials spell out a word, but he goes on to recommend making a word like **Joy** rather than **Sap**. An examination of the names of a thousand American students with this point in mind revealed two examples of **Mad**, a **Cad**, **Fat**, **Cat** and **Dad**. **Meg** was coincidentally a pet form of the first name, **Margaret**. Donald Earl Cline emerged as **D E Cline**. My own full initials, incidentally, announce to the world that I am quite a **Lad**.

Anyone who has initials that make up an unfortunate word should not despair. A famous example of a man who overcame such a difficulty is Sir Arthur Sullivan, of the Gilbert and Sullivan team. He began life, one would have thought, with something of a handicap, for his middle name of Seymour made him an **Ass**. Even this certainly did him no harm, so perhaps initials that form words, any words, really are lucky omens.

3 Nicknames and Role Names

Our less formal personal names

Apart from surnames and middle names, other names that can replace first names to some extent are nicknames and role names. The use of nicknames varies considerably. In some cases such a name will replace a first name for all but the most formal purposes. A person will be introduced to new acquaintances, or will introduce himself, by his nickname. In such a case the nickname will usually be a fairly neutral one, such as **Skip** or **Flakey**. A different kind of usage occurs when a name is used by only one speaker to the person concerned.

Love names

The 'love names' quoted on page 30, for instance, are probably in extremely restricted use. It is difficult to imagine some of them being spoken aloud when anyone else is present, and almost impossible to imagine them being used in the third person. It might be all right to tell **Twiddlepuss** that you love her when no-one else is listening, but surely no young man would remark to a friend or colleague that he had a date with Twiddlepuss that evening?

It is arguable, therefore, that such love names are not nicknames at all, but are the temporary name substitutes, or role names, that I discuss below. Nicknames, after all, are usually known to and used by at least a small group of people and can be used for third person reference.

Yet love names such as Twiddlepuss have more in common with nicknames than with the temporary substitute names which can occur in a complete conversation. In *Nicholas Nickleby*, for example, Mr Mantalini does not consistently address his wife by one love name. He uses a variety of terms ranging from the simple *my soul, my joy* or *my life* to the more artificial *my heart's joy, my soul's delight, my sense's idol, my existence's jewel*. Dickens even allows him to address Mrs Mantalini as *my essential juice of pine-apple*, *my cup of happiness's sweetener*, and on one notable occasion as *my gentle, captivating, bewitching, and most demnebly chick-a-biddy*.

These really are substitute names, not nicknames, and it is quite clear that Dickens did not like their fulsome use. When Mr Mantalini utters them we see how hypocritical they can be. In this respect, Dickens seems to have been in agreement with Congreve, who had earlier made one of his characters comment on the 'nauseous cant' used between husbands and wives. In *The Way of the World* Mrs Millamant objects violently to being addressed as *wife, spouse, my dear, joy, jewel, love* and *sweetheart*.

The objection is almost certainly to the insincere use of these expressions rather than to the names themselves. When Mr Mantalini addresses his wife as *my soul* we share the discomfort of Kate Nickleby, who is forced to listen to their conversation. We certainly have no such feelings when Romeo calls Juliet *my soul*, as he does on one occasion. He also calls her by such names as *dear saint, fair maid, my dear, love, my wife*, while Juliet refers to Romeo as *love, lord, sweet, husband*. No-one would accuse *them* of indulging in nauseous cant.

These terms are mostly taken from a general stock of endearments, available to any speaker for use with any partner. Since the names from *The Times* which I have quoted are not ordinary endearments, but at the same time are not normal nicknames, they deserve a description of their own. 'Love names' seems to suit them very well.

Nicknames

To return now to nicknames of the more usual kind, psychological studies in the U.S.A. and Britain have shown that the acceptance of a nickname is a sign of healthy social adjustment. If your first name is sending out the wrong signals for one reason or another, you might therefore consider replacing it permanently by your nickname, if you have managed to acquire one, that is. After all, there is something immediately reassuring about the person who says: 'My name's **Walter** but most people call me **Dizzy**.' The remark tells you that here is someone who likes to socialize and doesn't stand on formality. Even more than the first name, the immediate invitation to use a nickname indicates an easy-going wish for a friendly relationship.

The best-known nickname of Frank Sinatra (born Albert Francis Sinatra) is **The Voice***, but several others were suggested when the singer first became famous. They included* **The Lean Lark, The Croon Prince, The Sultan of Swoon, The Swami of Swoon, Dreamboat, The Larynx, The Mooer, Shoulders, The Bony Baritone** *and* **Angles***.*

In recent years many English people have taken to placing Valentine's Day messages in *The Times* on February 14th. In these the loved one is often referred to by a private 'love name' rather than by his or her first name. A selection of the love names that have occurred in the last year or so is given below:

Acorn	Face	Mummy Bare	Smiley
Andy Pandy	Fatty	Nodge	Snookums
Angel	Flop	Number Nine	Snoopy
Angelfish	Flopsy	Nunks	Snufkin
Ant	Fluff	Octopus	Spongelet
Aries	Fof	Old Digger	Squirrel
Baby Blue Eyes	Foxie	One-Tooth Jaws	Starfish
Baby Damelet	Freckles	Oodle	Stew
Babyface	Freebie	Opal	Sticks
Baby Gent	Fruitstack	Owl	Stinker
Bean	Fuzzypeg	Oz	Sugar Puff
Bear	Gazelle	Paddington	Superpip
Big Feet	Goatskin	Petal	Swaggles
Big O	Gollygobble	Phanty	Swiggles
Blooter Bucket	Gyppy	Philpot	Tablespoon
Boadicea	Happy Hippopotamus	Phonxay	Teaspoon
Bogfrog	Hoax	Pickles	Theeme
Boggets	Hog	Piggin	The Kicker
Bomber	Honeypot	Piggy	The One
Boo	Hunky Dory	Piglet	319
Boofs	Ickle	Piglit	Tickle
Booey	Irish Toad	Pinky	Ticktack
Bossy Banana	Jaybird	Pizziwig	Tiger
Brighteyes	Jellybean	Plumpernichol	Tigger
Budgie	Jerbibs	Poegface	Tiggo
Bummer	Jimjams	Pogel	Tish
Bundle	Joffa Woofer	Poggles	Toadies
Bunny	Kaffy	Pogo Mike	Tobes Doods
Bunnyfluff	Lamb	Pokey	Toes
Bunter	Little One	Poos	Toots
Bunting	Looby-Loo	Poozy Bear	Trot
Bunty	Maff	Pud	Trout
Buster	Maggot	Pudd'n	Twanks
Butter Mountain	Major Oak	Pumpkin	Tweets
Cat	Maxtable	Puppydove	Twiddlepuss
Cathykins	Merry Kent	Pussy	Walwus
Chick	Miaou	Pussycat	Weedie
Child Bride	Mini Beast	Raffles	Weeny
Chonk	Minty	Red Baron	Wellington Boot
Chou Chou	Miss Mo	Regina	Whiskey
Chubby Tubby Hubby	Miss Muffit	Road Runner	Widgie
Chucky Face	Moggo	Rotag	Wink
Chuzzer	Mooney	Sailor	Wol
Cookie	Moonface	Samuel Whiskers	Woody
Cubbles	Mousie	Sausage	Woozle
Cuckoo	Mrs Blues	Schnickelfritz	Woozloo
Cuddles	Mrs Drudge	Shaggy	Wuffie
Dawn Moon	Mrs Pudding	607	Wumpsey
Dobbin	Mrs Wuff	Sloppy Sex-Pot Lid	Wuzzie Bird
Dormouse	Muddy Bear	Smackeroo	Zuppy
Dumps	Muffin	Smasher	

Perhaps it is still only acceptable for men to imply such things when introducing themselves. It is rarer for women to admit to nicknames publicly, but this may be because fewer women have nicknames in the first place. A study of the nicknames in use at the Wallace Hall Academy in Dumfriesshire, Scotland, for example, and another based on English schoolchildren in Derby, both revealed that the boys had far more nicknames than the girls. Some boys were especially prone to nicknames, having up to five established names. This tendency to nickname males rather than females continues in adult working environments.

Nicknames have always been common in male strongholds such as the armed services. The Royal Navy, especially, has established certain traditions about them. Men with surnames such as White, Harris or Hall automatically become **Chalky, Bogey** or **Blinker**. Men from different cities or regions inherit nicknames such as **Dotty** (from Derbyshire).

Physical or mental characteristics also attract traditional nicknames, though these may vary in different parts of the English-speaking world. The American **Reddy** or **Redsy** will probably be **Ginger** in Britain. Such traditional nicknames are well treated in Julian Franklyn's *Dictionary of Nicknames*, and an excellent analysis of nicknames used by British schoolchildren is to be found in *The Lore and Language of Schoolchildren*, by Iona and Peter Opie.

Individual nicknames are arrived at in many different ways. A surname may be corrupted, for instance, to form a new name. Campbell becomes **Hannibal**, or Hewitt becomes **Chewitt**. If the surname is associated with something else, such as a commercial product, this can also lead to a name. Walker makes people think of Walker's Crisps, so **Crispy** becomes the nickname. Dustin Hoffman provides an example of how a first name can be corrupted to form a nickname. He has said that at school he was known as **Dustbin.**

The most individual nicknames of all are incident names. These arise from a chance remark, a slip of the tongue perhaps, or sometimes from a favourite expression. The person who keeps asking: 'D'you see?' finds himself permanently labelled **Juicy**.

In many parts of the world children are given incident names as their real names. One thinks especially of the African tribesman or the Indian brave who names his child after the first person or animal seen after the birth. This accounts for personal names such as **Sitting Bull**. But it is not necessary to go beyond our own society to find incident names. Many parents are influenced in their choice of a child's name by a song they happened to hear or a book they happened to read near the time of birth.

Nicknames, whether incident names or the various other types that I have described, are invariably colourful and amusing. It is tempting to fill many pages with examples, but I shall restrict myself to those shown on page 33.

They were gathered in California in 1969 by Patricia L. Pilling amongst the Yurok and Hupa Indians. Mrs Pilling tells me that the names are in very frequent use, and that 'real' names are often totally forgotten. Conversations amongst the men concerned must sound highly entertaining.

Nevertheless, nicknames are best left as nicknames. By that I mean that parents should not officially give their children names like **Amorous, Ace, Glass, Butter, Anvil, Champ, Emu, Rowdy, Feaster** or **Ham**. Unfortunately I have not chosen these examples at random. Far from being light-hearted nicknames, all were solemnly bestowed on children as their first names. Parents, sometimes, have a great deal to answer for.

Role names

All the names mentioned so far—surnames, with or without titles attached to them, middle names and nicknames—can be used instead of first names as terms of address. In many situations, however, we are addressed by role names. These have also been called 'personal name substitutes and modifiers'.

Role names may be used both by people who do not know our first name or surname and by those who do. In the latter case, the reason for addressing us as *sir* or *madam*, say, or *old man* or *darling*, instead of by our real name will usually be to make the speaker's attitude absolutely clear. He can convey an exact degree of politeness or friendliness, intimacy or detestation by the term he chooses. His choice of term may also reveal something about his own nationality, age, social class and profession.

To illustrate this point, consider the question: 'Have you found it yet?' That tells us nothing of the person who is asking the question, and nothing of the person being addressed. The addition of different role names to the basic question puts it immediately into many different contexts. Here are some examples:

Have you found it yet, Gramps?/Mummy?/dearie?/baby?/father?/ mate?/old boy?/you bloody fool?/buddie?/guv?/caddie?/you nosey bastard?/doctor?/ma'am?

Of these, *Gramps* interchanges with *Grandad* and *Gran'pa*, which are probably more usual forms. The particular name used depends to a large extent on family tradition. The other family role name, *Mummy*, is used by young children of both sexes and possibly by girls into their teens. There will often then be a change to *Mother*. Regional variants of this term include *Mum, Mom, Mam, Ma, Momma*. Formerly in polite circles it was *Mama*, stressed on the second syllable like its counterpart, *Papa*.

Father is at least as likely these days to be a professional title, used for a priest, as it is to be a family role name. *Baby* is used usually to a girl or

A selection of nicknames used by the Yurok and Hupa Indians in Northwestern California, gathered in 1968–69 by Patricia L. Pilling.

Addie Meat	Honeybee	Rat
Babe Merino	Horny	Renegade
Baby Doll	Horsemeat	Scatt
Big Doot	Islo	Scatter Hatter
Billy Winks	Jimmie Skunk	Scratch Mahatch
Black Snake	Jimmie To	Scrawny
Booboo	Jocko	Seadog
Boots	Junky	Senator
Boy Blue	Little Bonzo	Shaky Johnny
Buckaloo	Little Giant	Short Pants
Buffalo Nickel	Little Sack	Shosh
Bugs	Little Shoestring	Shraddy
Chuckles	Lizard	Silly Lilly
Chuffy	Longgone	Sireen
Clean Red	Luscious	Sleepy
Crying Lee	Man	Sly
Daipey	Marshmallow	Smith Creek
Dirty Red	Midget	Spider
Doodoo	Minnie Mouse	Squeaky
Duke City	Mo	Stoon
Elephant	Muchacho	Strawberry
Fada	Mumps	Stretch
Famous Amos	Nicodemus	Stumpy
Fido	Nimbles	Suds
Flea	Oh By God	Suesue
Flip	Okey Doakes	Super Beast
Flower Pot	Peachy Ed	Teddy Spaghetti
Frostie	Pearly Gates	Tinkerbell
Gets	Pee Wee	Toady
Gigi	Pinhead	Tokes
Gigs	Pook	Tweet
Grumpy	Popcorn	Two Feet
Gunny Sack	Pork	Watusi
Happy Hooligan	Putnuk	Weeps
Hardrock Dot	Rabbit	

> '*I think, father, I require a little time.*'
> '*Papa is a preferable mode of address,*' observed Mrs General. '*Father is rather vulgar, my dear. The word Papa, besides, gives a pretty form to the lips. Papa, potatoes, poultry, prunes and prism are all very good words for the lips: especially prunes and prism.*'
>
> *Charles Dickens*, Little Dorrit

woman, and by an American or Canadian speaker rather than an Englishman. I am told that those so addressed consider the term complimentary. A child of four or five who is addressed as *baby*, however, will always take it as an insult.

The other terms I gave as examples all give information about the speaker or the person addressed. *Guv*, for instance, is used by working men in Britain to middle-class strangers as well as their real 'governor', or employer. In Victorian middle-class families *Guv'nor* was often the name used by sons to address their fathers. I will leave you to decide for yourself what information is conveyed by the other role names I quoted. They deserve almost a book in themselves, for the English language is particularly rich in them, but I must confine myself here to a few general points.

It would be interesting to see psychologists turn their attention to the role names that come closest to being personal names. To what extent are parents induced to think of themselves in a certain way, for instance, by being constantly identified by 'mother' and 'father' names instead of by their own first names? Does a woman who is nearly always hearing herself called *Mom* or *Ma* partly lose track of her own individuality, which is far more closely bound up with her first name?

It may be comforting for young children to use the parental role names, but a switch to first name usage later might be to the parents' advantage. Apart from anything else, there comes a point when some role names can be too revealing. In this scene from *Love for Love*, Miss Prue is talking to her step-mother:

Miss Prue: Mother, mother, mother, look you here.
Mrs Foresight: Fie, fie, Miss, how you bawl. Besides, I have told you, you must not call me Mother.
Miss Prue: What must I call you then? Are you not my father's wife?
Mrs Foresight: Madam—you must say Madam. By my soul, I shall fancy myself old indeed to have this great girl call me Mother.

That was William Congreve nearly three hundred years ago making a point which many modern mothers would entirely understand.

Magic names

Another interesting study would lie in the name magic quality of titles such as *Doctor* and *Professor* when used as role names. Would patients feel as well after a chat with John or Mary as they do when they have just been talking to *Doctor*. Would students feel as awed by the wisdom of William or Ann as they are by that of the man or woman they call *Professor*? And how much more comforting it is for parishioners to talk to *Father*, instead of the Michael or Joseph who happens to be wearing a dog-collar.

In a far more negative way, name magic also plays a part in the practice of name-calling, which most of us indulge in when we are annoyed. Children, who quickly become experts in the art of insulting one another, have their magic formulae for warding off attacks:

> Sticks and stones may break my bones
> But names will never hurt me.

Such sayings merely testify to the fact that the use of insulting names *does* hurt.

The fact that insulting names do hurt us probably indicates that love names of the type quoted earlier have a positive influence on the person addressed. However strange the names may be in themselves, the person hearing them knows that they are meant to show affection. When her partner is annoyed with her, the girl called **Sugar Puff** in moments of intimacy is probably addressed once more by her first name.

Role names seem to me to become rather dangerous if they begin to impinge seriously on our personal view of ourselves. When a man who is David, say, begins to *think of himself* as *Doctor* or *Professor*, he is losing his

---

A name-calling contest can be good fun if one is merely a spectator. Shakespeare was well aware of this and provided a good example of a slanging match in Henry IV, Part I.

Prince Hal: *Why, thou clay-brain'd guts, thou knotty-pated fool, thou whoreson, obscene, greasy tallow-catch ... I'll no longer be guilty of this sin; this sanguine coward, this bed-presser, this horse-back-breaker, this huge hill of flesh—*

Falstaff: *'Sblood, you starveling, you eel-skin, you dried neat's tongue, you bull's pizzle, you stock fish. O for breath to utter what is like thee— you tailor's yard, you sheath, you bow-case, you vile standing tuck.*

(A 'bull's pizzle' was a bull's penis, once used as a flogging instrument. A 'tuck' was a slender rapier.) Basically, Hal is calling Falstaff fat, while Falstaff comments on Prince Hal's thinness.

sense of perspective. Those names describe only a part of what he is as a complete person. This applies also to the woman who allows herself to become *Mother*, though it is easy to see how this can happen. The 'mother' and 'father' names are exceptional because they occur in our most personal relationships and are persistently used for many years. They are very persuasive terms indeed.

But if there is any name with which an individual needs to identify, given the social customs that now prevail in the English-speaking world, it is not a role name but his or her own first name. First names are more important from a psychological point of view than any of the other names discussed in this and the previous chapter. As we have seen, we can all have many different personal names, but our first names are the most personal of all.

4 Name Magic

The supernatural powers of personal names

At the end of the last chapter I alluded briefly to name magic, a topic that concerns all personal names. It is something that has affected men and women throughout history in one way or another, and it certainly influences many people today. They are probably less consciously aware of it, however, than their ancestors would have been.

Name magic can be defined in various ways. A working definition is: 'the attribution of supernatural power to a name, or a belief in its extraordinary significance.' William Camden, an important writer on names in the seventeenth century, discussed one aspect of the subject, referring to 'the superstitious kind of divination called onomantia'. He used the Latin term for what we normally call onomancy.

Name omens

Onomancy is a way of foretelling future events and individual destinies by interpreting names as omens, either because of the meaning the names have or because of their supposed value in numerical terms. The latter system of divination is commonly called numerology. Camden says that name divination was 'condemned by the last general council', but it has been widely practised since the seventeenth century in various parts of the English-speaking world. At least one Canadian organization currently offers advice about changes of name—the idea being to make them more acceptable from a numerical point of view. And in a book published in New York in 1935, Mrs Charles B. Cochran remarked: 'since Numerology became so popular, I have known friends of mine who have altered the life-long spellings of their Christian names because the letters did not add up to a favourable number.' Mrs Cochran should have written—'since Numerology became popular *again*'. The followers of Pythagoras, the mathematical philosopher who lived in the sixth century B.C., made judgements about people according to whether they had an even or odd number of vowels in their names. By this reckoning I am decidedly 'odd' myself; perhaps you had better quickly check your own rating.

The ancient Greeks and Romans had various other beliefs about the magic of names and their meanings. The emperor Augustus, for instance, on the night before a sea-battle, is said to have met a peasant with a donkey. He demanded to know not only the name of the peasant, but also that of the donkey. The peasant turned out to be **Eutyches**, 'the fortunate one', and the donkey **Nicon**, 'victor'. Augustus went into battle supremely confident thanks to these omens and duly won, making himself master of the Roman world. It is not recorded whether his opponent, Antony, met a peasant or donkey before the battle, but he had certainly met a lady called **Cleopatra** some time previously. Her name seems to have proved unlucky for several men.

Camden tells us of a Gothic king, Theodatus, who also wished to have an indication of his success or otherwise in battle by means of name omens. In his case he was persuaded by a 'name-wizard' to shut up a number of pigs in a sty, after giving Roman names to some of them, Gothic names to the others. After a few days the pigs with Roman names, identified by their markings, were still alive, though showing signs of wear and tear. The pigs with Gothic names were dead. The name-wizard accordingly predicted the outcome of the battle.

In classical writings there are many references not only to the belief that names are omens of future events, but to the relationship between names and the natures of those who bear them. The third century Roman poet Decimus Magnus Ausonius stated: 'The supreme judge of the world bade that a man's name should be such as the character with which he created him.'

If the legend of St Hippolytus is to be believed, the Romans sometimes linked a man's name and fate in an extremely cruel way. Hippolytus was a Roman soldier guarding St Laurence and was inspired by his example to become a Christian. Arrested in his turn, his captors took note of his name, which meant 'of the stampeding horses'. It had been borne in Greek mythology by the son of Theseus. St Hippolytus was duly executed by being tied to wild horses which tore him to pieces.

A good name

Less drastically, most Romans had something in common with the English Puritans in believing that someone given a 'virtue' name—more likely to be 'happy' or 'strong' for a Roman rather than the 'humble' or 'patient' of the Puritan—would eventually live up to his name. For a Roman soldier to gain

In ancient times one way of 'interpreting' a name was to consider its anagram. The word that emerged when the letters of the name were re-arranged were thought to have special significance. Below are some anagrams of modern first names. While it is quite conceivable that a **Brian** may have a good *brain*, or that **Denis** *dines* regularly, it is rather more difficult to see the connection between *internees*, say, and a woman named **Ernestine**.

If you have plenty of time to spare you might like to experiment with your own full name to see whether a meaningful anagram emerges from it. **Leslie Dunkling** unfortunately leads to *dull senile king*, which I suspect will convince some that there is something in this theory of anagram-omens.

Alban *banal*	Elsa *seal*	Marian *airman*
Alfred *flared*	Enid *dine*	Mary *army*
Alister *retails*	Eric *rice*	May *yam*
Andrew *wander*	Ernest *nester*	Melissa *aimless*
Bertha *bather*	Ernestine *internees*	Miles *slime*
Brian *brain*	Freda *fared*	Mona *moan*
Carol *coral*	Gerald *glared*	Nancy *canny*
Clare *clear*	Glenda *dangle*	Olga *gaol*
Claud *ducal*	Gustave *vaguest*	Pat *apt*
Cordelia *cedar-oil*	Hortensia *senhorita*	Pepe *peep*
Cornelius *reclusion*	Ingrid *riding*	Piers *spire*
Daniel *nailed*	Kate *teak*	Rodney *yonder*
Dawn *wand*	Kay *yak*	Rosa *soar*
Delbert *trebled*	Lance *clean*	Rose *sore*
Delia *ailed*	Laura *aural*	Ruth *hurt*
Denis *dines*	Laurence *cerulean*	Saemus *amuses*
Dennis *sinned*	Leon *lone*	Silas *sails*
Dora *road*	Lewis *wiles*	Silvester *rivetless*
Earl *real*	Lois *soil*	Teresa *teaser*
Edgar *raged*	Lydia *daily*	Terrance *canterer*
Edwin *wined*	Mabel *blame*	Vera *rave*

favour with his general it helped if his parents had thought to call him **Victor** or **Valorous**. *Bonum nomen bonum omen*—'a good name is a good omen'— was a common Roman proverb.

This belief remained common for centuries. There is the well-known story of the French ambassadors who were sent to the court of King Alfonso in the thirteenth century to arrange a marriage between one of the Spanish king's daughters and Louis VIII. The elder daughter was the more beautiful, and it was taken for granted that she would be chosen, but when the ambassadors heard that her name was **Urraca**, while the younger daughter was **Blanche**, they immediately chose the latter. She was less beautiful in herself, but she had the better name. Urraca, 'magpie', would be an unpleasant sound to French ears, the ambassadors explained, and its meaning was not favourable. Blanche would be well received by the French populace because of its sound and meaning.

The French ambassadors were not merely comparing an ugly-sounding name with a more pleasant one. They knew that the majority of their countrymen really would believe that someone with a good name would be a good person. The 'goodness' of Blanche, incidentally, lay mostly in its meaning as a dictionary word. It was not merely a question, as it might be in modern times, of a name striking the correct fashionable note and having acceptable associations.

Blanche was perhaps something of an exceptional name for thirteenth century Frenchmen in that its meaning *was* immediately apparent. Most names being used at the time, both there and in England, no longer had such meanings. By the time Camden came to discuss first names in the seventeenth century he was forced to emphasize to his readers that names had originally not been 'vain senseless sounds' but meaningful words. He made a valiant attempt to say what those meaningful words had been, and did no worse than many a modern compiler of a baby-name book.

The Greeks and Romans, however, had needed no such explanations. Their own names revealed, or hinted strongly at, their meanings. In modern times we have a few meaningful word-names, such as **June**, say, or **Prudence**, but most names are like **Sarah** and **Catherine**—they remain merely 'names' until a reference book interprets them as 'princess' and 'purity'.

Name meanings as omens

That word 'purity', by the way, comes near to suggesting what **Blanche** meant to the French ambassadors. In their language it spoke of 'whiteness', 'cleanliness', 'beauty'. It is easy to understand why it seemed a good omen.

Most of us reveal a belief in some kind of name magic, but we do not generally think that a name's original meaning gives an indication of the

Name Magic in the Eighteenth Century

A famous passage on the subject of name magic occurs in the humorous novel, *The Life and Opinions of Tristram Shandy*, by Laurence Sterne. In volume one, published in 1760, Tristram Shandy tells us of his father's theories about first names:

'In respect to the choice and imposition of Christian names, he thought a great deal more depended than superficial minds were capable of conceiving. His opinion in this matter was that there was a strange kind of magic bias, which good or bad names, as he called them, irresistibly impressed upon our characters and conduct.

How many Caesars and Pompeys, he would say, by mere inspiration of the names, have been rendered worthy of them! And how many, he would add, are there who might have done exceeding well in the world, had not their characters and spirits been totally depressed and Nicodemus'd into nothing.

"I see plainly, sir, by your looks," my father would say, "that you do not heartily subscribe to this opinion of mine. Your son!—your Billy, sir—would you for the world have called him Judas? Would you, sir, if a godfather had proposed the name of your child, and offered you his purse along with it, have consented to such a desecration of him?

If I know your temper right, sir, you are incapable of it, you would have trampled upon the offer. Was your son called Judas, the sordid and treacherous idea so inseparable from the name would have accompanied him through his life like his shadow, and in the end made a miser and rascal of him, in spite, sir, of your example."

He was serious, and in consequence of it, he would lose all kind of patience whenever he saw people who should have known better, as careless and as indifferent about the name they imposed upon their child, or more so, than in the choice of Ponto or Cupid for their dog.

Jack, Dick and Tom my father called neutral names, affirming that there had been as many knaves and fools as wise and good men who had borne them. Bob was another which operated very little either way. Andrew was worse, he said, than nothing. William stood pretty high. Nick, he said, was the Devil.

But of all the names in the universe, he had the most unconquerable aversion for Tristram.'

(Abridged)

name-bearer's future. If we did, it would mean that the parents of a **Philip** would expect him to become a 'lover of horses', as his name implies. **Rebecca**'s parents would be waiting for the day when they could say: 'We always knew you would turn out to be "a snare" for some man.' Neither do we believe that certain names are either lucky or unlucky in themselves. In the seventeenth century it was commonly held that **John** was an unlucky name for any member of the royal family. **Henry** was thought of in a similar way in France.

I have been asking parents for many years to tell me why they chose one name rather than another for their child, and have received several thousand letters on the subject. Often parents refer to some kind of name book that purports to give the meanings of first names. It is quite clear, however, that the majority of parents do not choose or reject names on the basis of their original meanings. If they like a name instinctively, they may be pleased to see that the name once meant something pleasant, but they will not be worried to learn that **Paul** or **Paula** derive from a Latin word meaning 'small', or that **Cecilia**'s original meaning was 'blind'. If they like the names for other reasons they will use them, having no fears that the original meanings of the names will influence the development of the children.

It would be easy to find apparent exceptions to this rule. Somewhere there are parents, perhaps, who named their son **Neil** *because* they were told it meant 'champion', and that was what they wanted their son to become. Parents of a **Sophie** or **Sophia** might likewise have been struck by its original meaning of 'wisdom' and chosen it for that reason.

Such naming does happen on occasions, and I would personally not be all that surprised if children so named eventually went a long way towards fulfilling their parents' ambitions. Not because of any name influence, needless to say; simply because of those parental ambitions. If the parents really are so concerned with their child's athletic or academic achievements they will no doubt do all they can in the next few years to realize their dreams. It is their continued efforts which will produce the results, not the mere act of naming.

But if most of us do not think of personal names as omens, in the way that the ancient Romans and Greeks thought of them, I am quite sure that onomancy is still very much with us. I wonder how many people at racetracks have suddenly noticed that the name of a horse links with an event that recently occurred to them, or with someone they recently met. The professional punter may have learned to ignore such coincidences, but the average amateur finds it difficult to believe that he is not being given a sign from heaven, a command, almost, to back that particular horse. In a mild sort of way, it is Augustus again before the battle of Actium, meeting his peasant and donkey and being convinced of victory.

Name magic around the world

We can learn something about our own beliefs in name magic not only by going back into the classical past, but by looking sideways into other cultures. For this purpose we can turn to such books as *Magic In Names*, by Edward Clodd, and *The Golden Bough*, by Sir James Frazer. There we find that superstitious beliefs about names are clearly apparent, and of a wide variety, throughout the world.

Fairly common in many parts of the world, for instance, is the conviction that once someone knows your name, you are to a large extent in that person's power. This naturally leads to a reluctance amongst the people who hold this belief to reveal their true names. The Indians of Guyana, members of many African tribes, Australian Aborigines, hill tribesmen of the Malay peninsula, and many North American Indians are amongst those who share, according to anthropological reports, this fear of revealing their names to anyone who is not a member of the family. Some Indians have been known to ask foreigners to write a name at random on a piece of paper. The paper will then be shown to any other foreigner who asks the Indian to identify himself. The name on the piece of paper, as far as the Indian is concerned, serves perfectly well as a label. His real name is a different matter. It is inextricably bound up with his innermost self, and he values it as he values his life.

An example of how personal names can be regarded as something tangible and of great worth was mentioned by Frank Boas in a report published in 1898. This concerned the Kwakiutl Indians, of British Columbia. These tribesmen regularly pawned their names for a temporary period. Until they redeemed their pledge they considered themselves forced to remain anonymous or use other names. But getting their real names back again, as the tribal pawn-brokers well knew, was even more important to them than repossessing family heirlooms would be to us. Without the right to use their real names, they felt themselves to be without an identity.

A Kwakiutl Indian studying our society would soon note that we sometimes sell our names, or sell the right to use them for a certain period. We call it 'endorsing' a commercial product, and the name-magic inherent in the practice simply shows a different way of thinking. In our case we

> '*Change the name and not the letter*
> *Change for the worse and not for the better.*'
>
> *A common superstition in parts of England referring to a woman's change of name at marriage.*

obviously believe that certain names become powerful workers of magic and we are prepared to pay to have them inscribed on our sports goods or whatever.

It would be interesting to know how the Indian would react to another habit which is common in our society. We call it name-dropping, but he might well see it as the use of powerful names to bring ourselves some kind of social benefit.

Children and name magic

Even in countries where it is not considered to be a disaster of the first order to reveal one's real name, there is often a great reluctance to do so. The Fijians and Abipones apparently ask a friend to tell you their names rather than tell you themselves. As Clodd remarks, in *Magic in Names*, this inevitably makes us think of young children. They frequently have an instinctive dislike of answering a direct question about their own names, though they will willingly give the names of their brothers and sisters.

Clodd sees in this traces of primitive superstition; I see it as proof that many children think of their names as tangible possessions. Asking a child to tell you his name is like asking him to give you something he owns, an act which always makes him rather suspicious. It does not worry him to hear his name mentioned by a third person, however. There he recognizes that his possession is being talked about, but it remains his.

Older children in our society will sometimes amuse themselves by exchanging names. Girls in particular seem to like cementing friendships by temporarily assuming the name of the girl-friend they admire. I have come across the practice among modern schoolgirls, and it is clearly nothing new. Shakespeare refers in *Measure for Measure* to schoolmaids exchanging their names 'by vain though apt affection'.

Once again, this practice would be easily understood by natives in various parts of the world. An exchange of names signifies the establishment of a deep relationship. The eighteenth-century explorer Captain Cook was party to such an exchange with a man called Oree. The native became Cookee under the arrangement, and no doubt took his new name more seriously than Captain Cook seems to have taken his.

> *It occasionally happens that a woman marries a man whose surname is the same as her own maiden name. In some parts of England this was formerly thought to bestow healing powers on the woman concerned.*

Names are thought to be powerful instruments in the working of magic spells. The names of angels are especially useful. For those who would like to put name magic to the test, here are examples of an invocation and a spell which might improve your love life:

To excite love in a person:
Pour oil from a white lily into a goblet, recite the 137th Psalm over the cup and conclude by pronouncing the name of the angel Hamiel and the name of the person you love. Next write the name of the angel on a piece of cloth. Dip the cloth in oil, then tie it to your right arm.

At a suitable moment, touch the right hand of the person you love, and love will be awakened in his or her heart. The operation will be more powerful in effect if you perform it at dawn on the Friday following the new moon.

For men only:
Attach to the head of a girl's or woman's bed, near to the place where her head rests, a piece of virgin parchment on which you have written the names of Michael, Gabriel and Raphael.

Invoke these three angels to inspire (Doris, or whoever it is you yearn for) with a love for you equal to your own for her. She will not be able to sleep without thinking of you, and very soon love will dawn in her heart.

Perhaps a simpler way of weaving a name spell for romantic purposes is to repeat over and over again the name of the person you love while he or she is present. This is best done at night, and in a soft and tender voice. It is said to produce a hypnotic effect. As Shakespeare put it:

Juliet: Romeo!
Romeo: It is my soul that calls upon my name.
            How silver-sweet sound lovers' tongues by night,
            Like softest music to attending ears.
Juliet: Romeo!

Religious name magic

A change of one's own name to signify the birth of a new being in religious terms is a well-known practice, especially with entrants into religious orders. Converts to Christianity have also traditionally taken on new 'christian' names. The example of the former Cassius Clay, now Mohammad Ali, is there to show us that converts to other religions may also undergo a name change.

We may say that such name changes are merely symbolic, but the person concerned sees it as far more than that. The casting-off of the old name makes him feel that he has cast off a whole personality, one that was imposed upon him by outside events. By choosing a new name he also allows himself to choose the personality that is associated with it. There is an important principle here to which we shall return later, for it need not only be religious motivation which prompts the desire for a new personality.

In his *Tour Through the Island of Jamaica in 1823*, C. R. Williams told the story of a man who rather too willingly allowed himself to become a Christian convert. He changed his native name of **Quamina** to **Timothy**, and the local missionary regarded him as another soul saved. Soon afterwards Timothy's neighbour was heard complaining loudly that some money lent to the convert had not been repaid. 'Of course not', replied Timothy. 'The money was lent to Quamina, who is now dead. Timothy is not responsible for Quamina's debts.'

Perhaps this highly convenient way of thinking affects those members of our society who adopt an alias. Crimes committed by Tom Smith on Tuesday need not bother the conscience of the man who is Peter Gray by Friday. It is certainly not just for reasons of conscience that aliases are used, but there must be an element of name magic present when they are used. The shedding of one's real name allows the thought that one's innermost self has not been committed to the action.

Jewish name magic

Yet another illustration of the way we believe that a name *is* the person concerned is provided by the Jewish prayer for the sick. This is based on the principle that a person and his name are linked together in a spiritual way. An officially sanctioned change of name is therefore thought to be of great significance. I quote from *Hamadrikh, The Rabbi's Guide*, by Hyam Goldin:

> Even if it were decreed against him by Thy righteous court that he die of his present illness, lo, our holy Rabbis said that three things causes an evil decree passed on man to be cancelled, one of them being the change of the sick person's name. We fulfilled what they said and his

name was changed, and it is a different person. If the decree was passed on . . . , but on . . . it was not passed, it is now someone else that is not called by the former name. As his name was changed, so may the evil decree on him be changed from law to mercy, from death to life, from illness to a perfect cure to . . . , son of . . .

A Jewish correspondent tells me that one of his relations has acquired several additional names by this process.

Another interesting custom with many Jews is the avoidance of a name of a living relation when a child is named. The Ashkenazim believed, according to the Reverend Reuben S. Brookes in his *Guide To Jewish Names*, that such usage would 'rob the living of his full life'.

Not just the use, but the uttering of certain names, is strictly forbidden amongst many races. Frequently wives must not address their husbands by name, nor mention his name to others. The wife of a Mr Green, a missionary among the Kaffirs, is said to have created a scandal by referring to some fruit as 'too green'. By their rules she should have said 'not ripe', even though the word and not the name was being mentioned.

Names of parents-in-law are also taboo in various parts of the world, whereas to us they may merely be an embarrassment. There are those in our society who could never bring themselves to address their mother-in-law by her first name, for example, though Mrs followed by her surname may also seem wrong because of its formality. It is not easy to use one of the 'mother' terms to a mother-in-law, and there are few remaining possibilities. The difficulty, when it exists, is caused by the recognition of a special relationship which seems to demand a special name, though there is no established tradition as to what that name should be.

Name-giving rites

Mothers-in-law apart, it is clear that all personal names are matters of deep concern to people of all nations. If we wanted further proof of the way people everywhere attach the greatest possible importance to them we need only look at the different name-giving ceremonies. These occur at or near the birth, as with baptism, or perhaps later in life when new names are adopted as part of initiation rites. In every society, primitive or sophisticated, the bestowal of a personal name seems to be an occasion of formality and tradition. Once the name has been given, there is the common belief in the mystical relationship between the name and the person who bears it. The belief is so widespread that it would be very surprising indeed if we did not share it, and of course, we do share it. To take just one example, if you have a friend whose name is **Laurence**, say, and you notice that somone has written it as **Lawrence**, you tend to class this as a slight mistake of little importance. It is usually a different matter altogether when someone changes the spelling of your own name by even a single letter. It is as if they have been physically careless, treading on your toes while walking past you. Anyone who reacts like that to mis-spellings of his name, it seems to me, is thinking along the same lines as the native who believes that his name *is* himself. The name is being given that 'extraordinary significance' which indicates that name magic is at work.

Numerology

It may be that your concern with the spelling of your name extends to a belief in numerology. Browsing around the bookshops of New York recently I noticed a whole range of books on the subject. The one I eventually bought was called *Numerology Made Plain*, by Ariel Yvon Taylor, but I regret to say that it failed to live up to its title in my case.

The general principle of numerology, I agree, seems to be simple. Each letter is given a numerical value corresponding to its position in the alphabet. 'R' would be 18, but the two digits are added together to make 9, the highest number allowed in the system. It is important, it seems, to work out the total value of your name, then the separate values of the vowels and consonants. You arrive thus at a set of figures such as 5-7-7.

Having arrived at the numbers, it is necessary to have faith in your author's interpretation of what they mean, for if you are foolish enough to glance into a second book on the subject you will probably find not only a different method suggested for arriving at the numbers, but different views entirely on their significance.

By the Taylor method, **Sophia** and **Olivia** would both emerge with the set of figures 5-7-7, so their destinies would presumably be similar. So far, so good, for those names might seem to have something in common, making an appeal to the same kind of parents. I note, though, that the numbers 5-7-7 would also be produced by **Carlos** and **Sambo**, and at this point numerology and I part company.

Numerology is no doubt harmless enough, though I personally cannot arouse much enthusiasm for a name's so-called 'vibrations'. Name magic generally is of more interest. It influences us all in subtle ways, and it is important to be aware of that fact, especially when one is trying to look at names objectively. It is difficult to do this with one's own name at the best of times; it becomes quite impossible if a belief in name magic is getting in the way. One's name is a name, an identifying label which most people bear for reasons totally beyond their own control. It is like a suit of clothes or a dress which was chosen by somebody else, but which may fit very well nevertheless. If it does not fit, it can be changed for something that does.

It is worth stressing this point, for I have often found that even when people admit that their own name embarrasses them, they find it very difficult to do anything about it. They think of their name as if it were their skin, something they were born with and which they must keep until they die. That is allowing name magic to exert its influence in quite the wrong way. If your name is going to exert a supernatural influence on anyone, then let it be on someone else.

5 The Name Conquest

First names in the Middle Ages

Let us turn away now from sociological and psychological aspects of personal names in general. I want to concentrate on first names, and I begin with a brief sketch of their historical background, as far as English-speakers are concerned, that is. A convenient starting point is the time when first names actually become 'first' names instead of single, personal names. That also happens to be the time of the great 'Name Conquest'.

When the Normans conquered England in 1066, one result of their victory might have been a replacement of the English language by French. That didn't happen, of course, but there was at least one kind of linguistic take-over. The names that had been in use in England for centuries were quickly ousted by the names the Normans brought with them.

The traditional English names in use were not 'first' names, because no surnames or middle names yet existed. Englishmen in those days had one name only. If we give them their modern forms, they were names like **Ashwin** and **Hardman**, **Dodd** and **Kenward**, **Sweetlove** and **Woolmer**. Men of more recent Scandinavian descent might have names like **Hasting** and **Finn**, **Thorold** and **Orme**.

These names look fairly familiar to us because most of them survive today as surnames. Had it not been for the Name Conquest, however, we would have classed them mentally with such names as **Edith**, **Hilda**, **Mildred**; **Alfred**, **Edmund**, **Edward** and **Godwin**, Old English names which also survived the Norman invasion, but are still living as first names.

Norman names

There is ample evidence in medieval documents to show that in each succeeding generation following the arrival of William the Conqueror, Norman names rapidly replaced the English. Apart from the wholesale adoption of 'new' names such as **Alice, Maud, Matilda, Adela, Margery, Rosamond, Muriel, Olive, Emma**; **William, Robert, Richard, Geoffrey, Henry, Hugh, Ralph, Gilbert, Roger** and **Walter**, Englishmen also took on the Norman habit of using the same names over and over again.

Before that it had been the custom to create new names for children by permutating name elements. **Alfred** and **Edith** might call their son **Aldith**, for example. The Norman system was quite different. Names were passed on in the family, or children were named in honour of friends or famous people. A natural result of this practice was to reduce drastically the number of names in use and considerably increase the frequency with which these few names were used.

The Name Conquest provides a clear example of the imitation by a lower social class of the habits of the upper class. Perhaps the use of the new names by the English peasantry was politically necessary to some extent, as a sign that the new regime was accepted and, by implication, admired. Parents may also have turned away from the old names because they would have labelled the bearers as being of English, not Norman, stock—second-class citizens, in other words. Whatever the precise reasons, the naming habits of English-speaking people changed more drastically in a relatively short period after the Conquest than at any time before or since.

Christian names

Another Name Conquest was made about a hundred years later by the Church. For some time the Christian Church in western Europe had been urging its members to use the names of saints or biblical characters for their children. In the thirteenth century heed was at last taken of the Church's teachings. It is clear, in fact, from medieval art and architecture, that the saints in particular assumed great importance at this time. There was a sincere belief in their powers of protection and intercession, and the use of their names can perhaps be put down as further evidence of a belief in name magic.

Many established names, such as **Richard, Robert** and **William**, were fortunate in that they had also been borne by saints; had this not been the case they might well have been in danger. As it was, a flood of new names appeared. **John, Thomas, Paul, Simon, Peter, Matthew, Michael, Gregory, Philip, James, Laurence, Andrew, Stephen, Mark** and **Luke** were used in ever-increasing numbers, matched by female names such as **Mary, Anne, Elizabeth** and **Catherine**. Biblical names like **Adam, Solomon, Abraham, Daniel, David, Joseph, Isaac, Samuel** and **Saul** for the men, **Eva** or **Eve, Sara** or **Sarah, Susan** or **Susannah** for the women, also made their appearance at this time.

Maria, Queen of Aragon, gave birth to a son in 1207. Believing that the twelve apostles had interceded on her behalf to bring about the birth she decided to name her son after one of them:

> *Twelve waxen tapers she hath made*
> *In size and weight the same,*
> *And to each of these twelve tapers*
> *Hath been given an Apostle's name.*
>
> *From that which shall burn the longest,*
> *The infant his name should take,*
> *And the saint who owned it was to be*
> *His patron for his name's sake.*

James's taper lasted longest, and the son was named Jayme.

The one Christian name that was not used, and which has hardly ever been used in the English-speaking world, was that of **Jesus** himself. This compares strangely with the Moslem use of the Prophet's name, **Mohammad**, which is by far the most popular male name in the Islamic world. The Christian use of **Mary**, by contrast, exceeds the use by Moslems of **Fatima** and **Ayesha**, the names respectively of the Prophet's daughter and one of his wives.

In the mid-1970s **Joshua** is coming into fashion in the English-speaking world. Possibly parents who choose it are aware of the fact that it is a variant form of Jesus and use it for that reason. The name **Christian** is also being used increasingly.

By the end of the Middle Ages, around the year 1400, English parents wishing to name a child had in their minds a great many of the names that modern parents would consider. They were influenced, again like modern parents, by local name fashions when they came to make their choice. Dr P. H. Reaney has shown that a **Hamo**, for example, or a **Hamon** or **Hamond**, was seven times as likely to have received those names in Kent at this time than in another part of England. In a similar way, **Martin** was predominantly a Sussex name. Meanwhile, certain names were obviously considered to be 'safe' in all parts of the country. E. G. Withycombe, in her *Oxford Dictionary of English Christian Names*, tells us that by the end of the

*Rabbi Saul Kraft says that **Jesus** was changed from **Jehoshea** because it was an immigrant name.*

When the Bible was more widely and regularly read, biblical names had rather more meaning than they have today. Certain names immediately suggested the characters of the persons who bore them. An anonymous poet made use of this fact in his tribute 'To the pious memory of Dame Dorothy Selby.'

> She was
> In heart a Lydia, and in tongue a Hanna,
> In zeal a Ruth, in wedlock a Susanna,
> Prudently simple, providently wary,
> To the world a Martha, and to heaven a Mary.

Lydia (*Acts* xvi 16) extended hospitality to St Paul at her house in Philippi.

Hanna (1 *Samuel* i 13) 'spake in her heart; only her lips moved, but her voice was not heard.' She was Samuel's mother.

Ruth (*The Book of Ruth*) a kind and faithful woman.

Susanna (*Apocrypha*) falsely accused of infidelity but triumphantly proved innocent.

Martha (*Luke, John*) usually anxious and troubled about domestic matters. The patron saint of housewives.

Mary the reference is presumably to Mary, mother of Jesus, but Martha had a sister Mary who sat at the feet of Jesus listening to him while Martha bustled around.

Some male biblical names which have been associated with a definite character are:

Daniel an upright judge, a person of infallible wisdom

Jeremiah a doleful prophet

Jonah a person who brings bad luck

Judas a traitor

Samson a man of great strength

A doubtful person is still frequently described as a 'doubting **Thomas**' because of the story told of St Thomas in *John* xx 24–29.

Old English names (column 1). These are examples of Old English names which were still in use in London in the twelfth century. They are taken from Eilert Ekwall's *Early London Personal Names*. Had it not been for the Norman Name Conquest these would have been the names handed down to us but, with a few notable exceptions, they were replaced in the following two centuries by:

Norman names (column 2). These are some of the names that were popular amongst the Normans before they came to England, and which they introduced to English-speakers;

Women

OLD ENGLISH		NORMAN		CHRISTIAN	
Alditha	Godrun	Adela	Margery	Agatha	Gillian
Alveva	Golda	Adeline	Marjorie	Agnes	Helena
Edild	Goldburga	Alice	Matilda	Anna	Isabel
Edith	Goldcorna	Amice	Maud	Anne	Joan
Ediva	Goldhen	Avis	Millicent	Barbara	Joanna
Estrilda	Goldyva	Bertha	Muriel	Beatrice	Juliana
Ethelreda	Leofrun	Constance	Olive	Berenice	Juliet
Goda	Leveva	Emma	Oriel	Candace	Katharine
Goditha	Livilda	Emmeline	Rosamond	Catherine	Lois
Godiva	Milda	Jocelyn	Rosamund	Cecilia	Lucia
Godleva	Wakerilda	Joyce	Rose	Chloe	Lucy
		Laura	Sibyl	Clemence	Lydia
		Lauretta	Yvonne	Damaris	Madeleine
				Denise	Margaret
				Dorcas	Martha
				Dorothy	Mary
				Drusilla	Petronella
				Elaine	Priscilla
				Elizabeth	Rhoda
				Ellen	Sapphira
				Eunice	Susanna
				Euphemia	Tabitha

First Names in the Middle Ages

Christian names (column 3). The Church also made a Name Conquest, persuading the faithful to use biblical and saints' names. Those listed here are mainly from the New Testament, though a few popular saints' names are included. Common names from the Old Testament also came into use at this time. They are included in the lists on pages 68–9.

Men

OLD ENGLISH		NORMAN		CHRISTIAN	
Ailmar	Godman	Alan	Ivo	Adrian	Mark
Ailred	Godric	Amery	Jermyn	Ambrose	Martin
Ailsi	Godwin	Archibald	Joel	Andrew	Matthew
Albold	Goldwin	Arnold	Leonard	Anthony	Matthias
Aldred	Harding	Barnard	Lewis	Austin	Nathaniel
Alfred	Hardred	Bernard	Louis	Augustine	Nicholas
Alfric	Herbert	Bevis	Maurice	Barnabas	Pancras
Algar	Hereward	Brian	Morris	Bartholomew	Patrick
Alnod	Ingulf	Conan	Odo	Benedict	Paul
Alsi	Leofric	Denis	Oliver	Boniface	Peter
Alward	Leofstan	Drew	Otto	Christopher	Philip
Alwin	Mervin	Durand	Payn	Clement	Rufus
Alwold	Norman	Eustace	Piers	Cornelius	Sebastian
Bermund	Ordric	Everard	Ralph	Crispin	Silas
Bruning	Ormar	Fulbert	Raymond	Damian	Silvanus
Brunloc	Osbert	Fulk	Rayner	Fabian	Simon
But	Osmund	Geoffrey	Reynold	Felix	Stephen
Coleman	Sagar	Gerald	Richard	George	Sylvester
Derman	Saward	Gerard	Robert	Gregory	Thomas
Edgar	Sperling	Gervase	Roger	James	Timothy
Edmer	Swetman	Gilbert	Roland	Jason	Titus
Edric	Theodgar	Hamlet	Rolf	John	Urban
Edmund	Theodric	Hamo	Viel	Laurence	Valentine
Edstan	Theodulf	Henry	Walter	Lucas	Vincent
Edulf	Watman	Hugh	Warren	Luke	Zebedee
Edward	Wulfred	Humphrey	William	Marcus	
Estmar	Wulfric	Ingram			
Estmund	Wulmar				
Fromund	Wymar				
Gladwin	Wymond				

fourteenth century the five names **Henry, John, Richard, Robert** and **William** together accounted for over sixty per cent of Englishmen.

Girls' names

More male than female names occur in medieval records, and this is partly due to the fact that many male names were borne by women. **Philippa** rather than **Philip** might be written down in Church Latin if it referred to a girl, but this was only to satisfy the rules of Latin grammar. The girl concerned would actually have been *called* Philip. Records which are entirely in English make this clear. The spoken use of such feminine forms as Philippa was not to come until very much later.

When girls *were* given genuinely feminine names, their parents were inclined then, as they have been ever since, to seek out more exotic names for them than for their brothers. Names like **Camilla, Cassandra, Extranea, Grecia, Ismenia, Italia, Lavina, Leda, Melodia, Norma** and **Pavia** are to be found borne by English girls as early as the twelfth century. Several of these are still in use today, either in their Latin or English forms. Camilla, Cassandra and Norma were all to be found amongst students graduating in American universities in 1975. Melodia, in the form **Melody**, has long enjoyed a quiet but consistent popularity in America and Britain. It now names a character in a popular television cartoon series.

But I do not want to imply that every girl in the Middle Ages was given an unusual name. **Isabel, Juliana, Margaret, Mary** and **Matilda** were probably the five most frequently used girls' names at the end of the four-teenth century, but they would not have accounted for as many girls between them as the five boys' names already mentioned. There was less of a tendency to clothe girls in an onomastic uniform, as it were.

Pet forms

Just as uniforms make it difficult to distinguish individuals in a group, so the extraordinary commonness of a few names might seem to have made the identification of individuals difficult in the Middle Ages. But the English had taken over another naming habit from the Normans. If there were now countless Williams and Johns around, they mostly had by the fourteenth century a secondary name, one which was to settle down and become a hereditary surname. Nicknames must also have been common, and if these failed to individualize, there were the many pet forms of the standard names which provided variety.

There were far more pet forms in use at the time than there are today. Nowadays a man whose name is officially John might be called **Johnny** or **Jack**. In the Middle Ages, when the name had recently been introduced from France as **Johan** or **Jehan**, he could also have become **Jan, Jen, Jon**—and with the addition of -kin, **Jankin, Jenkin** or **Jonkin**. Other diminutive endings led to **Janin, Jonin, Jenin**, and to the feminine **Janet**. Johan also gave **Han** as a pet form, and this in turn led to **Hankin** and **Hancock**. The -cock ending seems to have been used in the same way as the -ny of Johnny, converting the name into a friendly form.

Jack as a pet form of John seems rather odd, but the form Jankin is said to be its origin. Pronounced by the Normans, Jankin is likely to have emerged as **Jackin**, and this in turn could have given Jack. The French name **Jacques** must also have been influential. It does not derive from the same name as John, but in terms of usage in France and England, the two names were roughly the same.

William also had more diminutive forms than today, though **Bill** does not seem to have been one of them. **Will** was obviously common; so too were **Wilkin, Wilkie, Wilcock, Wilmot, Willet**. We have clear evidence that all these various forms were used, for in most cases they became fossilized as surnames. I shall be discussing that topic further in the next chapter.

And in fact, very brief though this survey of name usage in the Middle Ages has been, I shall make that my cue to move on. In this book our interest is more in the use of first names in the last hundred years than in their use 600 years ago. It is worth making the point, however, that many of the names currently well-used in the English-speaking world have a very long ancestry indeed. They were already 'old' names when the Normans introduced them to English-speakers, or when our ancestors borrowed them from the Bible and Saints' Calendar. They were 'new' names to the English in the Middle Ages, but with 600 years of continual use they have become an essential part of our cultural background.

6 Super Names

Development and use of surnames

By the end of the Middle Ages, as we saw, there was a tendency to use a small number of names over and over again. Inevitably, as the population increased, secondary names came into use to distinguish the many **Johns** and **Williams** from one another. These secondary names were at first little more than nicknames, applying only to the individuals concerned, but slowly they began to be passed from one generation to the next. To describe the new kind of hereditary family names, the French term *surnom* was adapted as 'surname'. The sur- in surname is ultimately from the Latin word *super*, which can mean 'in addition' as well as 'above'. In a sense, then, we can all claim to have 'super names'.

Surnames are obviously fascinating in themselves, but this is not the place for me to deal in detail with their origins. I did in fact discuss the different categories of surnames and gave a great many of their meanings in my *Guinness Book of Names* (1974). I also gave there a full bibliography of books dealing with surnames, and included advice on how to trace the origins of rarer names. But there are at least two special ways in which surnames are linked to first names which justify a mention here. Firstly, there are the many surnames which actually contain a first name and mean 'descendant of' or 'servant of' the person named. These are names like Jones (**John**), Hobson (**Robert**), Parry (**Henry**), Watkins (**Walter**), and so on. Secondly, there are the names which we primarily consider to be surnames but which are used as first names. In this group are names like **Dwight**, **Dexter** and **Craig**. A few names, such as **Willis** and **Nelson**, fall into both categories.

First names in surnames

Surnames which are based on first names do not always make the original name obvious. Richardson may be easy to interpret as the 'son of **Richard**',

*John Wayne was born **Marion** Michael Morrison. The name was regularly used for boys in U.S.A. to honour General Francis Marion. The surname, like the girl's name, was a derivative of **Mary**.*

but Dixon and Higgins, say, offer less help. Dixon is another form of '**Dick**'s son', just as Nixon is '**Nick**'s son'. The spelling with 'x' represents a convenient shorthand form of that central cluster of letters.

As for Higgins, we have to remember that when surnames were coming into being, **Hick** as well as Dick was an accepted form of Richard. Hick has now died out as a name, though we still use it as a word to describe an unsophisticated provincial. A friendly form of Hick in the Middle Ages was **Hickin**, which in some dialects became **Higgin**. This led to Higgin's son or servant, Higgins for short. All this may seem a bit tortuous now, but to our medieval ancestors Higgins was as natural a development from Richard as Richards or Richardson.

Many other surnames derive from Richard in a similar way. The full name led to Richardes, Ritchard and Richarson. As **Rich** it gave a surname in that form, also Ritch, Riche and Riches. Dick produced everything from Dix, Deakes and Dickens to Diggin and Dicketts. Hick gave such names as Hickling and Hickmer, apart from the Higgins we have already seen. As if that were not enough, other forms of Richard—**Rick** and **Hitch**—produced a further crop of surnames, including Rickert, Rickett, Hitchcock, Hedgecoe and Hiskett.

It was mostly men's names which led to surnames of this type, but women's names could be used for illegitimate children, the sons and daughters of widows, and possibly the descendants of any woman who had assumed a special social importance.

There are some families who make a habit of using a particular first name in each generation, usually giving it to at least one child as a middle name. One can see the point of this wish for continuity in the case of women, who will normally give up their hereditary surnames at marriage. Many families, however, probably without being aware of it, are still using the first name of a remote ancestor because it happened to become fossilized as a surname. I provide on pages 60–61 further examples of these surnames which are first names in disguise.

Surnames as first names

But what of the reverse case, where a surname is given as a first name? The antiquary William Camden gave some of the arguments for and against the practice in 1605:

A great many of the surnames in use in the English-speaking world derive from first names. I show here some of the surnames produced by six common male names.

Henry	Fitzhenry	Harrison	Hendersen	Hendrix	Henrey
	Harrie	Harriss	Henderson	Hendry	Henrice
	Harries	Harry	Hendrey	Heneries	Henry
	Harriman	Heintz	Hendrie	Henery	Hinkins
	Harriot	Heinz	Hendrik	Henkin	Parry
	Harris	Henderix	Hendriks	Henn	Perry

Hugh	Fitzhugh	Hewkin	Howe	Huet	Huleatt
	Hew	Hewlett	Howes	Huetson	Hulett
	Hewat	Hewlins	Howett	Hughes	Hullett
	Hewell	Hewlitt	Howitt	Hughson	Hullot
	Hewes	Hews	Howkins	Hugo	Huot
	Hewet	Hewson	Howlett	Huison	Huson
	Hewetson	Hookins	Hows	Huitson	Husset
	Hewett	Hooson	Howson	Huitt	Hussett
	Hewison	Hoosun	Huchon	Hukin	Husson
	Hewitson	How	Huckin	Hukins	Huws
	Hewitt	Howat	Hue	Hulatt	Ugo

John	Fitzjohn	Jacketts	Janik	Jenkerson	Jinkinson
	Geen	Jacklin	Janin	Jenking	Jinks
	Genn	Jackling	Jannings	Jenkin	Joanes
	Hancock	Jackman	Jannis	Jenkins	Johncock
	Handcock	Jacks	Janos	Jenkinson	Johncook
	Hancox	Jackson	Jans	Jenkyns	Johnes
	Handel	Jacot	Janse	Jenn	Johns
	Hankin	Jacson	Jansen	Jenne	Johnson
	Hanking	Jagg	Janus	Jennens	Johnston
	Hankins	Jaggs	Jaxon	Jenness	Johnstone
	Hann	Jagson	Jayne	Jennett	Joinson
	Hendel	Jaine	Jean	Jennings	Jones
	Henkin	Jakeman	Jeanes	Jennins	Jonson
	Hinkins	Jakes	Jeans	Jennis	Jonsson
	Jackalin	Jan	Jecks	Jenns	Joynes
	Jack	Jane	Jeeks	Jenyns	Joynson
	Jacke	Janek	Jeens	Jex	Junkin
	Jackes	Janes	Jencken	Jeynes	Junkinson
	Jackett	Janet	Jenings	Jinkin	Junkison

Richard	Dekin	Dickason	Dicken	Dickerson	Dickey
	Dekins	Dicke	Dickens	Dickeson	Dickie
	Dick	Dickels	Dickenson	Dicketts	Dickin

Richard
continued

			Hitchmough	Richardson
Dickings	Digings	Higman	Hitchmough	Richardson
Dickins	Digman	Hiscott	Hix	Richarson
Dickinson	Dix	Hiscutt	Hixson	Riche
Dickison	Dixon	Hiskett	Hudd	Riches
Dickman	Dixson	Hitch	Hudden	Rick
Dickons	Dykins	Hitchcock	Huddle	Rickard
Dicks	Hick	Hitchcoe	Hudman	Rickardes
Dickson	Hicken	Hitchcott	Hudsmith	Rickards
Digan	Hickens	Hitchcox	Hudson	Rickeard
Digance	Hickes	Hitchen	Hutson	Rickerd
Diggan	Hickeson	Hitchens	Hytch	Rickert
Diggen	Hickin	Hitcheon	Ricard	Ricket
Diggens	Hicking	Hitches	Ricarde	Rickets
Digges	Hicklin	Hitcheson	Ricards	Rickett
Diggines	Hickling	Hitchin	Riccard	Ricketts
Diggins	Hickman	Hitching	Riccards	Ricks
Diggle	Hickmott	Hitchings	Rich	Ritch
Diggles	Hicks	Hitchins	Richardes	Ritchard
Diggon	Hickson	Hitchman	Richards	Rix

Robert

Dabb	Dobing	Hobson	Rabjohn	Robeson
Dabbs	Dobinson	Hopkin	Rablan	Robespierre
Dabinett	Dobson	Hopkins	Rablen	Robey
Dabson	Doby	Hopkinson	Rablin	Robin
Dobb	Dopson	Hopkyns	Robard	Robinet
Dobbe	Hob	Hopson	Robart	Robins
Dobbie	Hobb	Nobbs	Robarts	Robinson
Dobbin	Hobbes	Nobes	Robbens	Robison
Dobbing	Hobbins	Nopps	Robberds	Robjant
Dobbings	Hobbis	Nops	Robbin	Robjohn
Dobbins	Hobbiss	Rabb	Robbings	Robjohns
Dobbinson	Hobbs	Rabbatts	Robbins	Robkins
Dobbison	Hobday	Rabbets	Robcarts	Roblett
Dobbs	Hobdey	Rabbetts	Robens	Roblin
Dobby	Hobkinson	Rabbits	Robers	Robson
Dobbyn	Hoblin	Rabbitt	Roberson	Roby
Dobey	Hobling	Rabbitts	Roberts	Robyns
Dobieson	Hoblyn	Rabett	Robertson	Ropkins

William
(*Guillaume*
in its
French
form.)

Fitzwilliam	Wilcock	Wilkinson	Williamson	Willmot
Fitzwilliams	Wilcocke	Wilks	Williman	Willmott
Gellman	Wilcocks	Willament	Williment	Willot
Gelman	Wilcockson	Willard	Willimont	Willott
Gillman	Wilcox	Willcock	Willimott	Willson
Gilman	Wilcoxson	Willcocks	Willis	Wilman
Guillerman	Wilk	Willcox	Willitt	Wilme
Wellemin	Wilke	Willeson	Willman	Wilmot
Wellerman	Wilkens	Willet	Willment	Wilmott
Welliam	Wilkes	Willets	Willmes	Wilmsen
Wellman	Wilkin	Willett	Willmett	Wilmut
Welman	Wilkings	Willetts	Willmetts	Wilsen
Wilck	Wilkins	Williams	Willmin	Wilson

Whereas in late years surnames have been given for Christian names among us, and nowhere else in Christendom; although many dislike it, for that great inconvenience will ensue, nevertheless it seemeth to proceed from hearty good will, and affection of the Godfathers to shew their love, or from a desire to continue and propagate their own names to succeeding ages.

Camden was not necessarily objective in his comments, for the practice of using surnames in this way was mainly an upper-class habit in the sixteenth and seventeenth centuries. He himself was nothing if not diplomatic, and whatever his own views he would have been careful not to condemn aristocratic behaviour. He goes on, in fact, to say that the habit 'is in no wise to be disliked, but rather approved . . . in worshipful ancient families.'

He quotes the examples of men who had been given the names **Pickering, Grevil, Bassingburne** and **Calthorp** in honour of godfathers who made them their heirs. To further justify the practice, Camden adds: 'Besides the continuation of the name we see that the self-name, yea, and sometime the similitude of names, doth kindle sparks of love and liking among mere strangers.' Others have argued along these lines, but I am not sure that there is any evidence to support the claim.

No-one, presumably, would object to Camden's basic idea of keeping alive a family name that would otherwise die out. These days such a surname would simply become a middle name and there would be no problem. At the beginning of the seventeenth century, middle names hardly existed. Camden himself states firmly: 'Two christian names are rare in England.' If a surname was to survive in his day, in a family where there were no sons, it had to become the first name of a godson or nephew.

Extended use of surnames as first names

But Camden hints elsewhere that quite a different use of surnames as first names had already begun in England. 'Surnames of honourable and worshipful families are given now to mean men's children for christian names.' This, in Camden's view, is an 'inconvenience'. He presumably attributed the practice to a base motive—a wish to profit from a name that had high status value—rather than a wish to show regard for the person whose name was borrowed. Perhaps he simply did not like to see the names of noblemen being associated in any way with ordinary people.

Like it or not, some such names were later to become very common as first names, but it is unlikely that modern parents who give their children names like **Clifford, Desmond, Clive, Sidney, Rodney, Russell, Stanley** and **Leslie** think of them as surnames which are being used as first names. They have been first names in their own right now for several generations, and no-one would expect the bearers of such names to be connected in any way with the families concerned. With Rodney and Stanley, in fact, as with names like **Nelson, Jackson, Lee, Jefferson, Lincoln** and **Washington**, distant hero-worship coupled with a strong national pride was almost certainly the original reason for their use as first names, not a personal family tie. A different kind of admiration would originally have accounted for **Calvin, Luther** and **Wesley** being used as first names amongst the followers of those religious leaders, and for the use of **Homer, Byron, Milton** and the like amongst lovers of literature.

In the case of nationally famous people, the idea of using the surname as a first name will occur spontaneously to many parents. With a family like the Leslies, however, well-known in Scotland but not elsewhere, it is more difficult to understand why the name began to spread. In the case of Leslie, this had already begun to happen before Leslie Howard came on the scene, just as **Shirley** was already becoming popular in the U.S.A. before Shirley Temple appeared. The latter name, according to Charlotte Brontë in her novel *Shirley*, was first used by men after being converted from a surname. **Douglas**, on the other hand, put to use as a first name as long ago as the seventeenth century although before that it had been a Scottish surname, was formerly used for girls as well as boys.

Another surname turned first name which has undergone a sex-change is **Tracy** or **Tracey**. Dickens uses Tracy Tupman as a man's name, but it is now very firmly established as a girl's name and has recently enjoyed a remarkable popularity. In my view, incidentally, it is more likely to have come from the surname than from **Teresa** or **Theresa**, as some authorities will have it.

The creation of 'new' first names by transferring surnames continues all the time in the English-speaking world. Currently enjoying various degrees of popularity are **Scott, Curtis, Ryan, Ashley, Bradley, Clyde, Todd, Marshall, Craig, Glenn, Travis, Wayne** and **Cameron** for boys; **Kimberly** or **Kimberley, Stacy, Hayley** and **Kelly** for girls. All these are frequently enough used to make them familiar as first names, associated fairly clearly with one sex. In that respect they are as satisfactory as any other first names. They are also subject to the same drawbacks. Tracy and Tracey have been almost *too* popular in the last ten years, and once parents realize this they will quickly turn elsewhere. There will thus come a time

---

Some surnames have a rather dampening effect on the first names that precede them. The examples quoted below have an additional interest in that all were borne by contestants in the Miss America contest: ***Alberta Futch, Lorene Snoddy, Jenelle Strange, Flora Sleeper, Dulcie Scripture, Roberta Tarbox.***

A family's surname often influences the choice of first name in one way or another. The following examples are derived from various sources, mostly American, and all are authentic names. The influence of the surname on the first name seems to be especially marked.

Nancy Ancey	Goldie Goldfarb	Marybelle Merryweather
John B. A. Angel	Pink Green	Asia Minor
Cora Apple	Shade Green	Monte Montgomery
Etta Apple	Dyer Greene	Savage Nettles
Orange Apple	Gregory Grinn	Penny Nichols
Savage Bear	Early Guest	Boyle O'Boyle
Pleasure Bird	Sin Hall	Offing Offing
Truie Blue	Virginia Ham	Iona Outhouse
Charity Booth	Pearl Handel	More Payne
Alice Self Boss	Maine Hills	Precious Person
Shady Bower	Hard Hitch	Wilder Person
Lent Bride	Ima Hogg	Mince Pie
Tiney Bugg	Grove Hurst	Duck Pool
Duckworth Byrd	Lizzie Izabichie	Good Price
Christmas Carroll	River Jordan	Quentin Quay
Royal Chamberlain	Comfort Joy	Pearline Queen
Merry Christmas	Love Joy	Freeze Quick
Baker Cook	Tom Katz	Top Roe
Choice Cook	Pleasant Kidd	Rose Rose
Meat Cook	Winsome Kidd	True Scales
Golden Day	Gracious King	Annie Seed
May Day	Prince Knight	William Shake Spear
Rose Dew	Paschal Lamb	April Shivers
Parker Doreman	Moses Law	Silver Spoon
Louis Dorr	Rose Leaf	Love Spooner
May B. Dunn	Shanda Lear	Pearl Green Stone
Ireland England	Tiny Little	Fair Swann
Georgia Farmer	Handsome Lockett	Merry Tydings
Vinch Finch	Hope Lord	June Weed
Preserved Fish	Lorin Lorinsky	Crystal White
William Thrower Fitts	Juicy Love	Green Wood
Early Flowers	U. R. Low	Mollie Wollie
Grant Freelove	Strong Man	Love Wright
Pearly Gates	June May March	Since Wynn
Letcher Goforth	Waxes Merry	Tell C. Yelle

REGISTRATION DISTRICT _Easing..._

_18 45_ Birth in the Sub-district of _Easington_

No.	When and where born	Name, if any	Sex	Name and surname of father	Name, surname and maiden surname of mother	Occupatic of father
Columns:— 1	2	3	4	5	6	
399	Seventeenth of June 1845 Thornley	Streaker	Boy	James Smith	Ann Smith formerly Streaker	...

CERTIFIED to be a true copy of an entry in the certified copy of a Register of Births in the Di
Given at the GENERAL REGISTER OFFICE, LONDON, under the Seal of the said Office, th

This certificate is issued in pursuance of the Births and Deaths Registratio
purporting to be sealed or stamped with the seal of the General Register
relates without any further or other proof of the entry, and no certified c
force or effect unless it is sealed or stamped as aforesaid.

BXA173800

CAUTION:— Any person who (1) falsifies any of the particulars on this
false, is liable to prosecution.

Form A502M 51-4793 90M 11/74 McC

'Use of a maiden surname sometimes leads to a very unusual first name. Streaker Smith was
fortunate to be named in 1845, long before "streaker" acquired its modern sense.'

when a girl bearing one form or the other of this name will be clearly labelled
as having been born in the 1960s or 1970s, just as we now associate Shirley,
on the whole, with women born in the mid-1930s.

Advantages and disadvantages of surname first names

As for the many surnames converted to first name status by individual
families, each one must be judged on its merits. If **Robinson** Crusoe, for
example, were a modern businessman, his first name would be no problem
to him. His 'girl Friday' would probably call him **Bob**. Other surnames,
such as **Willis**, are similarly useful in suggesting familiar pet forms. With
some names it is actually quite difficult to know whether they are transferred
surnames or merely alternative forms of standard first names. Is **Morris**
really a Morris, or is he a **Maurice**? Is **Allen** simply a disguised **Alan**?
Mitchell is presumably not a **Michel**, but the use of that surname as a first
name is helped by the resemblance it bears to the French form of **Michael**.

> *Peter de Vries is one who amuses himself with what he calls 'paronomastic' names. The idea is to invent a suitable surname for a first name. A few examples:* **Eileen** *Dover,* **Gustave** *Wind,* **Lorne** *Order,* **Justin** *Case,* **Herbie** *Hind.*
>
> *Another humorist invented the surname Sexauer, so that he could tell the tale of a new employee, not known to the switchboard girl.*
>
> *Caller: Oh, hello. Do you have a Sexauer there?*
> *Girl: Sexauer! We don't even have a coffee break.*

Other names used as first names leave one in no doubt of their origin. Such names will not 'date' their bearers, but they will share the disadvantages of any first name that is rather unusual. We shall be discussing that subject later. On the credit side, perhaps, the use of an obvious surname as a first name may suggest that the bearer has a 'good' social background. As Camden made clear with regard to seventeenth-century usage, 'worshipful and ancient families' tended to use surnames as first names. Since then several American presidents have been known by such names, and the practice appears to be popular in American families of high social standing.

It is probably true to say that more surnames occur as first names in North America and Scotland than in England and Wales. The Scottish usage seems to be a natural development from using maiden surnames as middle names, thus half-converting them to first names. American usage, judging from the kind of names used in former times, once reflected the fierce national pride of people who were establishing a national identity. Some members of my own family, typical American immigrants, left England bearing names like **Joseph**, **William** and **Daniel**. Their grandchildren, however, bore names like **Jefferson** and **Madison**.

Surnames will obviously continue to be used as first names to some extent, and inevitably misunderstandings will occur on occasion. One of my correspondents once told me of an embarrassing experience which befell his aunt many years ago. His uncle's first name was **Smith**, and all went well until the Reverend J. Smith came to stay with them for a few days. The guest was shown into the parlour and talked with his host, Mr Smith Clarkson. When Mrs Clarkson came into the room she said thoughtlessly: 'Now, Smith, get the kettle on and let's have a cup of tea.' To her horror, the clergyman immediately rose to his feet and headed for the kitchen. He was perfectly reconciled to the idea of working for his keep.

At the age of ninety-two, my correspondent told me, his aunt still became agitated when she told this story. It perhaps makes the point that there will always be some slight danger in using a surname as a first name.

7 Reformed Names

First names in the seventeenth century

When almost any noteworthy event occurs in a country, it will be reflected to some extent in the first names of its citizens. *Concorde*, for instance, went into regular service from London airport in 1976 and was heard passing overhead by a mother giving birth to her child. The name of the aircraft immediately became one of the names of her child. As it happens, **Concorde** is not so unusual as a first name; the Latin form **Concordia** has occasionally been given to children.

Around the time that **Neil** Armstrong stepped onto the moon, many American parents chose his name for their sons in a personal commemoration of the historic event. In 1887 the vicar of Glossop, in England, reported that he baptized a girl **Jubilata**, 'because she was born in the year of the Queen's Jubilee'.

Revolutionary names

The greater the event, the more the names that will result from it. The American Civil War caused the surnames of many generals to be used as first names. In the Soviet Union the Revolution subsequently led many parents to name their sons **Vladimir** in honour of V. I. Lenin. It was not long before new names began to appear, similarly inspired by Lenin. They included **Lenian, Leniana, Vilen, Vilena, Vilenina, Vladilen, Vladilena, Vladlen, Lenina** and **Ninel**. The last of these shows a method of forming a 'new' name that has had a widespread appeal in the English-speaking world—an existing name is simply spelt backwards. The method is usually used to create trade names, boat names, house names and the like rather than first names, though **Senga** is popular in Scotland and I have come across names like **Azile**.

In the sixteenth century the great social revolution in England, as in many European countries, was a religious one. The English dispute with the

Protestants of the sixteenth and seventeenth centuries turned away from first names that did not have biblical sanction. The Old Testament now became a major source of names. The selection below shows the range it offered, though some of the names were obviously used more than others.

Men

Aaron	Barak	Gabriel	Job	Nimrod
Abdias	Baruch	Gad	Joel	Noah
Abednego	Barzillai	Gamaliel	Jonah	Obadiah
Abdon	Belteshazzar	Gershom	Jonathan	Obed
Abel	Benaiah	Gideon	Joseph	Omri
Abiasaph	Benjamin	Gog	Joshua	Onesiphorous
Abiathar	Benoni	Habakkuk	Judah	Pashur
Abiel	Bezaleel	Ham	Kish	Pelatiah
Abiezer	Boaz	Hananiah	Korah	Pharoah
Abimelech	Buz	Heber	Laban	Phineas
Abinadab	Cain	Heman	Lamech	Rahab
Abner	Caleb	Heth	Lemuel	Ram
Abraham	Canaan	Hilkiah	Levi	Reuben
Abram	Cush	Hiram	Lot	Samson
Absalom	Cyrus	Hosea	Magog	Samuel
Achan	Dan	Hoshea	Malachi	Saul
Adam	Daniel	Hur	Manasseh	Seth
Adlai	Darius	Ichabod	Melchizedek	Shadrach
Adonijah	David	Ira	Meshech	Shallum
Agabus	Ebenezer	Isaac	Methuselah	Shelah
Ahab	Eleazar	Isaiah	Micah	Shem
Ahaz	Elhanan	Israel	Michael	Simeon
Ahaziah	Eli	Jabez	Moab	Solomon
Amariah	Eliab	Jacob	Mordecai	Tobiah
Amaziah	Eliakim	Jael	Moses	Uri
Amnon	Elias	Jeduthun	Nabal	Uriah
Amos	Eliezer	Jehoash	Naboth	Vashni
Ananias	Elihu	Jehoiada	Nadab	Zachariah
Antipas	Elisha	Jehoiakim	Nahor	Zadok
Araunah	Elkanah	Jehoram	Nahum	Zarah
Asa	Elnathan	Jehoshaphat	Naphtali	Zebulon
Asael	Enoch	Jephthah	Nathan	Zechariah
Asher	Ephraim	Jeremiah	Nebuchad-	Zephaniah
Azariah	Er	Jeroboam	nezzar	Ziba
Baasha	Esau	Jesse	Nehemiah	
Balaam	Ezekiel	Jethro	Neriah	
Balak	Ezra	Joab	Nethaniah	

Women

Abigail	Athaliah	Hadassah	Maachah	Sarah
Abihail	Bathsheba	Hannah	Mara	Sarai
Abijah	Beulah	Hazelponi	Mehetabel	Sharon
Abishag	Bilhah	Hephzibah	Michal	Tamar
Achsah	Deborah	Jezebel	Milcah	Vashti
Adah	Delilah	Kerenhap-	Miriam	Zillah
Adnah	Dinah	puch	Naomi	Zipporah
Ahinoam	Eglah	Keturah	Rachel	
Aholibamah	Esther	Keziah	Rebekah	
Aphrah	Eve	Leah	Ruth	

The more extreme Puritans at this time turned to abstract 'virtue' or 'slogan' names. One or two of the examples given below were permanently accepted into the first name stock. Most, for obvious reasons, did not come into general use.

Abstinence	Fear-not	Increased	Remember
Accepted	Felicity	Job-raked-out-of-	Renewed
Amity	Fight-the-good-	the-ashes	Repentance
Arise	fight-of-faith	Joy	Resolved
Ashes	Fly-debate	Joy-again	Return
Be-courteous	Fly-fornication	Just	Safe-deliverance
Be-faithful	Forsaken	Kill-sin	Safe-on-high
Be-thankful	Fortune	Lament	Salvation
Charity	Freegift	Lamentation	Search-the-
Comfort	From-above	Love	scriptures
Confidence	Given	Make-peace	Seek-wisdom
Consider	Godly	Meek	Sin-deny
Constant	God-reward	Mercy	Small hope
Continent	Grace	More-fruit	Sorry-for-sin
Delivery	Gracious	More-trial	Stand-fast-on-high
Desire	Handmaid	Much-mercy	Steadfast
Diligence	Hate-evil	No-merit	Temperance
Discipline	Helpless	Obedience	Thankful
Donation	Help-on-high	Patience	The-Lord-is-near
Dust	Honour	Peaceable	The-peace-of-God
Earth	Hope	Perseverance	Tribulation
Elected	Hope-for	Praise-God	Truth
Experience	Hopeful	Prudence	Verity
Faint-not	Hope-still	Purify	Weep-not
Faith	Humble	Redeemed	Wrestling
Faith-my-joy	Humiliation	Reformation	
Fear	Humility	Rejoice	

Roman Catholic Church led to the establishment of the Church of England and ultimately to the emergence of the Protestant extremists known as Puritans.

The rejection of Catholic rites and practices included a rejection of the first names that the Church had recommended to its followers. The most obviously Catholic names were those of its own saints, men like **Augustine** and **Benedict**, women like **Barbara** and **Agnes**, revered by the Church but lacking the authority of scriptural sanction. Protestants generally, and the Puritans in particular, hastily turned away from such names. At first they replaced them with names from the Bible, especially the Old Testament. Later, some Puritans were to create their own distinctive names, aggressively proclaiming their beliefs.

Our ancestors in the sixteenth century named their children rather as we do. They chose names which would attract no undue attention in the society in which they lived. We tend to show by the names we choose that we are aware of current trends and taboos: at that time it was far more essential for parents to do so. For those who lived in Puritan communities, for example, to have continued to use the names of the non-scriptural saints would have been like English-speaking parents calling their son **Adolf** in the middle of World War Two.

Puritan names

Some Old Testament names were already familiar to the Protestant congregations. Since the Middle Ages the main stories from the Bible had been acted out annually in simple form for the benefit of the illiterate masses. **Adam, Eve, Noah** and the like were thus well-known, but with the need for new names to replace those that were disgraced, ministers dug more deeply into their Genevan Bibles. Children now became **Habakkuk** or **Shadrach**, **Keturah** or **Hephzibah**. So inappropriate were some of the names used at this time that it is difficult not to imagine a kind of biblical roulette being played. The Bible seems to have been opened at random and the first name that was seen immediately adopted.

Archie Armstrong, who was Court Jester to James I and Charles I in the early seventeenth century, wrote a Banquet of Jests and Merry Tales. *One of his stories concerns a Welshman who was reading the chapter in the Old Testament in which the generations of Adam are set out. The Welshman tried to cope with* **Cainan** *begat* **Mahaleel**, *who begat* **Jared**, *etc., but found 'the names very difficult that he could scarce reade them. And so saith he: "They begat one another to the end of the chapter."'*

This kind of blind acceptance did not become widespread. While unusual Old Testament names have continued to be used occasionally down to the present century, it is only the names of the more important figures which have been used a great deal. Consideration has also been given to whether a name 'fits in' with other names and words in English. **Kerenhappuch**, say, clearly does not fit in easily; **Rachel** and **Sarah** do.

The Bible was thus to prove unsatisfactory on occasions as a Naming the Baby book, but it almost certainly did better in general than the imagination of a few fanatical Puritan ministers. With the best of intentions, no doubt, some such men persuaded parents to use edifying slogans as their children's first names. A glance at the list of names on page 69 will show the results, a group of names acceptable only to those whose religious philosophy really was puritanical. Used within a tightly-knit community they may have become familiar and normal, but others saw the names as yet another example of the Puritans' eccentric behaviour. Most of the names did not survive for fairly obvious reasons. Some of the more reasonable abstract names, like **Mercy** and **Charity**, lived on, though Charles Dickens did those particular names, with their pleasant pet forms **Merry** and **Cherry**, an ill-service by portraying the Pecksniff daughters in *Martin Chuzzlewit* as highly unsympathetic.

Camden's 'usual names'

The Puritan names were used by only a small section of the community. For a more general picture of the names in the minds of Englishmen at the beginning of the seventeenth century we can turn to a book which, like all writers on personal names, I am compelled to refer to frequently: *Remains Concerning Britain*, by William Camden. In this he set down in 1605 a list of the first names 'most usual to the English nation'. I give his list in full, though without his explanations for the names, on pages 72–73.

Not all the names mentioned were being currently used in England when Camden wrote, neither does he differentiate between names that were occasionally used and those used a great deal. He presumably based his list on extensive reading, which in his case included many antiquarian works, as well as personal knowledge. He had been a schoolmaster at one time, so that he would have noted the names of his upper-class pupils.

The list of names must therefore be considered as no more than well-informed guess-work, a personal impression of the first names being used in England in the seventeenth century and before. Camden seems to have realized that the more unusual Puritan names, such as **Freegift** and **Reformation**, would not become part of the general name stock, for he dealt with them in a separate paragraph and omitted them from his main list. But he includes many Old English names, such as **Ethelstan** and

'Here will I set down alphabetically the names which we now call Christian names, most usual to the English nation . . .'

William Camden, *Remains Concerning Britain*, 1605

Aaron	Benjamin	Elmer	Giles	Jonathan
Abel	Bernard	Emanuel	Godard	Jordan
Adam	Bertrand	Engelbert	Godfrey	Joseph
Adelard	Blase	Enion	Godrich	Joshuah
Adolph	Bonaventure	Erasmus	Godwin	Josias
Adrian	Boniface	Ernest	Gregory	Julius
Aelward	Botolph	Esau	Griffith	Kenard
Alan	Brian	Ethelbert	Grimbald	Kenhelm
Alban	Cadwallader	Ethelred	Guy	Lambert
Albert	Caesar	Ethelstan	Hamon	Lancelot
Aldred	Caius	Ethelwold	Hannibal	Laurence
Alexander	Caleb	Ethelwolph	Harhold	Lazarus
Alfred	Calisthenes	Eusebius	Hector	Leger
Alphonse	Caradoc	Eustache	Hengest	Leofstan
Alwin	Charles	Eutropius	Henry	Leofwin
Ambrose	Christopher	Evan	Herbert	Leonard
Amery	Chrysostom	Everard	Hercules	Leopold
Amias	Clemens	Ezechias	Herman	Lewis
Ananias	Constantine	Ezechiel	Herwin	Lewlin
Andrew	Conrad	Fabian	Hierome	Lionel
Angel	Cornelius	Felix	Hilary	Ludovic
Anselm	Crescens	Ferdinand	Hildebert	Luke
Anthony	Cuthbert	Florence	Horatio	Madoc
Archibald	Cyprian	Francis	Howel	Malachias
Arnold	Daniel	Frederic	Hubert	Manasses
Arthur	David	Fremund	Hugh	Marcel
Augustine	Demetrius	Fulbert	Humphrey	Mark
Avery	Denis	Fulcher	Ingram	Marmaduke
Baldwin	Drogo	Fulke	Isaac	Martin
Balthazar	Dunstan	Gabriel	Israel	Matthew
Baptist	Eadulph	Gamaliel	Jacob	Maugre
Bardulph	Ealdred	Garret	James	Maurice
Barnabas	Ealred	Gawain	Jasper	Maximilian
Bartholomew	Edgar	George	Jeremy	Mercury
Baruch	Edmund	Geoffrey	Joab	Meredith
Basil	Edward	German	Joachim	Michael
Beavis	Edwin	Gervase	Job	Miles
Bede	Egbert	Gideon	Jocelin	Morgan
Bennet	Ellis	Gilbert	John	Moses

First Names in the Seventeenth Century

Nathaniel
Neal
Nicholas
Noel
Norman
Odo
Oliver
Original
Osbern
Osbert
Osmund
Oswald
Owen
Pascal
Patrick

Paul
Payn
Percival
Peregrine
Peter
Philbert
Philip
Posthumus
Quintin
Ralph
Randal
Raphael
Raymond
Reinfred
Reinhold

Reuben
Richard
Robert
Roger
Roland
Romane
Samson
Samuel
Saul
Sebastian
Sigismund
Silvester
Simon
Solomon
Stephen

Swithin
Sylvanus
Theobald
Theodore
Theodoric
Theophilus
Thomas
Timothy
Tobias
Tristram
Turstan
Uchtred
Urban
Urian
Valens

Valentine
Vincent
Vital
Vivian
Waldwin
Walter
Wilfred
William
Wimund
Wischard
Wolstan
Wulpher
Zachary

'Lest Women, the most kind sex, should conceive unkindness if they were omitted, somewhat of necessity must be said of their names.'

Abigail
Adeline
Agatha
Agnes
Alethia
Alice
Amabel
Amy
Anastasia
Anchoret
Anna
Arabella
Audrey
Aureole
Avice
Barbara
Beatrice
Benedicta
Benigna
Bertha
Blanche
Bona
Bridget
Cassandra
Catherine
Cecilia

Christian
Cicely
Clara
Denise
Diana
Dido
Dorcas
Dorothy
Douglas
Dousable
Douze
Dulcia
Eleanor
Eliza
Elizabeth
Emma
Emmet
Eva
Faith
Felice
Florence
Fortitude
Fortune
Frances
Francesca
Frediswid

Gertrude
Gillian
Gladuse
Goodeth
Grace
Griselda
Helena
Ida
Isabel
Jacquetta
Jana
Jane
Jenet
Joan
Joanna
Joyce
Judith
Julianne
Katharine
Kingburgh
Laura
Laurentia
Lettice
Lora
Lucia
Lucretia

Lydia
Mabel
Magdalen
Margaret
Margery
Mary
Matilda
Maud
Meraud
Millicent
Muriel
Nest
Nicia
Nicola
Olympias
Orabilis
Penelope
Pernel
Petronilla
Philadelphia
Philippa
Phyllis
Polyxena
Prisca
Priscilla
Prudence

Rachel
Radegunde
Rebecca
Rosamund
Rose
Sabina
Sanchia
Sarah
Scholastica
Sibyl
Sophia
Sophronia
Susan
Tabitha
Tace
Tamsin
Temperance
Theodosia
Thomasin
Ursula
Venus
Warburg
Wilmetta
Winifred

> '*1547 Ther was baptized by the midwyffe, and so buryed the childe of Thomas Goldham, called **Creature**.*' (*From the Parish Register of Staplehurst, England.*)

Hildebert, which by this time were only to be found in history books. The Norman importations such as **Bardolph, Beavis, Drogo** and **Maugre**; saintly names such as **Amyas, Basil, Blase, Kinborough, Bonaventure,** and Old Testament names like **Aaron, Abel** and **Ellis**—the latter being a form of **Elias**—were the names actually in use.

A commentary on Camden's names

Alexander would have been known to Camden, from his Greek studies, but the name was in any case already popular in Scotland, where it had named several kings. **Alphonse** was likewise a royal name in Spain, and must have been well-known in upper-class English circles. Names like **Baptist** and **Hercules** would have come in from France, where both are still used. The latter name is now well-known, of course, thanks to Agatha Christie's creation, **Hercule** Poirot. A name like **German** also looks more familiar, and reveals the reasons for its use, in the French form Saint **Germain**.

Elmer is perhaps a surprising name to see in an English list of such an early date. Camden explains it as a contraction of **Ethelmer**, 'noble and renowned'. This is substantially correct, and the name became a surname both as Elmer and Aylmer. The American use of Elmer as a first name is thought to derive from two brothers, officers in the Revolutionary Army, who bore that surname.

Another seemingly curious name to find listed for both men and women is **Florence**, but this was commonly used by both sexes in former times. As a male name it persisted until the present century in Ireland, where Florence or **Florry** was used to translate the Irish names **Finghin, Fitheal** and **Flann**. **Douglas** looks similarly out of place, but I have already mentioned its use for girls. It was originally a river name, like **Jordan**. The latter, used for boys, was introduced to England by returning Crusaders.

Welsh names occur in the list, notably **Cadwallader, Evan** and **Gawain**. The Welsh abbreviation of **Agnes**—Nest (for **Nesta**)—is given for the girls. The English at this time pronounced Agnes as **Annis** or **Anyes**, incidentally, and tended to link it with **Ann**. Another regional name is **Angel**, which was used for Cornishmen, though English people in general did not seem to want an English form of **Angelo**. Also Cornish at the time were the girls' names **Meraud** and **Tamsin**, the latter a feminine form of **Thomas** and now in far wider use.

Original would have been used by educated parents for a first son. **Postumus** can hardly have been used frequently. Once again it would have been used by the educated class, and would have referred to a child born after his father's death.

Pet forms of names are seen in **Bennet,** a colloquial version of **Benedict,** and **Garret**. The latter was for **Gerard,** which was pronounced in those days with a hard 'g' sound, as in the German form of the name, **Gerhard.** Liberated women should be especially interested in the name **Tace,** also found as **Tacy**. It derived from a Latin expression meaning: 'Be silent'. As it happens, **Silence** has also been used as a girl's name. The Bible does, after all, quote St Paul as saying: 'Let the women learn in silence, with all subjection.' Camden himself remarked that Tace was 'a fit name to admonish that sex'.

Perhaps we had better leave Camden's views on women aside and concentrate on his list of names. Together with the lists of Old Testament and Puritan names that I have given in this chapter, they show the naming situation as it was in England at the beginning of the seventeenth century.

The Restoration

From the Restoration (1660) onwards, first names in England showed no clear-cut national trends. The various layers of names, including the Old English and Norman, the biblical and saintly, the surnames turned first names and to some extent, the abstract quality names of the Puritans, all contributed to a general stock of names. The first name system, like the English language itself, had become a polyglot mixture and was willing to consider candidates for inclusion from any source. From now on, individual family preference could be shown in the choice of names, reflecting local fashion, perhaps, or simply a personal taste.

Meanwhile, there were those for whom the Reformation had been too important for it to be set aside under the new regime. A great many nonconformists, totally sincere in their beliefs, were prepared to make

---

*Cleveland Kent Evans has examined the Baptismal Records of Charles Parish, York County, Virginia from the year 1648 to 1699. The most frequently used boys' names in that period were **John, William, Thomas, James, Robert, Henry, Samuel, Richard, Edward, George, Anthony, Francis, Charles, Daniel** and **Peter**. The most popular girls' names for the same period were **Elizabeth, Mary, Ann, Sarah, Hannah, Frances, Elinor, Jane, Margaret, Dorothy, Catherine, Hope, Anna, Rachel** and **Susannah**.*

William Gosling is co-ordinating a study of English parish registers on behalf of The Names Society. *In the year 1700 the most frequently used names in England for baptisms were, for boys,* **John, Thomas, William, James, Richard, Robert, Joseph, George, Henry, Edward, Samuel, Charles, Edmund, Daniel** *and* **Benjamin**. *The girls were mostly named* **Mary, Elizabeth, Ann, Sarah, Jane, Margaret, Alice, Martha, Ellen, Catherine, Susan, Hannah, Esther** (*or* **Hester**), **Isabel** *and* **Dorothy**.

sacrifices and take great risks because of them. Religious persecution caused many such believers to flee to the New World, taking their doctrines and practices with them. They also took their ideas about names and naming. The children of Charles Chauncy, for instance, who died in New England in 1671, were **Isaac, Ichabod, Sarah, Barnabas, Elnathan, Nathaniel** and **Israel**.

The entertaining and authoritative writer on personal names, C. W. Bardsley, was encouraged by such examples to say in his *English Surnames* (1873) that the American and British first name systems became 'separate and distinct' from that time on. He was thinking, no doubt, of the familiar use of **Abe, Jake, Zeke** and the like in America, indicating the frequency with which such names were used. But these Old Testament names, in their full forms, could be found in countless English villages until the early part of the twentieth century. The differences in naming in the two countries have at no time become great enough to justify calling them 'separate' systems. The various name counts given in this book will make that clear.

There is some reason, nevertheless, for regarding Old Testament names as especially American. It is not just a question of frequency of usage in this case. We have to imagine those seventeenth-century settlers, faced with great hardships, exiles from their own country. It is then easy to see what Bardsley meant when he said: 'Their very life and its surroundings there but harmonized with the primitive histories of those whose names they had chosen. A kind of affinity seemed to be established between them.'

I think that's a marvellous thought—that 'kind of affinity'. Perhaps it is that which makes the names of famous Americans like **Abraham** Lincoln, **Benjamin** Franklin and **Noah** Webster seem so right. They are truly American names.

8 Pet Names

First names in the eighteenth century

A girl who is officially named **Elizabeth** might be known to her friends as **Liz, Lisa, Lizbeth, Beth** or **Betty**, to mention only a few possibilities. Since the eighteenth century it has been possible for any one of these pet names to have been given to a girl as an independent name. I refer to such forms as 'pet names', but because they are often shorter than the original names they are sometimes described as 'diminutives'. They could more accurately be called 'derivatives', or 'link names'. They are new names, based on a name that existed previously.

Baby language

Another expression that has been applied to forms like Betty is the learned word 'hypocorism'. The etymology of this word hints at baby language as a reason for such names, and in many cases the hint is no doubt justified. Children learning to talk are usually unable to cope with multi-syllable names like Elizabeth and may well pronounce a simplified form. Fond parents then use that form to the child, bringing a name like **Lillibeth** or **Izzy** into being.

Baby language is not the only reason for the development of the new name forms, however, so there is no need to describe them all as hypocoristic. 'Pet name' is rather more convenient, for it carries not only the suggestion of fond parenthood but of usage between friends and intimates. It speaks of

> *Tuesday Weld, the actress, was born on a Friday. She has explained that Tuesday was suggested by **Tu-Tu**, a childish corruption of her real name, **Susan**.*

Many old-established first names have a number of pet forms associated with them. In the eighteenth century pet names began to be accepted as first names in their own right, and their use has been increasing ever since. A selection of 'parent names', with their offspring, is given below.

Women

Abigail	Abbey, Abbie, Abby, Gail, Gale, Gayle	**Emily**	Emmie, Emmy
Adelaide	Adela, Adele	**Faith**	Fay, Faye
Alexandra	Alex, Alexa, Sandi, Sandy	**Florence**	Flo, Flora, Floss, Flossie
Amanda	Manda, Mandi, Mandy	**Frances**	Fanny, Fran, Franny
Angela	Angel, Angie	**Gabriella**	Gabbie, Gabby, Ella
Ann(e)	Annie, Nan, Nancy, Nannie, Nanny	**(Gabrielle)**	
		Georgina	Georgie, Georgia
Antonia	Toni, Tonia, Tonya	**Geraldine**	Gerri, Gerry, Jerrie, Jerry, Geralda
Arabella	Bella, Ella	
Barbara	Barby	**Gertrude**	Gertie, Gerty, Trudie, Trudy
Beatrice	Bea, Trixie, Trissie	**Harriet**	Hattie, Hatty
Belinda	Linda, Lindy	**Helen**	Ella, Ellie, Nell, Nellie, Nelly
Candace	Candi, Candy	
Cassandra	Cass, Cassie, Sandi Sandy	**Henrietta**	Etta, Hennie, Hetty
		Honora	Honey, Nora, Norah
Cecelia	Cecily, Celia, Cissie	**Isabel**	Bella, Belle
Charity	Cherry	**Judith**	Jodi, Jodie, Jody, Judy
Charlotte	Lotta, Lotte, Lottie, Lotty	**Katharine**	Cathy, Kathy, Kate
		(Catherine)	Katie, Katy, Kay,
Christina	Chris, Chrissie,		Kitty
(Christine)	Chrissy, Christa, Christie, Christy, Teena, Tina	**Laura**	Lori, Lorie
		Louise	Lou, Lulu
		Margaret	Madge, Maggie, Meg,
Cynthia	Cyn, Cindy		Maisie, Peg, Peggy
Deborah	Debbie, Debby	**Martha**	Marty, Matty
(Debra)		**Mary**	May, Minnie, Moll,
Dorothy	Doll, Dolly, Dot,		Mollie, Molly
	Dottie, Dothy, Dorthy	**Mathilda**	Mattie, Matty, Maud,
Edith	Eadie, Edie, Eda		Maude, Tilda, Tillie,
Edwina	Win, Winnie		Tilly
Elizabeth	Bess, Bessie, Beth,	**Miranda**	Mandi, Mandy, Randi,
	Betsy, Bette, Betti,		Randy
	Betty, Elisa, Elise,	**Nicola**	Nicky, Nikki
	Elsie, Elsa, Eliza,	**(Nicole)**	
	Liz, Lizzie, Lizbeth	**Patricia**	Pat, Patsy, Patti,
	Lisa, Liza		Patty, Tricia, Trish

Philippa	Pip, Pippa	**Susanna(h)**	Sue, Susan, Susie, Suzy
Priscilla	Cilla, Prissie		
Prudence	Prue, Prudie	**Teresa**	Tess, Tessa, Tessie,
Rachel	Rae, Ray	**(Theresa)**	Tracy, Tracey,
Rebecca	Becky, Reba		Treasure
Roberta	Bobbe, Bobbi, Bobby,	**Victoria**	Vicki, Vickie, Vicky,
	Rob, Robbi, Robbie		Vikki
Sabina	Bina	**Virginia**	Ginger, Ginny, Jinny
Sarah	Sadie, Sal, Sallie,	**Wilhelmina**	Mina, Wilma
	Sally, Sari		
Shirley	Sherri, Sherry, Sheryl		

Men

Abraham	Abe, Bram	**Herbert**	Herb, Herbie, Bert, Bertie
Albert	Al, Bert, Bertie		
Alexander	Al, Alec, Alex, Sandy	**James**	Jamie, Jem, Jim, Jimmie, Jimmy
Alfred	Alf, Alfie, Fred	**John**	Jack, Jock, Johnnie, Johnny
Antony	Tony		
(Anthony)		**Laurence**	Larry, Laurie, Lori
Arthur	Art, Artie	**(Lawrence)**	
Bartholomew	Bart	**Matthew**	Mat, Matt, Matty
Benjamin	Ben, Benjy, Benny	**Michael**	Mick, Mickey, Mike, Mitch
Bernard	Bernie, Barney		
Charles	Chas, Charley, Charlie, Chuck	**Nicholas**	Nick, Colin
		Oliver	Olly, Noll, Nolly
Christopher	Chris, Kit	**Patrick**	Paddy, Pat, Patty
Edmond	Eddie, Ned, Neddy	**Richard**	Dick, Dickie, Rich, Rick, Ricky, Ritchie
(Edmund)			
Edward	Eddie, Ned, Neddy, Ted, Teddy	**Robert**	Bob, Bobby, Rab, Rob, Robin
Francis	Fran, Frank, Frankie, Franky	**Theodore**	Tad, Ted, Teddy, Theo
Geoffrey	Geoff, Jeff	**Thomas**	Tam, Tom, Tommy
(Jeffrey)		**Walter**	Wally, Walt, Wat
Harold	Hal, Harry	**William**	Bill, Billy, Will, Willie, Willy
Henry	Hal, Hank, Harry		

informality and linguistic playfulness. If the term has a disadvantage, it is that it might seem to include both the love names we saw earlier—which are used in a petting situation—and the names of domestic pets. In this book 'pet name' will be used consistently to refer to the variant forms of a first name which were originally those used in informal circumstances.

Many first names carry with them as a kind of free bonus a variety of these pet names. A name like **Catherine**, for example, seems to offer a good bargain. The young lady bearing the name can be Catherine or **Cathy**, **Kate** or **Katie**, according to her own wish. Her first name is a whole block of names rolled into one.

That, at least, is the situation theoretically. In practice what is now happening more and more is that the pet names are becoming first names in their own right. Parents choose to register their daughters specifically as Cathy, Kate or Katie, pinning them down to those forms. As this happens, so it gradually becomes more difficult to say that Kate is simply a pet form of Catherine. The two names are beginning to stand alongside each other as equals much as **Barbara** and **Susan**, say, claim equal status with each other.

Pet names become first names

Cathy and Kate are borderline cases at the present time, hovering between the ranks of pet names and full first names. Many other names in use today, considered to be normal first names, would have been described as pet names by our ancestors. Two of the earliest names to establish themselves in this way were **Betty** and **Nancy**. By 1800 they were already appearing in baptismal registers far more frequently than old-established first names like **Dorothy** and **Matilda**. The names from which **Betty** and **Nancy** derived, Elizabeth and Ann, were at that time still amongst the most popular names for girls, and we can be sure that a great many girls who received the more formal names at baptism were actually known by the pet names. That must have been the case for centuries. The change that occurred in the eighteenth century was that pet names were at last officially accepted as names in their own right.

Before this time, clergymen and other officials would instinctively have 'corrected' such names. If parents had said that they wanted to call their

The first name of the actress **Bette** *Davis is not simply a fanciful variation of* **Betty**. *Miss Davis has explained that her mother was reading Balzac's* La Cousine Bette *just before her birth. The central character of that story is* **Lisbeth** *Fischer, called Bette for short. In French the pet name is pronounced Bet, not Betty.*

daughters Nancy, for instance, the clergyman would have nodded, but when it came to the baptismal ceremony, and to the entry in his register, he would have used Ann. It is unlikely that the parents would have argued about it. In earlier times ordinary people deferred to those who held official positions. For that matter, they still do to some extent. A young lady of my acquaintance called **Cherrilynne** tells me that she was meant to be called **Cheryl Lynne**. The registrar entered the two names as one by mistake, and this was accepted by her parents.

Apart from a certain awe with which officials were treated, ordinary people were in any case mostly at their mercy in former times when it came to anything that was written down. For the most part parents would have been illiterate. When they told their parish priest that they wanted their child to be **Peggy**, **Sally** or whatever, it was entirely up to him whether he decided to enter the names in those forms or as **Margaret** and **Sarah**. If he spoke the names as Margaret and Sarah during the baptismal ceremony, the parents would merely have considered this right and proper in the circumstances. Just as formal dress was appropriate for church, so formal language was suitable. Margaret and Sarah would have been thought of as Peggy and Sally in their Sunday clothes.

We have already seen, in our discussion of how surnames derived from first names, that a great variety of pet names were in use from the Middle Ages onwards. Men were addressed as **Gil**, or **Gib**, for instance, but were formally recorded as **Gilbert** when they married or died. The evidence of pet name usage comes in the surnames of their descendants, who were far more likely to be **Gibbs, Gibson** or **Gilson** than **Gilbertson**.

New status

It was during the eighteenth century that the pet names acquired a new status. Parish priests who were completing their registers now began to enter such names more and more as names in their own right. In the year 1700, for example, of 2500 girls whose baptisms are recorded in some two hundred English parish registers, only three are listed as Betty, though 441 girls were called Elizabeth in the same year. One Nancy occurs in the same sample, compared with 341 Anns. Margaret is given as the name of 114 girls, but there is no Peggy. Sarah occurs 167 times, Sally only once.

A hundred years later, the parish registers tell a completely different story. In 1800 Elizabeth is now the name given to 335 girls, but a further 82 are called Betty. Ann scores 360, but Nancy in her own right another 47. Margaret is down to 90 instances, but Peggy is now recorded 18 times. Sarah has become more popular, naming 224 girls, and 11 more are officially recognized as Sally. Other pet names granted full name status in the 1800 registers include **Bella, Eliza, Patty, Ally, Biddy, Elsie** and **Molly**. All

> *In search from 'A' to 'Z' they passed,*
> *And '**Marguerita**' chose at last;*
> *But thought it sounded far more sweet*
> *To call the baby '**Marguerite**.'*
> *When grandma saw the little pet,*
> *She called her 'darling **Margaret**.'*
> *Next uncle Jack and cousin Aggie*
> *Sent cup and spoon to 'little **Maggie**.'*
> *And grandpapa the right must beg*
> *To call the lassie 'bonnie **Meg**;'*
> *From '**Marguerita**' down to '**Meg**,'*
> *And now she's simply 'little **Peg**.'*
>
> > *An anonymous poem quoted in* By What Sweet Name?
> > *edited by Stephen Langton.*

had certainly been used for centuries in their spoken form; here at last their existence was acknowledged.

If we look at these names a little more closely there are those which present rather more of a puzzle than others. It is easy to see how **Isabella** leads to Bella, **Bridget** to Biddy, and how Eliza, Betty and Elsie derive from Elizabeth. Peggy and Sally do not so immediately reveal their sources. They reflect, however, typical sound changes that could occur in the spoken language. Margaret, to begin with, was lazily shortened to a single syllable, becoming **Mag**, **Meg** or **Mog** according to differences in dialect.

Rhyming names

Once these basic syllables are arrived at, they are played with in their turn. A frequent kind of change that occurs affects the initial letter and creates a rhyming form. Just as we might jokingly refer to someone as **Jimsy-Wimsy** or **Georgie-Porgy**, or create a rhyming phrase such as 'tricky **Dicky**', so our ancestors played with names in the same way. We have already seen some of the rhyming forms that made an early appeal to them: **Bob** for **Rob(ert)**, **Hodge** for **Roger**. **Peg** was a similar development from Meg.

Sally from Sarah went through an intermediate stage, **Sal**. Names with a first syllable ending in -r were often converted in this way. **Harry** became **Hal**, and **Mary** was **Mall**, or **Moll** in certain regional pronunciations. Then, just as Meg led to Peg and **Peggy**, so **Moll** and **Molly** led to **Poll** and **Polly**. An alternative source of Polly, however, is suggested by Charlotte Brontë in her novel *Villette*. The child in the book whose name is **Paulina** calls herself Polly.

A modern example of a rhyming name is **Wendy**, deriving from the phrase 'friendy-wendy'. The name was given currency by J. M. Barrie in his *Peter Pan* (1904) and quickly established itself.

It is quite clear that laziness in speech was not the key reason for the creation of pet names, for as we have seen, the new names were sometimes longer and more complex than the originals. There is a Hungarian proverb, it seems, which says that: 'A child that is loved has many names.' Perhaps that is relevant here. Pet names indicate a wish to create intimate, personalized forms of common names. They are names which arise naturally, of course, not because parents have sat down with the deliberate intention of creating a 'new' name. That is more a modern phenomenon amongst people who are literate. By this process Ann becomes **Annelle**, say, rather than **Nancy**. If we want to understand how our ancestors used names, we must constantly remember that they thought of them as sounds, not as spelled-out words.

Spelling pronunciations

We ourselves have in many ways become over-conscious of name-spellings. We are used to seeing the names **Henry, Agnes, Benedict** and **Augustine** in print, for instance, and we now pronounce them as they are spelled. Our ancestors would have been as amused to hear our spelling-pronunciations as we would be to hear someone say **Thomas**, pronouncing the 'th' as in 'thin'. Many Americans already pronounce **Anthony** with such a sound, though to British ears that is rather like pronouncing the 'b' in words like 'doubt' and 'debt'.

When Henry, Agnes and the rest were first introduced to English-speakers they were heard as **Herry** or **Harry**, and **Annis** or **Anyes**. The Normans pronounced the names according to their own conventions, which was very different from ours. A simple way of illustrating this would be to ask a Frenchman to pronounce a word like 'pain'. He will see it as his word for 'bread' and say something like 'pan'. You will certainly not hear the English word that sounds like 'pane'. The same Frenchman, asked to say the name Agnes, would quickly illustrate why Annis became the usual spoken form in English, until it was wrongly 'corrected' centuries later to correspond with the spelling Agnes.

Benedict and Augustine were likewise **Bennet** and **Austin** in normal usage. When we use them today it is in artificially reconstructed forms, for we mistakenly think that what were normal forms of the names are somehow corrupt. This would not have happened if the oral tradition had not been interrupted. If **Agnes**, for instance, had not suffered a long period of disuse, we would still be pronouncing it **Annis**. My personal view is that the name sounds far more pleasant in that form anyway.

I provide a list on pages 78–9 of some first names and their associated pet names. Some of the pet names are now very firmly established as names in their own right. No-one hearing a girl addressed as **Gail**, for instance, would automatically assume that she had been christened **Abigail**. It would be quite wrong to do so. An American girl born in the 1950s is sixty times more likely to have been named Gail rather than Abigail. Many parents who chose Gail for their daughters probably failed to connect the two names in their minds.

Advantages of full names

Yet in my view those girls who were actually called Abigail had by far the best of the deal. They can be known as Gail if they wish, or they might prefer to be known as **Abby**, especially if there are several other Gails in their social group. The choice is there for them to make. On certain solemn occasions they will use the full name, Abigail, with its centuries of history behind it. They have three very different names for the price of one.

Varient forms of a name also allow different attitudes to be expressed. As Tom Sawyer succinctly put it, when he asked to be called **Tom**, 'Thomas is the name I get whipped by.' Abigail would not be a whipping name, though as a child her mother's irritated call of 'Where are you, Abigail?' would have contrasted with the affectionate concern of 'Are you there, **Abby**?'

I believe we need a pet name system—names that have their associated pet forms—yet parents often go to great lengths to avoid a name that can be shortened or altered in any way. They pride themselves on finding a simple name, feeling that by doing so they have somehow fixed their child's identity. They have done nothing of the sort, for as the occasion demands, other names will be invented by their child's friends and intimates. If the new names cannot be based on the first name, they will be imported from elsewhere. Parents expect too much if they think they can hit upon one name, in one form, which will be suitable for both child and adult, addressed at different times by intimates, casual acquaintances and strangers. Using a name that has variant forms is one way of helping the situation.

Nevertheless, the use of pet names as first names has been increasing steadily in modern times. At first the pet names followed the fortunes of the names from which they derived. **Eliza** was popular in England but only because **Elizabeth** was still more popular. **Annie** and **Nellie** were used, but not as much as **Ann** and **Ellen** or **Helen**.

By the middle of the nineteenth century, however, **Lulu** had temporarily overtaken its original forms **Louise** and **Lucy** in the U.S.A., while **Fanny** had similarly passed by **Frances** in Britain.

Note that word 'temporarily'. It should serve as yet another danger signal,

> '*She was called in the Institution* **Harriet** *Beadle— an arbitrary name, of course. Now Harriet we changed into* **Hatty**, *and then into* **Tatty**, *because as practical people, we thought even a playful name might be a new thing to her, and might have a softening and affectionate kind of effect.*'
> *Charles Dickens*, Little Dorrit.

if one were needed, against the use of pet names as first names. **Elsie** and **Betty** for instance, have had their moments, being used more frequently than **Elizabeth**, but the pet names became dated, while Elizabeth itself sailed on unperturbed. **Lisa** recently overwhelmed it for a time, but that too is now receding.

Social-class aspects

Another aspect of pet names is suggested by pairs such as **James** and **Jim**, **William** and **Bill**. In England, especially, the pet forms suggest working-class men while the full names speak of men from the middle-class and upwards. Public figures such as entertainers and politicians manage to avoid such social-class associations when they become Jim or Bill, but the man in the street falls victim to them. A working-class boy who is Jimmy to his friends, for instance, would feel distinctly embarrassed if he were suddenly addressed as James by his teacher.

We shall return to the intricacies of the British social-class system and its effects on names in a later chapter. Meanwhile, it seems to me that for many reasons there are advantages in giving a child a full name rather than a pet name. An old-established first name, in its full form, is like a coin of high value. It can be exchanged for several smaller coins. If that is so, parents should surely think long and hard before giving a child a pet name. There are silver dollar names there for the asking.

9 Centennial Names

First names in the nineteenth century

The rise in status of pet names, which we have just been discussing, was a feature of the eighteenth century. By the beginning of the nineteenth century the stock of first names available to English-speaking people had thus been increased by another layer. Parents could choose biblical or saints' names, or the Germanic names brought to England by the Normans. A few of the 'virtue' names were established, and people were quite used to seeing surnames given as first names. Pet names had now won their battle for recognition by proving themselves an essential part of the living language.

Meanwhile, some of the oldest names known to English-speaking people, **Arthur, Albert, Edward** and the like, had miraculously survived the centuries. In North America they were being reinforced by European immigrants who arrived bearing names like **Alberto** and **Eduardo**.

With so many names available there was obviously great scope for individual choice in each family. The predominant naming custom, however, was still that of passing on to the next generation the names of parents, godparents, aunts and uncles. Sons, especially, were subject to this naming tradition which kept a relatively small number of names in continued use. With daughters it was considered more permissible for parents to indulge their romantic whims.

The proof of such statements is to be found mainly in name statistics, but also in comments in novels about how children were named. As the nineteenth century wore on, novelists themselves were to become important influences on naming habits. The names they chose for their heroes and heroines, especially those that were not already in common use, were often significant. Fictional characters at that time had something like the impact of television characters today.

Most popular names in the 1870s

On page 88 I provide lists of the most frequently used first names in the U.S.A. and England in the 1870s. The names concerned are certainly representative of those being used at that time in other English-speaking countries. It is worth beginning a more detailed analysis of name usage at this point because these are names which have been used within living memory. Most adults over forty have met people who were named at this time, so that they have personal associations with them. It is likely that the 'meanings' names have for us today began to formulate themselves a hundred years ago.

The English lists, I should mention, are based on the Registrar General's Indexes of Births for the year 1875. All social levels are represented. The American lists reflect the naming habits of whites, especially, and what was probably a select social class. They are based on the names of students who graduated in the year 1900 at universities all over the country. Given the normal age of students at graduation we can assume that most of them were born in 1877 or 1878. The social class bias need not worry us overmuch, for there is good reason to suppose that this section of society would have influenced the naming habits of the less privileged.

If we consider the men first, the names at the top of the lists provide few surprises. **William** and **John** are seen to lead the field, maintaining the commanding positions they had held for centuries. **Charles** had slowly but surely been rising to join them since its use as a royal name in the seventeenth century. In America its relationship with the Spanish **Carlos**, Italian **Carlo**, German and Scandinavian **Karl** may have helped it along.

Harry or **Henry**, **James** or **George** also had royal backgrounds, which no doubt helped their popularity in England. St George had also been patron saint of England since the fourteenth century, so that his name was slowly becoming more popular before King George I came to the throne in 1714. The fact that there was then a 'King George' on the throne for 116 years obviously established it firmly—in England, at least. There is little doubt that the name would rapidly have dropped from favour in the U.S.A. after the Declaration of Independence had it not also been the name of George Washington. He was able to counteract its associations with an unpopular king. As for Harry, Henry and James, by this time perhaps they were thought of more in America as the names of fathers and grandfathers than those of kings.

In both England and America the pet name **Frank** had become more popular than its full form, **Francis**. It seems clear that the word 'frank', with its pleasant meanings of 'openness' and 'sincerity', would have been at least partly responsible for the preference. 'Sissy' or 'cissy' was also being

Top Names in the 1870s

Men

U.S.A.
1. William
2. John
3. Charles
4. Harry
5. James
6. George
7. Frank
8. Robert
9. Joseph
10. Thomas
11. Walter
12. Edward
13. Samuel
14. Henry
15. Arthur
16. Albert
17. Louis
18. David
    Frederick
20. Clarence
21. Alexander
22. Fred
    Howard
24. Alfred
    Edwin
    Paul
27. Ernest
    Jacob
29. Ralph
30. Leon
    Oscar
32. Andrew
    Carl
    Francis
    Harold
36. Allen
    Herman
    Warren
39. Benjamin
    Eugene
    Herbert
    Lewis
    Maurice
    Richard
45. Clifford
46. Earl(e)
    Edgar
    Elmer
    Guy
    Isaac
    Leroy
    Stanley

ENGLAND AND WALES
1. William
2. John
3. George
4. Thomas
5. James
6. Henry
7. Charles
8. Arthur
9. Frederick
10. Joseph
11. Albert
12. Alfred
13. Walter
14. Harry
15. Edward
16. Robert
17. Ernest
18. Herbert
19. Sidney
20. Samuel
21. Frank
22. Richard
23. Fred
24. Francis
25. David
26. Percy
27. Edwin
28. Alexander
29. Peter
    Tom
31. Benjamin
    Harold
33. Daniel
    Isaac
35. Edgar
    Matthew
    Philip
38. Stephen
39. Andrew
    Sam
41. Abraham
    Christopher
    Oliver
    Willie
45. Allen
    Bertram
    Horace
    Leonard
    Ralph
50. Reginald
    Wilfred

(Variant spelling forms counted as one name.)

Women

U.S.A.
1. Mary
2. Anna
3. Elizabeth
4. Emma
5. Alice
6. Edith
    Florence
8. May
9. Helen
10. Katherine
11. Grace
12. Sarah
13. Ella
14. Clara
15. Mabel
16. Margaret
17. Ida
18. Jennie
    Lillian
20. Annie
    Edna
    Gertrude
23. Bertha
24. Laura
25. Minnie
26. Blanche
27. Bessie
    Elsie
29. Emily
    Martha
    Nellie
32. Marie
33. Lillie
34. Ethel
    Lulu
36. Carrie
37. Amelia
38. Agnes
    Frances
    Harriet
    Louisa
    Maud
43. Ada
    Lucy
    Rose
    Stella
47. Pauline
    Rebecca
49. Alma
    Belle
    Charlotte
    Dora
    Eleanor
    Esther
    Eva
    Fanny
    Ruth
    Sophia

ENGLAND AND WALES
1. Mary
2. Elizabeth
3. Sarah
4. Annie
5. Alice
6. Florence
7. Emily
8. Edith
    Ellen
10. Ada
11. Margaret
12. Ann(e)
13. Emma
14. Jane
15. Eliza
16. Louisa
17. Clara
18. Martha
19. Harriet
20. Hannah
21. Kate
22. Frances
23. Charlotte
24. Lily
25. Ethel
26. Lucy
27. Rose
28. Agnes
29. Minnie
30. Fanny
31. Caroline
32. Amy
    Jessie
34. Eleanor
35. Catherine
    Maria
37. Gertrude
38. Isabella
39. Maud
40. Laura
    Lilian
42. Amelia
    Esther
44. Beatrice
45. Bertha
46. Susanna
47. Lizzie
48. Henrietta
    Nelly
    Rebecca

*The principal royal names of England have been **William**, **Henry**, **Stephen**, **Richard**, **John**, **Edward**, **James**, **Charles**, **George**, **Albert** and **Philip**: **Matilda**, **Adela**, **Eleanor**, **Catherine**, **Margaret**, **Elizabeth**, **Anne**, **Jane**, **Mary**, **Adelaide**, **Isabella**, **Philippa**, **Victoria**, **Henrietta**, **Sophia**, **Charlotte**, **Wilhelmina** and **Caroline**.*

used in its modern sense by the 1870s, having derived from the habit of addressing an effeminate man as 'sister'. This may have acted against the final syllable of Francis. The use of **Frances** for girls, the name being pronounced in exactly the same way, must also have acted against it.

The special popularity of **Samuel** throughout the nineteenth century is evidenced in several ways. 'Uncle Sam' became established by mid-century as the symbolic American, the name humorously expanding the letters U.S. The legend that it derives from the name of Sam Wilson, a contractor to the U.S. government, seems to be impossible to stamp out, though there was no need for the name to refer to a particular person. The only other name that might have been used at this time because it began with S was **Stanley**, but Samuel had been established longer and was being used far more frequently.

In England Charles Dickens published his immensely successful *Pickwick Papers* in 1836–37. Both the hero and his servant are named Samuel, though the former is invariably addressed as Mr Pickwick and the latter as Sam. The novel provides interesting proof that the name was acceptable at all social levels at this time.

American preferences

With **Louis** we come to the first name in the male lists which shows a marked difference in English and American usage. Imported into Britain in the eleventh century, **Lewis** became the normal form of the name. It was used especially by Welshmen to translate **Llewelyn**. Taken directly to America centuries later by the French themselves, Louis was retained as such in Louisiana, St Louis and the like. As the name that had been borne by eighteen French kings, one of whom was made a saint, it is easy to see why Louis was incorporated into place names by the French settlers, many of whom must have borne the name themselves. In terms of the English-speaking world, both forms of the name have been far more used in America than England over the last hundred years.

Clarence is another such name. It scraped into the top twenty in the U.S.A. for boys named in the 1870s, but was almost unheard of in England at that time. It reached its minor peak in England at the turn of the century, and that may well have been the direct influence of American usage. Writing in 1939, the English academic Ernest Weekley remarked that the name had come to be considered 'pretentious', and was rapidly being dropped by those who bore it.

Clarence was an invention of the nineteenth century, deriving ultimately from the title of the Duke of Clarence. This in turn represented the Latin *dux Clarenciae*, referring to the Duke of Clare (in Suffolk). The curiously half-translated title had been bestowed in the fourteenth century on several unlucky people, all of whom met unfortunate ends. The first of these was **Lionel**, third son of Edward III, who was dead at thirty. In spite of the bad reputation it had gained, the title was revived in 1789 for the future William IV.

Clarence House was built in London as a royal residence in 1825. It was possibly from that source that the novelist Maria Edgeworth took the name of Clarence Harvey, the hero of her novel *Helen*, published in 1834. One must then assume that the novel was well read in the U.S.A. during the following years, and that the name was borrowed from there. Alternatively, the name could have been taken directly from the title Duke of Clarence at a time when **Duke** itself was being taken over as a first name. Yet another possible source is Shakespeare, for in some of his plays the dukes bearing this title are addressed simply as Clarence. Whatever its source, there is plenty of evidence on all sides that the name was popular amongst both whites and blacks.

American heroes

Another 'American' name of this period was **Howard**. It is always assumed by English writers on names that Howard was borrowed from the surname of the British noble family, but the fact that it was used mainly in the U.S.A. in the nineteenth century points strongly to a local hero. Oliver Otis Howard, the Union general in the Civil War, later founder-president of Howard University, seems a likely candidate. H. L. Mencken is amongst those who seem to have missed the point on this name. Mencken was misled by his own incorrect statement that 'by the middle of the seventeenth century Percy, Howard, Sidney and Cecil had become common given names in England'. He was wrong about all four names as it happens, but to stay with Howard for a moment, it was not until the 1960s that it reached its peak of popularity in England. By this time it had been imported from America and was certainly not connected in anyone's mind with the surname of an aristocratic family.

The American hero **Paul** Revere must have been largely responsible for the many American Pauls who were named in the nineteenth century. The name was known at that time in England, but it was hardly used at all there until the 1950s. Paul Revere's famous ride occurred in 1775, but the publication of Longfellow's poem on the subject in 1863 must have given added impetus to the name's usage in the U.S.A.

European names in America

The more frequent use of **Oscar** in America as compared with England can be put down to the influence of Scandinavian immigrants. The name was not generally popular in England when Oscar Wilde was named in 1854. Wilde's father was a surgeon who attended King Oscar of Sweden, and the naming in that case was a special kind of name-dropping. The Oscar Wilde scandal was later to kill off the name almost completely, both in England and the U.S.A.

The American 'top fifty', it will be seen, includes other 'immigrant' names such as **Carl** and **Herman**. These survived a change of country and language because they were easily assimilated by English-speakers. Names like **Gottfried, Dietrich, Knut, Nils, Anders** and **Gunnar**, also brought in from Germany and Scandinavia, were less fortunate. It is recorded that teachers were given to renaming the children of immigrants for their own convenience. A Knut, say, would be forced to become **Kenneth** for school purposes. The children so treated no doubt remembered the indignity they had suffered when they came to name their own offspring and chose 'safer' names.

The remaining 'American' names in the top fifty male list are **Warren, Eugene, Earl, Elmer** and **Leroy**. The first of these we can associate with General Joseph Warren, who died a hero at Bunker Hill. Elmer has been discussed previously as a similar surname transfer, and Earl as a transferred title. Leroy exists as a fairly common French surname, and it is tempting to derive it from the surname of a person as yet untraced rather than think of it as a constructed phrase meaning 'the king'.

Eugene is something of a mystery name. All books on first names blithely explain it as meaning 'well-born' in Greek, and say that it was made famous by Prince Eugene of Savoy, 1663–1736. It seems strange, however, to say that the use of a name in the U.S.A. in the 1870s derived from a European prince who died 150 years previously. Just as I suggested that Clarence might have been introduced by a novel published in 1834, so it may be significant that the novel *Eugene Aram* was published in 1832. This was by Bulwer Lytton, and took up a story already celebrated in verse by Thomas Hood. Eugene Aram was a gifted and gentle schoolmaster who agreed, because of his extreme poverty, that a murder should be committed by an acquaintance. Aram afterwards suffered extreme remorse and was eventually executed.

To modern ears Eugene Aram hardly sounds like a hero to emulate. His story might well have appealed to nineteenth-century readers, however, because of its highly moral tone, and the name would have been in the air, as it were, because of the literary works. Whatever caused the name to be used in the U.S.A., at any rate, failed to produce a similar response in England. Men there were being named **Percy, Matthew, Philip, Oliver, Horace** or **Wilfred** instead.

English names

Percy was not unknown in nineteenth-century America, but it had nothing like the success it enjoyed in England from 1840 onwards. The Romantic poet Percy Bysshe Shelley was so named in 1792 because of vague connections with the Percy family. The poet's fame was if anything augmented by his tragic death in 1822, so that his name would have been in people's minds.

The fame of Horace Walpole and Horatio Nelson presumably accounted in turn for the use of Horace in the nineteenth century. As for Oliver, it had recently been re-introduced to England by Dickens's *Oliver Twist*, after a period of disgrace caused by the name's association with Oliver Cromwell. **Wilfred**, finally, may owe its appearance amongst the top names to literature, for Sir Walter Scott's *Ivanhoe* was published in 1820. The hero of the book was Wilfred of Ivanhoe.

I have been concentrating in the above remarks on names that were being used more in one part of the English-speaking world than another towards the end of the nineteenth century. It would be quite wrong, however, to give the impression that English and American families were using completely different names. To begin with, over 60% of the names occurring in the American top fifty for the 1870s occur in the similar list for England. Over 90% of the names would have occurred if the English list had been extended to a hundred names. Name *preferences* in the two countries differed, as the lists reveal, but the names being used were largely the same.

Girls' names

This overwhelming general agreement continues when we turn to the girls' names. The English list contains 65% of the names in the American list,

At one time an 'Oliver's skull' in English slang was a chamber-pot, the reference being to Oliver Cromwell. There was perhaps another allusion to him in expressions like 'Oliver's in town', meaning that the nights were moon-lit. By the end of the nineteenth century London Cockneys were referring to a fist as an 'Oliver'. This derived from rhyming slang, and Oliver Twist.

though in a different order. Once again, many of the remaining names that were being used in the U.S.A. were also current in England though not in the top fifty.

A few differences between English and American usage were marginal. American parents preferred **Helen** while English parents plumped for **Ellen**. Americans liked **Anna** and **Annie** but not **Ann** or **Anne**. The English put Annie first, then Ann/Anne, with Anna very definitely in third place. An American **Katherine** or **Lillie** was more likely to be **Catherine** or **Lily** in England, but here we must remember that the lists group together alternative spellings under the spelling form that predominated in that country. There were also American Catherines and English Lillies at this time.

Some of the names popular in America in the 1870s but not at that time popular in England crossed the Atlantic in the next decade or so. **May**, for example, which had begun as a pet form of **Mary** but had been reinterpreted by many as the name of the month, had noticeably increased in use in England by 1900. The same is true of **Ida, Grace, Eva**, and to a lesser extent, **Blanche, Bessie** and **Stella**.

Elsie was by far the most successful transplant, taking England by storm at the turn of the century. It had been set on its way by Longfellow, who made Elsie the central character of his *Golden Legend*, published in 1851. By 1896 it had assumed a less dignified poetic form in a popular British music-hall song:

Elsie from Chelsea, I thought of nobody elsie
But Elsie from Chelsea. Nobody elsie for me!

Perhaps because of such treatment, but more likely because of its own popularity, the name had almost completely disappeared again by 1935, leaving its bearers stranded with a name that proclaimed its age-group very clearly.

Alma and Edna

Names that took rather longer to reach Britain included **Alma** and **Edna**. Of these, Alma is usually explained as a reference to the Battle of Alma in the Crimea, which took place in 1854. Some English children were undoubtedly named because of it. Writing in 1863, Sophy Moody commented: 'It will be in the recollection of all how many a fatherless babe but a few years back was baptized in tears by the name of Alma.' Tragic instances of this kind would clearly not be enough to make the name generally popular, and this did not happen in Britain until the 1920s, some time after the name had been popular in the U.S.A. The name's use there must have derived from the Latin word *alma*, occurring in the familiar phrase *alma mater*. This in turn

The names shown below did not reach the American or English top fifties in the 1870s, but were being regularly used.

Men

Aaron	Cyril	Hubert	Luther	Reuben
Adam	Dan	Hugh	Mark	Roger
Adolph	Denis	Irving	Marshall	Roland
Algernon	Donald	Isaiah	Martin	Rowland
Alvin	Douglas	Israel	Marvin	Seth
Ambrose	Dwight	Jack	Max	Sherman
Anthony	Edmund	Jesse	Michael	Solomon
Amos	Eli	Job	Moses	Spencer
Archibald	Elias	Joe	Nathan	Stuart
Augustus	Elijah	Jonah	Noah	Theodore
Ben	Emmanuel	Jonathan	Norman	Timothy
Bernard	Ephraim	Joshua	Orville	Victor
Bertie	Eric	Josiah	Oswald	Vincent
Bertram	Gerald	Julian	Otto	Wallace
Cecil	Gilbert	Lawrence	Owen	Wilbur
Charlie	Gordon	Lee	Patrick	
Chester	Gregory	Leslie	Percival	
Christian	Hartley	Lionel	Ray	
Cornelius	Hector	Luke	Raymond	

Women

Abigail	Daisy	Janetta	Mercy	Rosanna
Adelaide	Della	Jemima	Mildred	Rosalind
Adeline	Diana	Johanna	Millicent	Rosetta
Agatha	Dinah	Josephine	Miriam	Rosina
Alberta	Donna	Julia	Muriel	Ruby
Amanda	Dorothy	Kathleen	Myra	Sabina
Angelina	Drusilla	Kezia	Nancy	Sadie
Ava	Eda	Lavinia	Naomi	Selina
Barbara	Emmeline	Leah	Nora	Sibyl
Betsy	Eveline	Lena	Norma	Susan
Betty	Evelyn	Lettice	Olive	Sybil
Bridget	Flora	Lois	Olivia	Sylvia
Cecilia	Georgia	Lorraine	Pamela	Teresa
Celia	Georgiana	Lottie	Patience	Theresa
Christabel	Georgina	Louise	Philippa	Ursula
Christiana	Helena	Lydia	Phoebe	Viola
Christina	Hephzibah	Mabel	Phyllis	Violet
Christine	Hester	Madeleine	Polly	Virginia
Cicely	Hilda	Maggie	Priscilla	Winifred
Clare	Irene	Margery	Rachel	Winnie
Clarice	Isabel	Marian	Rena	
Clarissa	Ivy	Marion	Rhoda	
Constance	Janet	Matilda	Rosa	

was a title applied to several Roman goddesses, with the meaning 'bounteous mother', but in America, especially, it was used to describe one's former school or university.

Alma was actually used on rare occasions in England long before the Crimean battle, as it had every reason to be. The poet Spenser established the name in his *Faerie Queene*, published in the sixteenth century. He based it on the Italian word meaning 'soul' or 'spirit' and made Alma the Lady of the House of Temperance, defended from her enemies by Prince Arthur. The name thus had a sound literary pedigree and the most respectable of origins, all of which only goes to show how irrelevant such factors are. Far more important to the image the name evokes today is the fact that after reaching its peak of popularity in the 1920s, both in the U.S.A. and England, the name was hardly used thereafter. It thus became another label which stated its bearer's age.

Edna is probably another name introduced by literature. The novelist Charlotte Yonge, who was later to write a *History of Christian Names*, made Edna a character in *Hopes and Fears*, published in 1860. She presumably took the name from the Apocrypha, but it is strange in that case that she did not mention it in her own study of names. The name may have been discovered independently in the U.S.A. by those using the Bible as a name source, but it is most unlikely, as several writers have suggested, that it is a contraction of **Edwina**. This feminine form of **Edwin** was never much used, and then only *after* Edna had made its mark in the U.S.A.

The later spread of Edna to England was helped by its use as a pen-name by the best-selling novelist Edna Lyall. By 1925 Edna was a common girl's name, too common for the taste of many. It fell very rapidly from favour and joined the ranks of rather embarrassing names, for it would be a rare occurrence today to meet an Edna who was younger than fifty.

Ella, Lulu and Carrie

A few names popular in the U.S.A. in the 1870s remained permanently American. **Ella** had been used in England in the Middle Ages, and a few highly educated parents may consciously have been reviving the Norman name. The other names surrounding Ella, however, show how well its sound and form matched the taste of the time. It fitted in smoothly with **Emma** and Edna, **Stella** and **Belle**, **Nellie** and **Eleanor**.

Weekley 'conjectured', as he put it, that Ella was a pet form of **Ellen**, but we have already seen that Ellen was not much used in America at this time. More likely sources are from **Arabella** or **Isabella**, and the possibility of a pet name from Eleanor should not be discounted.

Lulu and **Carrie** are other American pet names that failed to take root in any serious way in England. Lulu, usually from **Louisa**, rapidly disap-

> lulu *one that is remarkable or wonderful* (*slang*). Webster's Dictionary

peared when **Louise** came into favour as its replacement. The popular song, 'Lulu's Back In Town', shows that the name made quite an impact for a time, but perhaps not every bearer of the name was pleased to be associated with the Lulu of the song. **Carrie** survived rather better, and has recently enjoyed a new popularity.

Only one name very popular in England at this time but not in the U.S.A. seems to have later made the Atlantic crossing in the other direction. **Jane** became more popular in America as the century wore on, though it declined temporarily in England. Many other names shown in the English list but missing from the American top fifty were in fact being used in the U.S.A., but less frequently. This is certainly true of **Hannah, Kate, Amy** and **Jessie**.

Less popular names

As we saw on page 17, the top fifty names in any one year account for 50% of the names given to girls and 61% of the names given to boys. Obviously what happens as we leave the top fifties is that more and more names occur which are given to fewer children. I give examples of such names on page 94 in order to give a more complete picture of the names being used a century ago in the U.S.A. and England. Apart from these less popular, but still common, names about one child in a hundred then, as now, received a decidedly individual name. In the 1870s, for instance, there were girls called **Etna, Goldie, Ambrosina, Euphemia** and **Salome**, while boys were to be found who had received the names **Napoleon, Buddy, Plato** and **Celestial**. I shall be dealing with these more unusual names in a later chapter; meanwhile, I hope it is clear why I have concentrated so much on the names that occurred in the top fifties. These were not only the names which most people received: they were also the names which by virtue of being fashionable became associated with a particular period.

Thus, the girl who was **Minnie**, say, at the turn of the century, bore a form of the name **Mary** which was very much in fashion at that time. As she grew older her name unfortunately gew older with her. The girl called **Etna** may have avoided such 'dating', but she was not much better off. In her case she would have been made aware all her life that her name was something of a curiosity. The parental task of finding one's way through the naming maze was clearly as much a problem a hundred years ago as it is now.

10 Name Spells

Spelling variations of modern first names

We move on now into the twentieth century and I shall shortly be considering separately the use of first names in some of the different countries that make up the English-speaking world. Before I turn to a regional discussion, however, there are some general points to be made about the names in use today. One of these concerns the tricky question of how names are spelt. Which is correct, for instance: **Catherine, Katharine** or **Kathryn**; **Stephen** or **Steven**; **Ann** or **Anne**; **Alan, Allan** or **Allen**? Does it matter which one is used?

I have asked similar questions on countless occasions when addressing audiences of various kinds, and have come to know what answers to expect. There will be those who say that all the forms mentioned are legitimate alternatives, so that all are correct. Some will argue that Kathryn and Steven are modern inventions, and are not genuinely acceptable versions of those names. A few will advance the theory that Kathryn, Steven and Allen are the American spellings of Catherine, Stephen and Alan or Allan in Britain. One or two people will suggest that Ann was the former spelling of a name which has now officially become Anne. As to whether it matters how you spell a name, nearly everyone will say: 'Yes, it does matter.'

The few examples I have given so far simplify the matter, of course. A great many variants are likely to occur. I have noted, for example, in addition to the forms given above: **Catherin, Catharine, Catharin, Cathrine, Cathrin, Cathryn, Catheryn, Catheryne, Katherine, Kathrine, Kathrin, Katheryn, Katheryne**. Of these I would say that by frequency of use, Catherine, Katharine, Katherine and Kathryn have established themselves as acceptable alternative spellings, though purists might accept only the first two. Forms like Katheryne fall into what can be called the 'deliberately exotic' category. Parents spelling the name that way probably know that they are varying the normal spelling. When we get to

> *Names are sometimes mis-spelt by the official who registers them. Worse mistakes can be made. The following entry is in the Parish Register of Hanwell, Middlesex: '1731. Daughter. **Thomas**, son of Thomas Messenger and Elizabeth his Wife, was born and baptized Oct 24, by the midwife at the Font called a boy, and named by the godfather Thomas, but proved a girl.'*

Cathrin, Kathrin, etc., one wonders whether this is still true. Such forms look suspiciously like simple mis-spellings.

Fancy spellings

To give them the benefit of the doubt I usually call anything which is not an accepted form a 'fancy' spelling. Or to be precise, on the analogy of **Nanci** as a now common alternative to **Nancy**, I call them *fanci* spellings.

That last sentence has some point to it when the words are in print, but not when they are spoken. That is true also of variant spellings of a name. The bearers of the various forms of Catherine, for example, probably all say their names in the same way. If there were sixteen young ladies present, each spelling her name in one of the ways shown, it would be very difficult indeed to distinguish by sound which girl used which form. Some Katherynes may pronounce the last part of their name to rhyme with 'dine' rather than 'din', but I have never met them. Such a pronunciation would not surprise me, however. Those whose surname happens to be spelled **Smythe** instead of **Smith** often turn it into quite a different sounding name, though from a historical point of view both are exactly the same.

Let us return to our sixteen young ladies. Do they all have the same name, or does each have a different name? Does the change of even a single letter convert one name into another? My question, really, is: what is *a* name? The question is a very simple one, but the answer certainly isn't.

For the moment I will argue that one name can have many different spelling forms. To support this view I can say that language, including names, consists mainly of speech, not writing. All words are primarily sounds, and it is only a secondary form when they are written down. This secondary form is usually fixed by convention, though the conventions may vary from country to country. The American 'color' is the British 'colour', and so on.

Spelling conventions

This fixing of the spelling conventions did not happen overnight, and there are still many words which have more than one acceptable form. It would be possible to write about the Czar of Russia, or the Tsar, or the Tzar. Dictionaries give their approval to all three, just as they agree that 'gaol' is as correct as 'jail'. Nevertheless, the 'fixing' process of words is well-nigh complete. Words which have alternative spellings are the exception, not the rule.

The conventional spelling of a word has often come about almost by chance. There is little logic in the fact that we spell 'cough' and 'dough' in much the same way, although they represent very different sounds. Nor is there much logic in spelling 'feat' and 'feet' differently when they sound alike. Given this lack of a system, it is hardly surprising that many people have problems with spelling.

A child might write about 'a feet of bravery'. His teacher would quite rightly say—'he is using the word "feat" but he doesn't know how to spell it yet.' The context would have made it perfectly clear which word was intended, and if the child had said the phrase aloud, nothing would have been noticed. In my view we have a similar situation when the name which I normally think of as **Catherine** is written as **Kathryn**.

There are several possible reasons for varying a name's spelling. The main one, I suspect, is a wish to catch the eye in the way that a *fanci* spelling undoubtedly does. Advertisers have long been using the technique, and perhaps the brand names they have invented have had a widespread effect on our attitude to spelling in general.

Anyway, if what is important is that the unit of sound remains the same, then all sixteen spellings of Catherine refer to one name. We must not ignore other factors, however. **Leslie** and **Lesley** also sound the same, but they are two names if they refer to a man and a woman respectively. For that matter, **Robin** is in itself two names, as Leslie can be, because it can be both a male and female name. A similar phenomenon is found in a word like 'lead', which becomes different words in phrases like 'a lead pencil' and 'lead me to the altar'.

Historical reasons for spelling variants

Like many other names Catherine has different spelling forms not only because of deliberate whim or ignorance. In its passage through the centuries it was used in many countries and was adapted to the spelling conventions of the language spoken there. The name that seems to have begun in Greece as **Ekaterina**, a form still preserved in Russia, became **Katerina** in Latin. Later it was thought that the name must derive from a Greek word *katharos*, 'pure', so the spelling was adjusted to **Katharina**. In Italian the name became **Caterina**, while in French it was **Caterine**, later 'corrected' to **Catherine**. Early English forms were **Katerine**, later

Initial harmony is sought for by some parents. Elsdon C. Smith quotes the example of the Mayards, of Abbeville, Louisiana, who named their children **Odile, Odelia, Odalia, Olive, Oliver, Olivia, Ophelia, Odelin, Octave, Octavia, Ovide, Onesia, Olite, Otto, Ormes** *and* **Opta.**

Katherine or **Katharine.** The pet form **Kateline** led to the Irish **Kathleen** or **Cathleen.** Meanwhile, the Danish version of the name had become **Karen.**

Kathleen and Karen are naturally considered to be names in their own right, but Katharine and Catherine are seen to be basically the Latin and French forms of the same name. I do not want to make too much of that point, however. It is the pronunciation of the two forms which makes them one name.

Yet I understand the argument that runs the other way. This insists that a name is not simply a sound, but is a composite mixture of sound and spelling. In modern times there is a lot of truth in this, for most of us today see as well as hear our names a great deal. A girl who is a Catherine and sees the name Katharine may therefore say: 'That is not me.' Only if the surname that follows the name makes it clear that she is intended will she reluctantly accept that this is a form of her name.

There are no signs that first names which have been in use for hundreds of years are settling into single conventional spellings. If anything, the reverse is true. The spelling **Steven** was virtually unknown in the U.S.A. until the 1930s; it is now more frequently used than **Stephen. Debra** is now a very common form of **Deborah,** though until the 1940s it would have been considered a hilarious mis-spelling.

The 1870s

If we return to the names of the 1870s for a moment, I said earlier that I had counted certain name forms as individual names. Those treated in this way were on the whole normal alternatives rather than fancy spellings. **Alan,**

Another example of 'initial harmony', also mentioned in Treasury of Name Lore, *concerns the Hickok family, of Bellingham, Washington. They ensured that their children would be forced to spell out their names all their lives by coming up with* **Zarnell, Zane, Zorin, Zellum, Zale, Zolund, Zerrill, Zatha, Zorina, Zelpha** *and* **Zella.**

Allan and **Allen**, for instance, have been variously used to represent the French **Alain** for hundreds of years. The American preference in the 1870s was Allen, so it appears in the lists in that form. By the 1930s the name was back in favour in both the U.S.A. and Britain, this time as Alan. It will therefore take that form in later lists.

I separated **Lewis** and **Louis** in the 1870s list, however, counting them as two names. Here I was assuming that Louis was normally pronounced Louie, whereas Lewis was given its final -iss sound. **Ann** and **Anne** have always sounded the same, so they were counted together. On the whole, the number of names incorporated in this way was very small at this period. The need to block names together becomes far more essential, and creates far more problems, when the fancy name spellings begin to proliferate in the present century.

Let us look more closely, then, at what present-day namers are doing when they come to spell the names of their children. Many of the changes they make fall into recognizable patterns which can be briefly described.

-ie/-y variations

A favourite target for a change in spelling, for instance, is the -ie or -y termination of names like **Julie** and **Nancy**. Both of these are pet forms, from **Julia** and **Ann** respectively, and a great many other names are converted into friendly forms, as we have seen, in a similar way. With some the -y ending is normal: **Terry, Sally, Peggy, Polly, Harry, Penny**, etc. Others usually take -ie, as in **Bonnie, Sadie, Connie, Jamie**. Many more are found with both forms in almost equal numbers: **Johnny** and **Johnnie**, **Vicky** and **Vickie**.

It is probably the latter examples which lead many people to believe that either ending will do for any name. Amongst American students one therefore finds **Terrie, Peggie, Barrie, Wendie, Tobie, Kathie** and many more. It could be argued that **Sallie, Pennie** and **Merrie** make name forms of the words 'sally', 'penny' and 'merry', and that there is real point to the change. What really does convert the words to names when they are written down, however, is the initial capital letter.

Bonnie and **Bonny**, as it happens, are both acceptable spellings of the dictionary word, as well as the name. The word is still used in Scotland, especially, as a general term of appreciation. Applied to a girl the meaning is 'plump and pretty'. Such, at least, was the meaning when the old poets talked of 'a bonny lass'. In those days plumpness was not thought to be the terrible evil which we now seem to think it is.

Julie obviously does change its character when it is spelled **July**, as happens occasionally. Anyone seeing it in that form would naturally

The examples on this page show what can happen to ordinary names when they are spelled oddly. All are authentic names taken from official records.

Agniss	Ednar	Lettuce	Roda
Albatina	Elce	Lewisa	Rolph
Albirt	Eleazar	Lezlie	Rosanner
Algeenon	Elyzabeth	Loes	Roza
Allon	Erbert	Lylah	Rueben
Alster	Feargus	Lynas	Rufas
Ambrows	Freada	Mabal	Saidee
Amon	Glawdys	Magge	Secilia
Aubary	Godfry	Magnes	Seelia
Bazel	Gordan	Maranda	Sibbill
Benjaman	Harray	Marrey	Sidny
Betcy	Henery	Maurra	Silus
Betrice	Herbut	Maybel	Soloman
Brigett	Herrmann	Meriar	Stuert
Carry	Hillery	Merina	Thresa
Charle	Ileen	Mille	Trever
Chora	Isia	Mrrya	Treza
Clarance	Ivon	Murial	Ursella
Daffeny	Jimima	Osker	Violer
Dasey	Jobe	Pammala	Whillie
Daved	Jona	Pearcy	Whinney
Denjes	Joney	Pheabe	Willifred
Dorathy	Josephene	Phelix	Winnafred
Eanoc	Judeth	Precilla	
Ebbaneza	Launa	Purcy	
Edger	Lennord	Reta	

pronounce it as the name of the month. If one goes back far enough in linguistic history, July and Julie derive from the same source, but I would certainly treat them as separate names in modern times.

The occasional choice that genuinely exists between -ie and -y in pet names causes some namers to vary the two elsewhere. This leads to **Emilie, Hilarie, Amie, Melodie** and the like. In some cases these spellings restore the names to their medieval forms, but this hardly helps the modern bearers of the names. One can be quite sure that they will constantly have to correct people who give them their usual written form. This does not happen with **Mary** and **Marie**, and their compound forms **Rosemary** and **Rosemarie**, for the change in spelling alters the pronunciations and creates new names.

-ey/-y variations

The -ie/-y ending of pet names and full names has other rivals. One of these is -ey, which leads to pairs like **Tracy** and **Tracey, Beverly** and **Beverley, Lesley** and **Leslie**. Less common forms are **Tracie** and **Lesly**. Those names where -ey is the usual ending naturally become vulnerable. **Audrey** is seen as **Audrie** and **Audry, Wesley** as **Weslie** and **Wesly, Harvey** as **Harvie** and **Harvy**. Further evidence of the general confusion is seen in **Jeffry, Shelly, Bradly, Amey, Ronney, Garey, Rickey, Salley, Abbey, Nancey, Betsey, Kenney, Bonney** and **Sadey**.

The next complication is caused by Greek names like **Zoe, Phoebe** and **Chloe**. Here the sound represented by -y, -ie and -ey takes the simple form -e. For many name-spellers this grants a licence for **Sydne** instead of **Sydney, Bobbe** instead of **Bobbie** or **Bobby, Monte** instead of **Monty**, and so on. Some namers feel that the single -e is not enough to ensure that the name is pronounced correctly. After all, **Anne** is still **Ann** rather than **Annie**, and how would one deal with **Lesle**? Doubling the 'e' leaves no-one in doubt, and **Bettee, Nancee, Leslee** find their way into the name lists. Other examples include **Margaree** and **Marjoree, Connee, Randee, Julee** and **Jamee**. A few genuine -ee names, such as **Andree** and **Renee**, are alongside them, presumably retaining their French -ay pronunciation. They may, however, be forced to become **Andray** and **Renay** in the future, just as Zoe has been forced to become **Zoey** or **Zowey** in some instances.

The use of **Leigh** as a feminine form of **Lee** in recent years has opened up the possibility of a new range of spellings, and I have so far seen a **Beverleigh, Gayleigh** and **Merrileigh**. Somewhere there is a girl called **Lesleigh**, I feel sure, but I have not as yet come across her. On the other hand, I *have* seen yet another variant, **Lesli**.

Names in -i

The final -i for -ie, -y, -ey, -e and -ee is becoming more popular each year. Linguists would no doubt explain names like **Terri, Vicki, Kerri, Patti, Randi, Judi, Nanci, Mandi, Nicki, Betti, Penni, Candi** and similar examples as back formations from the -ie forms. As we shall see later, they can also be seen as part of a general interchange of 'i' and 'y'. The model for such names could well have been provided by pet names common in Europe—**Heidi, Trudi, Mitzi** and the like. In recent times the influence of Walt Disney's popular film, *Bambi* (1942), cannot be discounted. American place names such as **Missouri, Corpus Christi, Miami, Cincinnati** and **Mississippi** must also have helped to make -i names familiar.

The number of such names has increased dramatically in recent years, for Mencken, writing in 1948 and listing a large number of unusual names, found only one example of an -i spelling. Significantly it was the name of a girl, **Tomi**, where the -i converted a male name to female use. The suffix is used in this way with **Tobi, Toni, Kenni** and **Bobbi**, all names of American girls born in the 1950s.

It is very noticeable that the names of girls take on fancy spellings far more often than boys' names. This must partly be a reflection of the attitude that has prevailed for centuries, namely that boys should have traditional names with no frills, while girls could be treated more frivolously. But as the lists of names quoted in earlier chapters have made clear, there was for a long time a genuine shortage of girls' names. Standard sources such as the Bible offered far more suggestions for boys' names. If the range of girls' names was to be extended, variations in spelling offered one way of doing it.

The -i names mentioned above certainly do no harm, and in many instances manage to give a modern look to an old name. Changes of meaning resulting from the new ending are rare, though **Juli** from Julie or Julia does acquire the same possible meaning that we saw with the form July. *Juli* is the name of that month in German, and we already have the name **Avril**, 'April', to show that a French month-name can become an English first name.

There is also a grammatical difference, technically speaking, between **Cherie** and **Cheri**, both of which are given as girls' names. The removal of

---

'*April, April, laugh thy girlish laughter;*
Then, the moment after
Weep thy girlish tears.'

William Watson

the -e in this case converts a feminine form into a masculine one in French, but the answer to that is that the names are being used in an English-speaking context. There, as we have seen, -i seems to have become an accepted feminine ending in first names.

The possibility that -i names show a general i/y interchange is suggested by an internal spelling change in many names. Usually this is from 'i' to 'y', leading to names like **Lynda, Janyce, Lyonel, Allyson, Dyane, Franklyn, Alvyn, Borys, Elysa, Francyne, Judythe, Phyllip, Dennys, Marcya, Celynda, Martyne. Clide,** from **Clyde,** is the only instance I have so far found of the reverse process. The former change is nothing new, for **Sidney, Silvester, Silvia** and the like have been written as **Sydney, Sylvester** and **Sylvia** for centuries. An interesting reversal is **Sybil** for the more correct form **Sibyl.**

Name extensions

'Y' gets further use as an unnecessary intrusion into names such as **Jane, Dale, Gale, Thane, Lanc** and **Wade,** converting them into **Jayne, Dayle, Gayle, Thayne, Layne** and **Wayde.** The influence of well-established names such as **Wayne** has perhaps contributed to this habit of building names into longer versions of themselves, and 'y' is in any case not the worse offender. That distinction must go to the silent 'e'.

The French form of **Anne** alongside its English counterpart **Ann** caused an early confusion between the two. In more recent times, **Jean** has been under attack from **Jeanne** and **Carol** from **Carole.** Many namers now seem to feel that a final silent 'e' is necessary for form's sake, so that we find **Faye, Lynne, Bettye, Carolynne, Earle, Karle, Judythe, Gaye, Jaye, Jeane, Paule, Alane, Nancye, Robbye, Teddye.**

Another way of extending a name is to double one or more consonants, especially the final one. This again is a centuries-old habit. The name **Ann,** after all, could be perfectly well represented (and in earlier times often was) as **An,** but we have come to expect the double-letter spelling. Perhaps this is why **Glenn, Wynn** and **Lynn** are more frequently found than **Glen, Wyn** and **Lyn,** while **Donn** and **Jann** are occasionally to be found alongside **Don** and **Jan.** The extra -n on **Joann, Jilliann** and **Deann** creates new names, equating them more with **Joanne, Julianne** and **Deanne.** Internally a

---

Harry C. Thompson is reported to have practised his own kind of family name extension. The number of syllables in his daughters' names reflected the order in which they were born. Jean was followed by Nancy, Eleanor and Marylouise.

double 'n' can occur in **Danna** for **Dana, Dennis** for **Denis, Dianna** or **Dianne** for **Diana** and **Diane**. **Jennifer** has long been an accepted form of **Jenifer**.

Almost any consonant can be doubled in order to create an alternative form of a name. A few examples are **Robbin, Todd, Greggory, Nikki, Gillian, Kimm, Terrence, Douglass, Violett, Evva**. Inevitably, though, a few instances are found of single consonants where two are expected—**Casandra, Mathew, Jery**.

c/k/s interchanges

As one might expect, 'c' is the consonant most likely to be played with in other ways by the fancy spellers. The fact that it can represent both a 'k' and an 's' sound does not go unnoticed. Perhaps influenced by the old-established Catherine and Katharine spellings, **Karol, Erika, Konnie, Kandace, Karla** and **Kraig** all occur together with the more frequent **Carol, Erica, Connie, Candace, Carla** and **Craig**. 'C' replaces 'k' in **Caren** and the popular **Marc**, though the latter may simply be an importation of the French form of **Mark**. **Synthia** and **Cydni** show other possible variations.

The 'ck' combination is likely to be altered, as the names **Fredric, Dominik** and Nikki typify. The co-existence of **Eric** and the Scandinavian **Erik** inevitably leads to examples of **Erick**. As for 'ch', it can be replaced by 'k': **Kristine, Kristopher**; by 'c': **Cristine, Cristopher**; or by 'sh': **Sheryl, Sherie, Roshelle, Sharlotte**.

Other fairly regular changes occur, and the potential permutations are almost endless. There are common pairs of names, for instance, such as **Geoff** and **Jeff, Gerald** and **Jerald, Gill** and **Jill, Gerry** and **Jerry**. This presumably accounts for the less common variants **Gean** and **Jean**. There is also a group of female names which are found as **Deborah** or **Debora, Sarah** or **Sara, Leah** or **Lea**. This in turn leads to rare instances of **Emmah, Sheilah** and **Dina**, where **Emma, Sheila** and **Dinah** are the expected forms.

Abnormal variants

The interchanges I have described above are frequent enough to be 'normal', and it is easy to understand how the variant forms arise. Most of the examples somehow suggest that they are deliberately changed spellings. One may disagree with that practice in principle, perhaps, but one can at least see some kind of pattern emerging in the new forms. Rather more worrying are names such as these: **Ileene, Everlyn, Jacalyn, Macksine, Micheal, Urvin, Valorie, Dustan, Deberah, Johnathan, Mathue,**

Madlynne. No doubt they sound perfectly all right, as **Eileen, Evelyn, Jacqueline, Maxine** and so on, but they look like awful mis-spellings of well-established names.

When I see such forms I find myself imagining a young man who is attracted by a girl's voice on the phone and arranges to meet her. He forms a picture in his mind of the beautiful **Madeleine** he is to meet, only to find a **Mad Lynne** waiting for him. He hastily takes to his heels.

I'm exaggerating, I know, but I am not alone in finding some spelling variations quite acceptable while others cause a distinctly negative reaction. In my view, anyone who bears a name that is spelt in an ugly way should quickly change it to its normal form. While it really doesn't matter in the least if you are an **Ann** or **Anne, Tracy** or **Tracey, Stephen** or **Steven**, it may matter a great deal if you are a **Moorean**, say, or a **Kennith**. These forms of the names look wrong, and that is important. It has been shown time and again that when people think there is something strange about a name, they extend that judgement to the person who bears it.

Correcting a name to its normal spelling-form is the simplest kind of name change to make. The name, after all, remains basically the same. All one is doing, one can say, is restoring the harmony between a name's sound and its appearance, and what possible harm can that do?

11 Adam's Rib

The creation of feminine first names

In the last chapter I touched upon another general theme apart from the ways in which a name can be spelled. It concerned the naming of women. It is worth exploring that topic more fully before making a regional survey of first name usage. Women's names have certain characteristics that set them apart, especially in modern times.

Link names

A great many names used for girls are of the type known as link names. They are based on an existing name but add an extra element. The male name **Paul** serves as a base, for example, for the new names **Pauline** and **Paulette**. These can in turn be made into the 'Latin' forms, **Paulina** and **Pauletta**. Established female names such as **Ann** can likewise be transposed into new names by the addition of suffixes, giving names like **Annette** and **Annelle**.

As a glance at the top fifties for the 1870s will show (page 88), **Harriet, Louisa, Pauline, Charlotte, Henrietta** and **Caroline**—all based on male names—were already popular. Feminine adaptations come to mind for almost all the names in the boys' lists. There is not a single boy's name there, however, that derives from a girl's name or, for that matter, from another boy's name. The formation of new names based on existing male or female names has always brought names into being for girls, not boys.

The habit of creating link names in this way was borrowed directly from countries such as France, Spain and Italy. Some of the suffixes used in those counties have taken on a life of their own in the English-speaking world. Other suffixes have been created by English-speakers, as we shall see. I deal briefly with the more important name-forming elements below.

-a

When girls' names were written in early records and documents in their Latin form, **Ann** became **Anna**, **Mary** became **Maria**, and so on, by the normal rules of Latin grammar. The girls concerned, however, continued to be called Ann and Mary. It was only in the eighteenth century that the Latin forms became fashionable as English names. Anna was now actually addressed as Anna, and the way was clear for a whole series of new name forms to be created. Names that had come into English as **Eve, Sophie, Louise** and **Claire** now became more popular as **Eva, Sophia, Louisa** and **Clara**. They were still popular in these forms at the end of the last century. Other names with a Latin look in use in the 1870s were **Amelia, Sara, Laura, Stella, Alma, Emma, Bertha, Lydia** and **Ada**. Not all of these were genuine Latin forms. Some Hebrew names fitted naturally into the scheme of things by ending in -a, as with Sara, **Rebecca** and **Martha**. **Elizabeth** offered the pet form **Eliza** as its contribution to the -a fad, and its Spanish form **Isabel** was converted into **Isabella**.

The -a ending for a girl's name has remained popular to the present day, and it has understandably come to be thought of as an indicator in itself of a feminine name. No-one is in doubt about the sex of **Paula, Roberta, Ricarda, Alberta, Carla, Frederica, Martina, Erica, Philippa,** etc. Less commonly one sees the ending used to convert male names in examples such as **Ronalda, Davida, Leona, Shauna, Melvina**. **Adriana** was a Shakespearian character, but the name does not seem to have made a general appeal. In **Norma** and **Rona** we perhaps have back-formations from **Norman** and **Ronald**.

A curious use of this suffix is in names that are already feminine, but which the namer apparently wants to make more so. This produces names like **Dawna, Gaila** and **Lilliana**. **Lynna** is more understandable, since **Lynn** can be both a male and female name.

-ia

A slight variation of the -a ending is used for the sake of euphony in **Marcia, Patricia, Victoria, Alicia, Amelia, Antonia, Georgia, Virginia, Eugenia, Eulalia, Olivia, Lavinia, Felicia** and **Lucretia**. These are all normal forms, but the suffix is made to look rather odd in a name like **Tonyia**. This seems to be an attempt to arrive at a new name which sounds like **Sonia** or **Sonja**. The -ia is more in harmony in **Alysia** and **Lynthia**, two examples of modern names. In **Pamelia**, which occasionally occurs, we seem to have a blend of **Pamela** and Amelia.

Of the names mentioned above, Marcia is frequently re-spelled as

One way of extending the range of names for girls was to form link names, adapting boys' names by adding a variety of suffixes.

Adrian	Adrienne, Adrianne
Alan	Alaine, Allene, Alana, Alanna, Lana
Albert	Alberta, Albertine, Albertina
Alexander	Alexandra, Alexandria, Alexandrina, Alexia
Alfred	Alfreda, Freda
Alvin	Alvina, Alvena, Alva
Andrew	Andrea, Andreana, Andreena, Andrena, Andrene, Andrewina, Andriene, Andrina, Andrine, Dandy
Antony	Antonia, Antoinette
Augustus	Augusta, Gussie
Bernard	Bernadette, Bernette, Bernardine, Bernardene, Bernarda, Bernice
Cecil	Cecilia, Cecelia, Cicely, Celia, Celine, Celinda, Celynda, Cecile
Charles	Carla, Karla, Carlotta, Charlotte, Charlene, Charleen, Carol, Carole, Caroline, Carolina, Carrie, Carolyn, Carolynn, Karol, Karole, Cary, Caryl, Carolee
Christian	Christiana, Christine, Christina, Christa, Kristine, Kristin, Kristina
Claud	Claudette, Claudine, Claudia, Claude, Claudina
Clement	Clemence, Clemency, Clementina, Clementine
Constantine	Constance, Connie, Constantia
Daniel	Danielle, Danna, Danetta, Danette, Danella
David	Davida, Davina, Davidina, Vida
Denis	Denise, Denyse, Denice, Dionysia
Edwin	Edwina, Winnie
Eric	Erica, Erika, Ricky, Rika, Riki, Rikki
Ernest	Ernestine, Ernesta, Erna

Eugene	Eugenia, Eugenie, Genie
Felix	Felicia, Felicity, Felice
Francis	Frances, Francine, Francelle, Francella, Francene, Francesca, Frankie
Frederick	Frederica, Fredella, Freda
George	Georgette, Georgina, Georgiana, Georgeann, Georgia, Georgie, Georgine, Georgene
Gerald	Geraldine, Geraldina, Jeraldine, Geralda, Geraldene
Henry	Harriet, Harriette, Henrietta, Henriette
Jacques	Jacqueline, Jacquelyn, Jacquetta
James	Jamesina, Jacoba, Jacobina, Bina, Jamie, Jaime
John	Jane, Jean, Joan, Janet, Janette, Janetta, Jeanne, Jeannette, Jayne, Janice, Janis, Joanne, Joanna, Jana, Janna, Jeannine, Johanna
Joseph	Josephine, Josepha, Josie, Josephina
Julius	Julia, Juliana, Julianne, Julie, Juliet, Juliette, Juli, Jillian, Julian, Julietta, Liana, Liane, Leanne
Laurence	Laura, Lora, Laurel, Loretta, Lorraine, Lauren, Lauri, Laurie, Loren, Laraine, Laureen, Loralie, Lorinda, Lorine, Lauretta, Laurencia
Leslie	Leslie, Lesley, Leslee, Lesly, Leslye
Louis	Louisa, Louise, Louella, Luella
Lucius	Lucia, Lucy, Lucasta, Lucetta, Lucine, Lucille, Lucinda, Lucilla, Lucette, Lucina, Luciana
Marcus	Marcella, Marcelle, Marcia, Marsha, Marcelline, Marcie, Marcy
Michael	Michaela, Michele, Michelle, Micheline, Michelina, Michelene, Micha
Nicholas	Nicola, Nicole, Nichole, Nichola, Nicolette, Colette, Nicoletta
Patrick	Patricia, Patrice
Paul	Paula, Paulette, Pauline, Paulina, Paulene
Peter	Petra, Petrina
Philip	Philippa, Pippa
Richard	Ricarda, Richenda
Robert	Roberta, Robina, Robena, Robertina, Robyn, Robin
Ronald	Ronalda, Rona, Ronnie
Stephen	Stephanie, Stefanie, Stevie, Steve
Thomas	Thomasin, Thomasine, Thomasina, Thamasin, Tamasine, Tamsin, Tammy
Theodore	Theodora, Thea, Dora
Victor	Victoria, Victorine
William	Williamina, Wilhelmina, Wilma, Billie
Yve	Yvonne, Yvette, Evonne, Evon, Ivonne

> *A rare case of a male name being derived from a female name occurred in France in the sixteenth century, where Ann was apparently treated as the male form of Anne and bestowed on **Ann** de Montmorency. His godmother was Anne, Duchess of Brittany.*

Marsha to match its normal pronunciation. The pet name **Tricia**, from Patricia, is likewise frequently found as **Trisha**. I have as yet seen no examples of **Patrisha**, but I would consider it a normal development.

-e

Whereas -a and -ia are primarily Latin, -e is the normal French feminine ending. **Anna, Louisa** and the like thus become **Anne** and **Louise** in French. At the present time, French forms are more in favour than the Latin, but if 'older' names are resurrected in a fashion turn-about of the future, we shall probably see a return to the -a names.

Meanwhile, the familiarity of such pairs as **Louise** and **Louis, Denise** and **Denis, Justine** and **Justin, Cecile** and **Cecil** inspires some namers to add an -e to other male names in order to convert them. **Ronalde** and **Allene**, for instance, are made to change their sex by this means, though a French name ending in -en would be more likely to become -enne, as in **Adrienne, Vivienne, Marcienne**. Some genuine French feminine forms have not managed to establish themselves with English-speakers. **Paule** and **Claude**, for example, have failed to replace the Latin **Paula** and **Claudia**, which are perhaps felt to indicate the bearers' sex more clearly.

-ette

This French diminutive ending originally meant 'small', and is used in that way in words like 'kitchenette' and 'cigarette'. It has long been felt to be an indication of feminity, however. Genuine French names using the suffix include **Annette, Arlette, Jeannette, Paulette, Henriette, Bernadette, Georgette, Claudette**, but it has also been used by English-speakers to create names like **Donette, Lanette, Rowlette, Arnette, Glynette, Harriette** and **Janette**. **Juliet** is sometimes seen in its French form, **Juliette**, but the example of Juliet and **Harriet** has also led to the occasional formation of names like **Charlet** and **Carolet**.

The Latinized version of -ette, naturally, is -etta, and this provides alternative forms for most of the names taking -ette. In addition, **Claretta, Floretta, Maretta, Danetta, Junetta, Veretta** and **Wanetta** occur amongst lists of American students. The -etta form is probably more usual

> *Our word 'jacket', describing the article of clothing or the paper cover of a book, is a form of the name Jacquette. The word originally described the coat worn by the typical French peasant, whose name in the Middle Ages was frequently Jacques.*

than -ette in **Rosetta, Henrietta** and **Jacquetta. Charlotte,** by the way, is not a mistaken form of **Charlette** or **Charletta,** but shows the diminutive form of a separate ending, -ot, formerly common in France.

-elle

This has become a formative suffix in English though it is not one in French. The mistake probably arises because of French names like **Danielle, Noelle, Gabrielle** and **Michelle,** which are feminine forms of names already ending in -el. The alternative spellings **Daniele, Noele, Gabriele** and **Michele** occur in French, because it is the final -e, as we have seen, which really changes the sex of the names.

The popularity of **Belle** at the end of the last century must also have helped establish -elle as a suitable suffix for a girl's name. We may wonder in passing why Belle and not **Bella** was used in view of the fashion at the time for the -a ending. The names from which it derived, such as **Isabella** and **Arabella,** would have made it quite natural. Belle may have been preferred because it was already an English word, occurring in phrases like 'the belle of the ball'.

The influence of French names in -elle has caused some modern namers to turn **Rachel** into **Rachelle, Adele** into **Adelle.** Full proof of its use as an independent suffix, however, is seen in **Roselle, Janelle, Lovelle, Annelle, Francelle, Richelle, Ozelle.** The -ella form is naturally to be found as well, giving names such as **Marcella, Fredella, Rosella, Joella, Ronella, Suella, Majella.** In some cases these could be blended names which include the independent name **Ella.**

Other variations of -elle include the occasional -el, as in **Terrel, Arnel. Laurel** as a girl's name is probably a transferred flower name or surname rather than a new formation from **Laura.**

-ine, -ina

With -ine we come to a Greek suffix used to create feminine titles and names. A Greek hero properly became a Greek heroine from a grammatical point of view. In Latin, -ine became -ina, and the co-existence of the two forms has naturally led to many pairs of names. But while **Georgina** and

Georgine, **Josephina** and **Josephine, Geraldina** and **Geraldine**, etc., are all in use in both forms, one of the two usually predominates. **Bettina** easily leads **Bettine**, for instance; **Georgina** is far more frequent than Georgine. By contrast, Josephine, Geraldine, **Ernestine** and the like are far more usual than the forms in -ina.

The fact that both forms of the suffix are alive and well is seen in modern names like **Norina, Michalina, Celina, Carina, Dixine, Charline, Elmerine** and **Audine**. With **Celine** and **Nadine** we are probably dealing with names imported directly from France, where -ine is also in use.

–een

Doreen, Noreen and **Kathleen** are the English forms of Irish names. They provide a model to some namers who make up names like **Nadeen** and **Laureen**. Kathleen has had a great deal of influence because of its special popularity and has given rise to imitative names like **Kayleen, Arleen, Joleen** and **Loleen**.

–ene

Even more frequently found are names in -ene. With the exception of **Marlene**, which was a direct import from Germany, most of the examples seem to indicate that this suffix has come into being as a mixture of -ine and -een. It does not sit all that easily on names, as the following will demonstrate: **Carolene, Charlene, Arlene, Shirlene, Gaylene, Jolene, Karlene, Bernardene, Georgene, Michalene, Jeannene, Verlene, Margene.** In most of these the desired sound could have been achieved, and perhaps should have been achieved, by using the -ine or -een form.

–ice, –issa

The best known example of a feminine name ending in -ice is probably **Clarice**, as it is in its French form, **Clarissa** as it becomes in Latin. **Anice, Ellice** and **Janice** are amongst other girls' names of this type, Ellice also being found as **Ellissa**. The biblical name **Candace** is pronounced and sometimes written as **Candice** or **Candis**. **Alexis** might therefore be taken as a name belonging to this group, but it is an independent name that was formerly used for men but has now been taken over as a girl's name.

A name that was probably influenced by the Latin -issa is **Vanessa**. This was invented by Jonathan Swift, who based it on the parts of the surname and first name of Esther Vanhomrigh. Vanessa in its turn has helped to bring names like **Rhodessa** into being, and has caused the occasional adaptation of **Theresa** as **Theressa**.

*An English journalist a few years ago claimed to have discovered a young lady called **Anita Belly** who was running keep-fit classes.*

–*ita*

Names with the Spanish diminutive ending -ita have come into use recently in the English-speaking world via the U.S.A. The most popular is **Anita**, but also to be found are **Dorita, Adelita, Marguerita, Juanita, Laurita, Venita, Lupita, Carmita, Cherita** and **Marita**. The variants in -eta which are sometimes listed have probably been influenced by Germanic names such as **Agneta**.

Linda

When we come to **Linda** it hardly seems right to speak of a suffix, though historically it would be correct to do so. **Linda** happens to be the Spanish word for 'pretty', and it is obviously tempting to derive the name from that source. It is not that simple. Linda was first used in English because it occurred as a suffix in many German names, spelt *linde* but pronounced -linda. Scholars argue about the original meaning it had in German, but are apt to favour a derivation from *Lind*, 'serpent'. In some of the names that occur in Germanic legends, such as **Gerlind**, this is so. But *Lind* also had a far more pleasant meaning in German, similar to the early meanings in English of the word 'lithe'. Before this came to mean 'flexible' or 'supple' it meant 'gentle', 'agreeable', 'pleasant'.

All these different meanings derived from an original sense of 'slow moving'. Slow movement in a person was matched with gentleness, but it is easy to see how the same word could be applied to a snake. A snake, incidentally, was often taken to be a symbol of wisdom, so the use of the name with this meaning would not have shocked our ancestors. **Ophelia** happens to be a similar name, based on the Greek word *ophis*, 'serpent'.

By the 1950s Linda was immensely popular throughout the English-speaking world, both as an independent name and as a name element. **Rosalinda** and **Belinda** came back into use at this time, and names like **Melinda** or **Malinda, Earlynnda** and **Celynda** were used. The influences of Linda was also to be seen in **Larinda, Florinda, Marinda**, and probably in **Mindy. Cindy**, the pet form of **Cynthia**, benefited from the surge in interest. **Glenda** was an indirect derivative, inspiring in its turn **Gwenda, Kenda, Ronda, Sheilda, Jonda** and **Johnda**. Meanwhile, while the

second half of Linda was helping to form new names, its first syllable, taking
the spelling form Lyn, was becoming part of many other names.

Lyn

The popularity of **Lyn** as a name or name element seems to have paralleled
that of Linda. By the 1950s it had certainly invaded traditional names,
turning them into **Jacquelyn, Jacalyn** or **Jaclyn, Carolyn, Gwendolyn,
Jocelyn, Kathlyn**. **Marilyn**, unknown until a tentative appearance in the
1930s, became extremely popular. It was surrounded by newcomers such as
**Jeralyn, Daralyn, Angelyn, Marlyn, Rivalyn, Bevelyn, Ethelyn,
Arlyn, Ossilyn, Sherilyn**. **Franklin** and **Merlin** became girls' names
simply by being re-spelt as **Franklyn** and **Merlyn**.

As a separate name Lyn (or **Lynn, Lynne**) was almost certainly thought
to be a pet name from Linda, but it was well-established as a man's name in
North America before being taken over by the girls. The name is by no
means alone in being sexually ambiguous as a result. Relatively modern
names such as **Lee** and **Leslie** have proved to be particularly vulnerable to
take-over bids. Male pet names such as **Terry, Jackie, Bobbie, Billie** and
the like are also being increasingly used for girls.

Flower and tree names

For first names to change their sexual allegiance is nothing new, but the
wholesale borrowing of male names for female use is a modern phenomenon. The same is true of the ready use of suffixes to form new feminine
names. At the turn of the century the range of female names was extended
by using flower and tree names. In the top fifties of the 1870s, **Rose** and **Lily**
were already to be found, and perhaps these had something to do with
starting the fashion. As it happens, the earliest use of Rose as a personal
name derived from a word *hros*, which had nothing to do with the flower. It
became the modern word 'horse'. Lily was likewise a pet name from
Elizabeth, not the flower name. A long established first name which really
did mean 'lily' originally, however, was the Hebrew **Susanna**.

Whatever the reason for the use of botanical names, they caught the
public imagination. **Hazel** quickly became popular in the U.S.A.; **Violet,
Ivy, Olive** and **Daisy** in Britain. Other names that followed in all the
English-speaking countries were **Blossom, Bryony, Cherry** (also a pet
name from **Charity**), **Daffodil, Daphne, Fern, Heather, Holly, Iris,
Laurel, May** (also a pet name from **Mary**), **Myrtle, Pansy, Poppy,
Primrose, Rosemary, Snowdrop, Viola**.

The first appearance of such names was an occasion for much comment.
An English clergyman was moved to write in 1890:

It was my good fortune recently on a railway journey to make the acquaintance of a perfect nosegay of children, all members of one family, and all justifying the sweetness of the names that had been given them—**Daisy, May, Lily, Violet** and **Olive**. There had also been a sixth, **Pansy**, but she, I was informed, had been transplanted to a better and brighter garden than any on earth.

There is, I may mention, a strong prejudice existing in some minds against naming children after flowers, on the grounds that the children so called are supposed, like flowers, to be short lived. I hope my little travelling companions may, at any rate, belie the superstition.

A general improvement in the infant mortality rate probably helped rid people of the superstition mentioned, an interesting further instance of a belief in name magic.

Jewel names

Just as **Rose** and **Lily** may have suggested an extended use of flower names, so **Margaret** may have inspired parents to use further jewel names. **Pearl**, which translates Margaret's original meaning, began to be used as a first name at the turn of the century. In the minor fashion for such names that followed it was joined by **Beryl, Ruby, Opal, Crystal**—and, to a lesser extent, by **Amber, Coral** (and **Coralie**), **Amethyst, Jet, Onyx, Jade** and **Diamond**. Beryl was certainly the most popular of these, and although it has now virtually disappeared it was no doubt in some way responsible for the **Cheryls** and **Sheryls** who came afterwards.

A music-loving American couple have named their daughter Amanda-Lynn.

Blended names

The search for new feminine names continues, of course. Currently fashionable as a way of forming new names is the practice of putting two names, or parts of them, together to form one new name. In their full form such names emerge as: **Patricia-Jo, Donna-Lynne, Kathleen-Louise, Helenmarie, Billijean, Jomarie**, etc. The commonest first element is usually a form of **Mary**, and since **Ann(e)** is by far the commonest middle name, that becomes the typical second element: **Maryanne, Mary-Jean, Marylouise, Marijane, Maryruth, Maribeth, Marilena, Maryjulie, Maripat, Maryellen, Marykathryn; Ruthann, Leighann, Janann, Barbara-Anne, Beth-Ann, Bettyanne, Julieann, Sarah-Anne, Chris-anne, Martha-Ann**.

Eldon C. Smith reports on a family who have made use of the blended name idea to achieve family unity. The seven daughters were named **Marybeth, Marykay, Marysue, Marylynn, Maryjean, Marypat** and **Maryrose**.

Other blends are what Mencken called 'collision forms', where parts of one or both names are used to form the new name: **Cynjo, Marjean, Marlisa, Rosanita, Leanna, Rhodora, Nellora, Cherilyn**. Some blended names occur in both their full forms and 'collision' forms: **Leanne** is found as well as **Lee-Anne**, for instance, and Cherilyn also occurs as **Cheryl-Lynn**.

The practice of using blended names has no doubt been copied from France or other European countries, where they are commonly used for both girls and boys. But in some parts of the English-speaking world there has long been a habit of addressing a child by both first and middle name. This is an especially convenient custom when the first name is a common one. Several **Johns** can thus be distinguished by their own names, rather than as John One, John Two, John Three, as some teachers thoughtlessly call them.

And with that I must move on from a general discussion about the formation of new names to a detailed survey of their use in different countries. In this chapter I have tried to show that in a twentieth-century Garden of Eden **Eve** would have been more likely to become an **Evelyn**, or **Eve-Lynn**. Perhaps, as Adam's rib, she would have been made to show her status in a name like **Adamine, Adamelle, Adamene, Adamette** or **Adama**. She could also have been named Linda, after the serpent, or have taken the name of one of Eden's flowers. Meanwhile, a modern-day **Adam** would simply have been named Adam, for the name is currently much in fashion. Such is the curious difference between male and female names in the English-speaking world.

12 Stately Names

The first names of white Americans

In this chapter I shall be concerned with the use of first names in the U.S.A. this century. All of the names so far discussed in this book are, of course, American names in a sense. They are part of the common stock of names shared by all the English-speaking countries, used in the U.S.A. as they are everywhere else. I want to take a closer look in this chapter and the next, however, at the first names which perhaps have a special right to be called American, either because they originated in the U.S.A. or because they have been used there more consistently this century than in the other English-speaking countries.

Most of the names I discuss in this chapter have been used by both black and white Americans, but my comments here on usage relate particularly to the habits of the whites. I shall deal with the separate history of the names of American blacks in the next chapter.

Place names as first names

Let me begin, then, with the name **Virginia** as an example of a typical American name. It is clearly American in being an important place name, the state having been named in honour of Elizabeth I, the Virgin Queen. In August, 1587, the first child born in America of English parents was also named Virginia, rooting the name yet again in American soil, but this time as a first name. It is hardly surprising that the name later became popular with American parents.

A surge in popularity seems unlikely at the present time because attitudes to 'virginity' have changed so drastically in recent years. The name has probably become slightly embarrassing, though any young woman who bears it can make use of the pet forms **Ginnie** or **Ginger**. Ginger Rogers was responsible for making the latter form of the name famous.

> *'Georgia?' his mother said. 'Why in the world would a mother want to give her daughter such an outlandish name?'*
>
> *'Georgia's named for a whole state.'*
>
> *'How'd thee like to be called Ohio?' his mother asked. 'Thee was born there.'*
>
> Except For Me And Thee, *by Jessamyn West*

In America the first name use of Virginia was undoubtedly influenced by the place name, and in that respect one can compare **Georgia** and the Canadian **Alberta**. Georgia is still used more in the U.S.A. than anywhere else, though the fame of the song 'Sweet Georgia Brown' has had some effect on the name's spread to other English-speaking countries.

The other state names are used on rare occasions, as when twins were named **Okla** and **Homa** some years ago, and the practice is sometimes extended to include county names. **Kent, Leicester (Lester), Warwick** and **Norfolk** are among those that have been used as first names—the latter in the famous case of Norfolk Howard, formerly Joshua Bug, who announced his change of name in *The Times* of 26 June 1862. Only a few state or county names lend themselves easily to this kind of transferred use. The English county name of **Middlesex**, for instance, would hardly be suitable as a first name.

As we shall see in the next chapter, the names of British towns such as **London, York** and **Richmond** were once fairly common as slave names. These did not become part of the normal American names scene, however.

Beverly, Beverley

Some well-known American first names are actually place names in disguise. An example that comes immediately to mind is **Beverly**, which is especially American when spelt that way. The name is now well used in other English-speaking countries but is usually spelt **Beverley**.

Beverley was in fact the original spelling of a place name in Yorkshire, England, but in making the journey to the U.S.A. it dropped the last 'e'. The next stage in the name's development occurred at the turn of the century. At that time it was widely reported in the press that President Taft had been spending some time at Beverly Farms. This seems to have been enough to convert Beverly overnight into a 'high class' name, similar to Ritz, say, or Savoy. It was therefore borrowed as a name for many other places, including the Los Angeles suburb of Beverly Hills.

The association of Beverly Hills with movie stars probably suggested the use of the name to Beverly Baine, a star of silent movie days. Either she, or

The Top Fifty First Names For Girls–USA

Based on university students, mainly middle-class whites, born in the years shown. The 1975 names are drawn from newspaper birth announcements. Variant spelling forms are shown as one name.

1900	1925	1950	1975
1. Mary	1. Mary	1. Mary	1. Jennifer
2. Ruth	2. Barbara	2. Susan	2. Amy
3. Helen	3. Dorothy	3. Deborah	3. Sarah
4. Margaret	4. Betty	4. Linda	4. Michelle
5. Elizabeth	5. Ruth	5. Patricia	5. Kimberly
6. Dorothy	6. Margaret	6. Barbara	6. Heather
7. Catherine	7. Helen	7. Nancy	7. Rebecca
8. Mildred	Elizabeth	8. Catherine	8. Catherine
9. Francis	9. Jean	9. Karen	9. Kelly
10. Alice	10. Ann(e)	10. Carol(e)	10. Elizabeth
Marion	11. Patricia	11. Ann(e)	Julie
12. Anna	12. Shirley	12. Kathleen	Lisa
13. Sarah	13. Virginia	13. Elizabeth	Melissa
14. Gladys	14. Nancy	14. Janet	14. Angela
15. Grace	15. Joan	15. Margaret	Kristen
Lillian	16. Martha	16. Cynthia	16. Carrie
17. Florence	17. Marion	17. Pamela	Stephanie
Virginia	18. Doris	18. Dian(n)e	18. Jessica
19. Edith	19. Frances	19. Sandra	19. Christine
Lucy	Marjorie	20. Jane	Erin
21. Clara	21. Marilyn	21. Judith	Laura
Doris	22. Alice	22. Gail	Nicole
23. Marjorie	23. Eleanor	23. Christine	23. Stacy
24. Annie	Catherine	24. Sharon	Tracy
25. Louise	25. Lois	25. Donna	25. Andrea
Martha	26. Jane	26. Janice	Ann(e)
27. Ann(e)	27. Phyllis	27. Kathy	27. Rachel
Blanche	28. Florence	Lynn(e)	Karen
Eleanor	Mildred	Rebecca	Wendy
Emma	30. Carol(e)	30. Marcia	30. Christina
Hazel	31. Carolyn	31. Joan	31. Amanda
32. Esther	Marie	32. Martha	Mary
Ethel	Norma	33. Ellen	33. Christy
Laura	34. Anna	Marilyn	34. Danielle
Marie	Louise	35. Laura	35. Jodi
36. Julia	36. Beverley	36. Cheryl	36. Shannon
37. Beatrice	Janet	37. Joanna	Tanya
Gertrude	38. Sarah	38. Sarah	38. Alison
39. Alma	39. Evelyn	39. Carolyn	Lori
Mabel	40. Edith	Theresa	Robin
Minnie	Jacqueline	41. Jean	Theresa
Pauline	Lorraine	42. Michelle	42. Emily
Rose	43. Grace	Paula	Susan
44. Fanny	44. Ethel	Robin	Tara
45. Agnes	Gloria	45. Virginia	45. Heidi
Carrie	Laura	46. Vicki(e)	Jill
Edna	47. Audrey	47. Beverly	Tonya
Evelyn	Esther	48. Suzanne	48. Tammy
Harriet	Joanne	49. Helen	49. Kathleen
Ida	Sally	50. Brenda	Erica
Irene		Denise	Kara
Miriam		Ruth	Melanie

more likely, the general aura of luxury that quickly became associated with Beverly Hills, commended the name to others. By 1925 Beverly had become one of the top fifty American first names. It was to remain so throughout the next twenty-five years.

The name also spread to Britain, Canada, Australia and New Zealand. In Britain, where the name first began to appear in the 1950s, it re-assumed its original spelling of Beverley. By 1960, when Beverly was already fading rapidly in the U.S.A., Beverley was at the height of its success in Britain. Then came a reversal of fortune, and it fell away as rapidly as it had climbed.

The difference in usage brings about an unusual situation, for it means that American Beverlys are almost always older than British Beverleys. All concerned are probably too young as yet to worry about such a detail, but in another twenty years a few Beverlys may be tempted to replace that missing 'e'.

Shirley

The -ley of the place name Beverley, if one goes back far enough in time, was probably an Old English word *lecc*, 'stream', while the first part of the name meant 'beaver'. **Shirley**, another English place name that was eventually to become a popular first name, looks as if it might have a similar origin, but here the -ley was a 'lea', an open place in a wood. The first part of the name has different origins according to whether one is explaining the meaning of the Northern English Shirley or the place of the same name in the South of England. In any case, the original meaning is not important. Shirley was only taken into the first name system after it had become a surname, and that was its immediate source.

It was in the mid-1930s that Shirley Temple made this name world famous, but it was already very popular in the U.S.A. some years earlier. It was the twelfth most popular name for girls born in the late 1920s, yet a count of the names of college students who were born between 1910 and 1915 shows no trace of it. Something made the name become fashionable around 1920.

This sudden interest can hardly have been due to Charlotte Brontë's novel, *Shirley*, which was published in 1849. It is more likely to have been caused by an American Shirley family which had achieved prominence, or to have come from one of the places in the U.S.A. named for such a family. Shirley in Massachusetts, for example, was named in honour of William Shirley, governor of the state in the eighteenth century.

Shirley is another example of a name that became too popular too quickly. While it may not be clear what started the name on its way in the 1920s, causing Shirley Temple's parents to choose it along with many other young parents at that time, the impact of the child star on the name can easily be seen in all the English-speaking countries. As her films appeared, so the name went to the top of the popularity polls.

There was then, however, an embarrassed reaction. It was as if hundreds of women had appeared on the streets wearing exactly the same dress. Shirley quickly dropped away, and could easily have left thousands of girls with a name that would always show to which generation they belonged. Fortunately it enjoyed something of a revival in the mid-1950s—in Britain, at least—and the name's image was rejuvenated.

Martha, Eleanor, Esther

Another American name is **Martha**. It is American by usage not origin, for as a name with a respectable New Testament background it was formerly used everywhere. In the U.S.A. however, it has only begun to go out of fashion in the last decade or so. In Britain and elsewhere the name was fading away very rapidly at the turn of the century and has hardly been used since then. To Americans, therefore, the name is still relatively young. Most other English-speaking people would expect a Martha to be at least sixty years old.

The name's survival in the U.S.A. was certainly influenced by its association with Martha Washington, the first First Lady. She was able to give it the prestige that in England was normally reserved for royal names. The biblical Martha's role as patron saint of housewives may also have helped the name's image in the past, but the same change of attitudes that has affected Virginia has not been kind to housewives, either.

Eleanor and **Esther** are two more names which were more used in America at the beginning of the century than elsewhere in the English-speaking world. Eleanor was relatively popular in England in the 1870s, but it dropped into the background after that. In the U.S.A. its far longer survival was probably influenced by Eleanor Roosevelt. The name was less used in America after 1930, but was taken up in Scotland at about the same time.

Esther was another survivor into the 1930s, having virtually disappeared long before then in England, though not in Scotland. According to official figures published by the New York City authorities, the name was even more popular in New York at the beginning of the century than in the country as a whole. The Department of Health records show it in seventh place for girls born in 1898, which certainly reflects a local rather than a national preference. The novel *Esther Waters*, by George Moore, was published in 1894 and may have had some influence on the name's general use around that time, but this hardly explains why it suited American rather than English taste.

The New York City usage hints strongly at a Jewish fondness for the

The figures given below indicate in which year a name reached the American top fifty and the rank that was attained. Variant spelling forms are included under the main spelling.

	1875	1900	1925	1950	1975		1875	1900	1925	1950	1975
Ada	43					Dian(n)e				18	
Agnes	38	45				Donna				25	
Alice	5	10	22			Dora	49				
Alison					38	Doris		21	18		
Alma	49	39				Dorothy		6	3		
Amanda					31	Edith	6	19	40		
Amelia	37					Edna	20	45			
Amy					2	Eleanor	49	27	23		
Andrea					25	Elizabeth	3	5	7	13	10
Angela					14	Ella	13				
Anna	2	12	34			Ellen				33	
Ann(e)		27	10	11	25	Elsie	27				
Annie	20	24				Emily	27				42
Audrey			47			Emma	4	27			
Barbara			2	6		Erica					49
Beatrice		37				Erin					19
Belle	49					Esther	49	32	47		
Bertha	23					Ethel	34	32	44		
Bessie	27					Eva	49				
Betty			4			Evelyn		45	39		
Beverly			36	47		Fanny	49	44			
Blanche	26	27				Florence	6	17	28		
Brenda				50		Frances	38	9	19		
Carol(e)			30	10		Gail				22	
Carolyn			31	39		Gertrude	20	37			
Carrie	36	45			16	Gladys		14			
Catherine	10	7	23	8	8	Gloria			44		
Charlotte	49					Grace	11	15	43		
Cheryl				36		Harriet	38	45			
Christina					30	Hazel		27			
Christine				23	19	Heather					6
Christy					33	Heidi					45
Clara	14	21				Helen	9	3	7	49	
Cynthia				16		Ida	17	45			
Danielle					34	Irene		45			
Deborah				3		Jacqueline			40		
Denise				50		Jane			26	20	

Girls' Names Most Frequently Used in the USA

Name	1875	1900	1925	1950	1975
Janet			36	14	
Janice				26	
Jean			9	41	
Jennie	18				
Jennifer					1
Jessica					18
Jill					45
Joan			15	31	
Joanna				37	
Joanne			47		
Jodi					35
Judith				21	
Julia		36			
Julie					12
Kara					49
Karen				9	27
Kathleen				12	49
Kathy				27	
Kelly					9
Kimberly					5
Kristen					14
Laura	24	32	44	35	19
Lillian	18	15			
Lillie	33				
Linda				4	
Lisa					13
Lois			25		
Lori					38
Lorraine			40		
Louisa	38				
Louise		24	34		
Lucy	43	19			
Lulu	34				
Lynn(e)				27	
Mabel	15	39			
Marcia				30	
Margaret	15	4	6	15	
Marie	32	32	31		
Marilyn			21	33	
Marion		10	17		
Marjorie		23	19		
Martha	27	24	16	32	
Mary	1	1	1	1	31

Name	1875	1900	1925	1950	1975
Maud	38				
May	8				
Melanie					50
Melissa					11
Michelle				42	4
Mildred		8	28		
Minnie	25	39			
Miriam		45			
Nancy			14	7	
Nellie	27				
Nicole					22
Norma			31		
Pamela				17	
Patricia			11	5	
Paula				42	
Pauline	47	39			
Phyllis			27		
Rachel					27
Rebecca	47			27	7
Robin				42	38
Rose	43	39			
Ruth	49	2	5	50	
Sally			47		
Sandra			19		
Sarah	12	13	38	38	3
Shannon					36
Sharon				24	
Shirley			12		
Sophia	49				
Stacy					23
Stella	43				
Stephanie					16
Susan				2	42
Suzanne				48	
Tammy					48
Tanya					36
Tara					42
Theresa				39	38
Tonya					47
Tracy					23
Vicki(e)				46	
Virginia		17	13	45	
Wendy					27

The Top Fifty First Names For Boys – USA

Based on university students, mainly middle-class whites, born in the years shown. The 1975 names are drawn from newspaper birth announcements. Variant spelling forms are grouped under the main spelling.

1900	1925	1950	1975
1. John	1. Robert	1. John	1. Michael
2. William	2. John	2. Robert	2. Jason
3. Charles	3. William	3. James	3. Matthew
4. Robert	4. James	4. Michael	4. Brian
5. Joseph	5. Charles	5. David	5. Christopher
6. James	6. Richard	6. Steven	6. David
7. George	7. George	7. William	7. John
8. Samuel	8. Donald	8. Richard	8. James
9. Thomas	9. Joseph	9. Thomas	9. Jeffrey
10. Arthur	10. Edward	10. Mark	10. Daniel
11. Harry	11. Thomas	11. Charles	11. Steven
12. Edward	12. David	12. Gary	Eric
13. Henry	13. Frank	13. Paul	13. Robert
14. Walter	14. Harold	14. Jeffrey	14. Scott
15. Louis	15. Arthur	15. Joseph	15. Andrew
16. Paul	16. Jack	16. Donald	16. Mark
17. Ralph	17. Paul	17. Ronald	17. Aaron
18. Carl	18. Kenneth	18. Daniel	18. Benjamin
19. Frank	19. Walter	19. Kenneth	Kevin
20. Raymond	20. Raymond	20. George	20. Sean
21. Francis	21. Carl	21. Alan	21. Jonathan
22. Frederick	22. Albert	22. Dennis	22. Timothy
23. Albert	23. Henry	23. Douglas	23. Ryan
Benjamin	24. Harry	24. Gregory	24. Joseph
25. David	25. Francis	25. Edward	25. Adam
26. Harold	26. Ralph	26. Timothy	Richard
27. Howard	27. Eugene	27. Peter	27. Paul
28. Fred	28. Howard	28. Larry	28. Jeremy
Richard	29. Lawrence	29. Lawrence	Thomas
30. Clarence	30. Louis	30. Philip	30. Charles
Herbert	31. Alan	31. Frank	31. Joshua
32. Jacob	32. Norman	32. Craig	32. William
33. Ernest	33. Gerald	33. Scott	33. Peter
Jack	34. Herbert	34. Brian	Nathan
35. Herman	35. Fred	35. Roger	Todd
Philip	36. Earl	36. Christopher	36. Douglas
Stanley	Philip	37. Patrick	Gregory
38. Donald	Stanley	38. Carl	38. Patrick
Earl	39. Daniel	39. Gerald	Shane
Elmer	40. Leonard	Terry	40. Kenneth
41. Leon	Marvin	41. Kevin	41. Edward
Nathan	42. Frederick	42. Randall	Nicholas
43. Eugene	43. Anthony	43. Raymond	43. Chad
Floyd	Samuel	44. Anthony	44. Anthony
Ray	45. Bernard	45. Andrew	45. Justin
Roy	Edwin	46. Frederick	Keith
Sydney	47. Alfred	47. Arthur	47. Bradley
48. Abraham	48. Russell	48. Eric	48. Donald
Edwin	Warren	Howard	George
Lawrence	50. Ernest	Walter	50. Dennis
Leonard			
Norman			
Russell			

name, and if that can be said of Esther, it can also be said of **Gloria**. In 1925 Gloria was the sixth most popular name for a girl born in New York though in the country as a whole the name only managed to scrape into the bottom ranks of the top fifty. Writing in 1939, from a British viewpoint, Professor Weekley said: 'Of late Gloria has been used by film-stars and millionaire heiresses.' He was thinking, no doubt, of Gloria Swanson as one of the former, though Gloria de Haven and Gloria Grahame also began to appear on screens in the early 1940s.

The earliest appearance of the name was in a theatrical setting, *You Never Can Tell* by Bernard Shaw. This was published in 1898, the year of Gloria Swanson's birth. By 1920 Miss Swanson was established as a Mack Sennet bathing beauty and was making the name famous. Its use spread to England and elsewhere, but it was not destined to become generally popular. The name is now rarely used, and of the women bearing it those born in Britain are usually younger than their American counterparts.

Transplanted names

This time-lag in the use of names is not uncommon. It can often take a full generation for a name to be transplanted from one English-speaking country to another. A good instance of this is provided by **Hazel**, which reached its peak of popularity in the U.S.A. at the turn of the century, though it was then practically unknown elsewhere in the English-speaking world. Later, however, as the use of the name declined in the States, so it increased elsewhere.

The name was at its most popular in Britain in 1950, especially in Scotland, yet it is rarely found amongst American or Canadian university students who were born at that time. Once again, then, we have a name which will evoke one image for North Americans and quite a different one for the British. It makes the point yet again that the meaning of a name depends on its usage in a particular country, and has little or nothing to do with its original meaning.

A more recent example of the time-lag phenomenon is seen in **Helen**. Having remained a favourite American (and Scottish) name for a hundred years, Helen at last began to fade away in the 1950s. It was only then, having remained in steady but unspectacular use over the same period, that the name really began to come into its own in England. By 1971 it had reached nineteenth place, and by 1975 it had climbed to sixth position. It will be interesting to see whether this outside opinion, as it were, causes American parents to change their minds and re-introduce the name. For the moment, American Helens will find that their name has a much younger image almost anywhere else in the English-speaking world than it has at home.

Ellen rose in America as Helen fell, but exactly the opposite happened

The figures given below indicate in which year a name reached the American top fifty and the rank that was attained. Variant spelling forms are included under the main spelling.

	1875	1900	1925	1950	1975
Aaron					17
Abraham		48			
Adam					25
Albert	16	23	22		
Alexander	21				
Alfred	24		47		
Allen (Alan)	36		31	21	
Andrew	32			45	15
Anthony			43	44	44
Arthur	15	10	15	47	
Benjamin	39	23			18
Bernard			45		
Bradley					47
Brian				34	4
Carl	32	18	21	38	
Chad					43
Charles	3	3	5	11	30
Christopher				36	5
Clarence	20	30			
Clifford	45				
Craig				32	
Daniel			39	18	10

	1875	1900	1925	1950	1975
David	18	23	12	5	6
Dennis				22	50
Donald		38	8	16	48
Douglas				23	36
Earl(e)	46	38	36		
Edgar	46				
Edward	12	12	10	25	41
Edwin	24	48	45		
Elmer	46	38			
Eric				48	11
Ernest	27	33	50		
Eugene	39	43	27		
Floyd		43			
Francis	32	21	25		
Frank	7	19	13	31	
Fred	22	28	35		
Frederick	18	22	42	46	
Gary			12		
George	6	7	7	20	48
Gerald			33	39	
Gregory				24	36
Guy	46				

Boys' Names Most Frequently Used in the USA

Name	1875	1900	1925	1950	1975
Harold	32	26	14		
Harry	4	11	24		
Henry	14	13	23		
Herbert	39	30	34		
Herman	36	35			
Howard	22	27	28	48	
Isaac	46				
Jack		33	16		
Jacob	27	32			
James	5	6	4	3	8
Jason					2
Jeffrey				14	9
Jeremy					28
John	2	1	2	1	7
Jonathan					21
Joseph	9	5	9	15	24
Joshua					31
Justin					45
Keith					45
Kenneth			18	19	40
Kevin				41	18
Larry				28	
Lawrence		48	29	29	
Leon	30	41			
Leonard		48	40		
Leroy	46				
Lewis	39				
Louis	17	15	30		
Mark				10	16
Marvin			40		
Matthew					3
Maurice	39				
Michael				4	1

Name	1875	1900	1925	1950	1975
Nathan		41			33
Nicholas					41
Norman		48	32		
Oscar	30				
Patrick				37	38
Paul	24	16	17	13	27
Peter				27	33
Philip		35	36	30	
Ralph	27	17	26		
Randall				42	
Ray		43			
Raymond		20	20	43	
Richard	39	28	6	8	25
Robert	8	4	1	2	13
Roger				35	
Ronald				17	
Roy		43			
Russell		48	48		
Ryan					23
Samuel	13	8	43		
Scott				33	14
Sean					20
Shane					38
Stanley	46	35	36		
Steven				6	11
Sydney		43			
Terry				39	
Thomas	10	9	11	9	28
Timothy				26	22
Todd					33
Walter	11	14	19	48	
Warren	36		48		
William	1	2	3	7	32

> *'Was this the face that launched a thousand ships,*
> *And burned the topless towers of Ilium?*
> *Sweet Helen, make me immortal with a kiss!'*
>
> *Christopher Marlowe*, Dr Faustus
>
> *'Only once have I encountered a face with that same strange beauty*
> *which has been immortalised for getting the navy quickly out to sea in an*
> *emergency; and she was not called Helen, but Marlene.'*
>
> *G. B. Stern*, A Name To Conjure With

elsewhere. Both names derive from the same source, so perhaps an Ellen and a Helen should feel that they have the right to use either form. In that case, in years to come, when the ages of both names will be more apparent, the 'h' should be dropped in the U.S.A. but sounded elsewhere.

The Ellen-Helen variation is a minor example of differences in name usage in different countries, but it is probably worth being aware of such factors. Just as there are some items of clothing which are fashionable in one's own country, but which are not quite right when worn abroad, so some names change their image when they travel. If a minor adjustment will put things right, why shouldn't it be made?

Names abroad

Further examples of women's names that are younger in Britain than in the U.S.A., owing to later adoption, are **Joanne, Jacqueline, Lorraine, Louise, Marilyn, Michelle, Paula, Sally**. A rare instance of a name that is younger in the U.S.A. is **Kathleen**. This Irish name became popular in Britain, probably in imitation of American usage, but faded away more quickly. All the other names mentioned needed the time-lag before reaching British shores, and all are entitled to be called American names because their use in modern times clearly began in the U.S.A.

Even more American, in a sense, are the names **Laura, Lois, Nancy** and **Vickie**. Laura has retained a remarkable hold on the affections of American parents, both white and black, and is still felt to be as fitting a name for a baby girl as it is for a young, attractive woman or a dignified old lady. The name has been used in other English-speaking countries, but not by any means to the same extent. The name formerly had the pet form **Lolly**, but this seems to have died out.

Lois was especially popular in America around 1925, but this was one name which failed to catch on in Britain. Its slightly unusual spelling in relation to its pronunciation, a factor often present in names of Greek origin,

Victoria, Sharon, Lorraine, Henrietta, Gale, Doris, Diana, Dagmar, Dixie, Christy and *Alma have all been used as automobile names, reports M. W. Martin, of Ohio.*

probably acted against it. The same cannot be said of Nancy, and it is astonishing that a name which returned to America in force in the 1950s should so far have failed to make a come-back with British or Australian parents. It was certainly taken up again in Canada without any problems, though the Canadians have not been quite as enthusiastic about it as Americans in recent years. There is as yet no sign of its spreading overseas, but it can be predicted fairly confidently that it will happen in the near future.

Vickie, finally, in all its variant spelling forms, remains primarily American for the moment, though there are signs of stirring interest in the other countries. The name will actually be heard a good deal in Britain in years to come, but as the pet form of **Victoria** rather than as a name in its own right. Victoria has come very much into fashion there in the 1970s. This is slightly strange, for in the first part of Queen Victoria's reign, her name was very rarely given in baptism to ordinary British girls, though it was used to some extent in the U.S.A. A favourite name at that time, however, was **Elizabeth**. With the popular Queen Elizabeth II now on the throne, the name Elizabeth is steadily declining in use, while Victoria comes into her own. The balance is perhaps redressed on the male side, for **Philip** remains far more popular than **Albert**.

Male American names

If we stay now with men's names we can quickly mention the more important of those names which have remained primarily American this century, and those where American usage was later imitated elsewhere.

Mainly American are names such as **Earl, Elmer, Larry** and **Lawrence, Howard, Leon, Leroy, Lewis** and **Louis, Marvin** and **Eugene**. American exports to the rest of the English-speaking world include **Carl** (or **Karl**), which is now fading fast in the States but arriving in a big way in England, **Craig, Daniel, Gregory, Maurice, Paul, Russell, Scott** and **Warren**. These 'exported' names usually reached Canada first, then were adopted some time later in the other English-speaking countries. In modern times the time-lag that always occurred before a name crossed the Atlantic does not necessarily apply. New names seem to appear simultaneously in different parts of the English-speaking world, and it is very difficult to say exactly where they begin.

Other men's names that may seem to be more American than anything else include **Dennis, Frank, Frederick** and **Walter**. These survived longer in the U.S.A. than elsewhere. This is not to suggest that all are in frequent use at the present time, but Dennis, for instance (in that spelling rather than **Denis**), was being well used in America in the 1950s, by which time its use in Britain had dropped away dramatically.

Influence of the movies

In the 1920s and 30s the main way in which names were exported from America was by means of movie stars. Many of the stars themselves adopted names which seemed to have the right image at the time, and the publicity machine of the industry then spread those names world-wide. The publicity merely exposed the names, however, like a shopkeeper offering goods for sale. It could not change naming habits by forcing names down parents' throats. **Errol** Flynn's name was once as well known as that of **Elvis** Presley today, but neither Errol nor Elvis has come into general use. Something about those two names has failed to appeal to the public at large.

There is in any case a tendency nowadays to avoid the names of actors and actresses and to use instead the names of the characters they play. Dustin Hoffman did far more for the name of **Benjamin** when he played a man of that name in *The Graduate* than he did for **Dustin**. Grace Kelly had a lot to do with making **Tracy** popular when she played Tracy Samantha Lord in *High Society*. Tracy was the name that made a great impact, though **Samantha** was certainly helped along. It is just possible that the film also helped to launch **Kelly** as a first name, adding a new dimension to the use of movie stars' names.

These days television continues to expose names to a wide public in all the English-speaking countries, but it is not enough to say—in explanation of a name's popularity—that it derives from a television series. For every name that does come into general use because of television there are twenty more television names which remain well known, but are not used to name children.

Regional variations in name usage

I speak of 'general use', and throughout this chapter I have been discussing names that have been used throughout the United States at one time or another this century. With nationwide communications what they are the country is one as never before, but there is obviously not a complete sameness of language and behaviour in all fifty states. The top twenties I list for the main states (pp. 137–145) are based on students attending universities in those states, not on births there, but the lists do give some kind of guide to the way local fashions influenced naming in the 1950s. The majority of students in a state university come from the state itself, or one that is nearby.

The differences between the names used in the North as compared with the South are less marked than one might suppose. The most popular names at any one time tend to be the same in all parts of the U.S.A. Independent evidence to this effect comes in the name collections of Professor Puckett, to which I shall be referring more fully in the next chapter. His counts of the most popular names for white children born in the South between 1910–1915 show variations in the order of preference revealed by the top fifty for the country as a whole at that time, but not different names being used. **Hugh** and **Milton** were used by Southern parents then rather more often than by Northern parents, and **Raymond** and **Clyde** were temporarily Southern names. The latter soon travelled Northwards, however. Southern girls at this time were likely to receive the names **Lucille, Ruby, Josephine** and **Marguerite** more often than their cousins in the North, but these were the only noticeable differences. The other top names were being used extensively all over the country.

I must emphasize that I am dealing here with the names most frequently used. These are the names the ordinary person does not tend to notice because they *are* so ordinary. Thus an American from the North who visits the South, or *vice-versa*, will especially take note of the occasional individual he meets who has an unusual name. The fifty other people he meets who have perfectly normal names will fail to register in his memory. When he goes back home he will tend to say that the names used in the place he has just visited are different, because the unusual names he happened to come across will spring into his mind.

Most of us also have a tendency to make generalizations which are based on very little evidence. An American who has met only six or seven Englishmen will tend to assume that all Englishmen bear those names. Needless to say, English people often have odd ideas about American names, because the small number of Americans they have met happened to have less common names. The statements I am constantly making in this book relate to actual facts, as revealed by objective name counts—not by subjective impressions. The reality of the situation may well be at variance with your own ideas about it.

'Dated' American names

The pattern revealed by the names that have reached the American top fifty this century strongly supports the view that names come and go, and that in doing so many become 'dated'. I indicate below a few examples of names that have been affected in this way.

Name-bearers probably born before 1905:

Ada	Belle	Edna	Harriet	Maud	Sophia
Agnes	Bertha	Emma	Hazel	May	Stella
Alma	Bessie	Eva	Ida	Minnie	
Amelia	Blanche	Fanny	Lillian	Miriam	
Annie	Carrie	Gertrude	Lucy	Pauline	
Beatrice	Clara	Gladys	Mabel	Rose	

Abraham	Edgar	Herman	Leon	Maurice	Sydney
Clarence	Floyd	Isaac	Leroy	Oscar	
Elmer	Guy	Jacob	Lewis	Ray	

Name-bearers probably born before 1930:

Audrey	Edith	Esther	Florence	Marion	Norma
Doris	Eleanor	Ethel	Grace	Mildred	

Alfred	Earl	Ernest	Marvin
Bernard	Edwin	Herbert	Warren

Many more names than those mentioned above have a young or old image, depending on whether the name was rising or falling in popularity in the early 1950s. At that time **Alice** and its derivative **Alison** were both being used, for example, with Alice being chosen by American parents five times as often as Alison. This might seem to make Alice a safely 'young' name, but the reverse is true. In the 1970s Alison has come into fashion, while Alice has almost completely disappeared. An Alice born in 1950 will therefore find that most of her namesakes are older women; those of Alison will be younger girls. The inference is obvious: any Alice born in the 1940s or 50s would do well to think of becoming an Alison when she reaches forty. With the younger name she can go back to being thirty again.

Names which seem to be destined to become dated in the future include **Dorothy, Evelyn, Gloria, Irene, Jacqueline, Julia, Frances, Louise, Joanne, Lois, Lorraine, Marie, Marjorie, Phyllis** and **Sally**. An interesting test would be to ask youngsters of twelve or thirteen to assign a date to names. They have grown up amidst a new set of names altogether, and their ideas concerning names can act as warning signals. The men, incidentally, might like to try the test with names like **Eugene, Francis, Fred, Harry, Henry, Jack, Leonard, Louis, Norman, Ralph, Samuel** and **Stanley**.

Alicel, in Oregon, is one of many American towns named in honour of a woman. It took its name from Alice Ladd. The most frequently-found name of this type is Marysville.

Names that avoid 'dating'

What, then, of names that manage to avoid this dating process? They are of two kinds: long-established names that make a continued appeal to generation after generation; names which have never been used often enough at one time to become closely associated with that period. The latter can be names which have been used continuously, but sparingly, for centuries; they can also be new names, ad-hoc inventions which give no clues as to when they were brought into being.

The select band of names which manages to survive in spite of immense popularity is very small indeed. **Ann** or **Anne**, **Catherine** or **Katharine**, **Elizabeth, Laura, Mary** and **Sarah** can claim membership of the group, which **Helen, Margaret** and **Martha** have recently left. Mary, almost certainly, will be the next to go. The name's remarkable consistency over the centuries is now gravely threatened. The names that have come in to replace it, such as **Jennifer** and **Michelle**, are unlikely to become permanent replacements. The mood of the times is not in favour of long-standing favourites, but of names which reflect the fashion of a particular period.

The American men's all-time name club has also lost some of its members recently, waving goodbye to **Arthur, Carl, Frank, Frederick, Howard** and **Walter**. Names still eligible for membership at the moment are **Charles, David, Edward, George, James, John, Joseph, Paul, Robert, Thomas** and **William**. George is likely to be the next to go, perhaps allowing **Richard** to take its place. **John, Joseph, Thomas** and **William** are all rather shaky. It remains to be seen, by the way, whether the political happenings of the last few years have damaged Richard's reputation. This has certainly not been the case in Britain, where detailed studies show that the name rose slightly in popularity between 1971 and 1975.

Eve and Eva

For a name to survive the centuries, be instantly recognizable as a normal first name while avoiding a date-tag, it has to have played a quiet background role for a long time. **Eve** offers an interesting example of such a name—in that form, especially. We must consider **Eva** to be an independent name, one which emerged from obscurity in relatively modern times when Little Eva of *Uncle Tom's Cabin* caught the public's imagination.

But within living memory Eve, the most feminine of all names, has hardly been used anywhere in the English-speaking world. It has appealed far more to Europeans, being popular in such countries as Sweden, Poland, Hungary and Czechoslovakia. As names go, Eve seems to fulfil every possible requirement, being easy to say and spell, clearly indicating its sex, and

> *Adam and Eve are registered brand names in the U.S.A., associated with cigarettes. Many other first names have similar trade connections.* **Kathy** *is linked with lingerie,* **Joan** *with candy,* **Lynn** *with shoe-polish,* **Dennis** *with chicken and turkey products,* **Brenda** *with shampoo. A check on the* Trade Names Dictionary, *published by Gale Research, may reveal unsuspected commercial aspects of your own name.*

having an impeccable biblical background. Perhaps the growing fondness for **Adam** at the present time will cause parents who have that name in mind for a son to switch to Eve if they have a daughter. They could hardly do better.

New names

The other kind of name which fails to date its bearer is the 'new' name. Often it is of the kind we saw in the previous two chapters, brought into being by re-spelling a traditional name or by adding a suffix to it. Such names may not date, but all too often they have other disadvantages. In attempting to be novel they are likely to be so in the wrong way, attracting the kind of comment that would come the way of a person wearing outlandish clothes. Each name of this type must be judged on its individual merits, of course, and some new inventions are highly successful, but the decision to invent rather than to stay within established limits must not be taken lightly.

America has led the way with new names, with **Almita** and **Charlena**, **Delisa** and **Jerlene, Lovette, Velda** and **Melvina**. The list is endless, for such names may be borne by only one or two people in a generation, or by no-one else at all. A small number of parents have always favoured such names, for many new 'inventions' are to be found in the parish registers of long ago. The American example of using such names this century has not necessarily caused them to be imitated elsewhere, but it has perhaps contributed to a general wish for newness of one kind or another. Name fashions now change far more rapidly than ever before and there is a ready acceptance of previously unknown first names such as **Kerry** and **Hayley**.

New names are an essential part of the American scene, giving it a breadth unparalleled in the English-speaking world. Equally American, however, are all those traditional names which the country as a whole has taken to its heart. The origins of the names are varied, their histories very different, and they have come to the U.S.A. by many routes, but all have shown that they have a right to stay. They have been made American citizens by popular acclaim, and that is no mean achievement.

Variant spelling forms are grouped under the main spellings.

Arizona

1. Mary	1. John
2. Linda	2. David
Patricia	3. Michael
4. Deborah	4. Robert
5. Susan	5. Richard
6. Catherine	6. Steven
7. Ann(e)	William
8. Barbara	8. Thomas
Carol(e)	9. James
10. Nancy	10. Charles
11. Elizabeth	11. Mark
12. Cynthia	12. Gary
13. Christine	13. Jeffrey
Margaret	14. Donald
15. Pamela	15. Ronald
16. Dian(n)e	16. Daniel
17. Jane	17. Peter
Judith	18. Bruce
Laura	Joseph
Sandra	20. Al(l)an
	Dennis
	Douglas
	George

Arkansas

1. Mary	1. James
2. Deborah	2. John
3. Linda	3. William
4. Karen	4. Robert
5. Barbara	5. David
6. Judy	6. Thomas
Nancy	7. Charles
8. Brenda	8. Michael
Carolyn	9. Larry
Patricia	10. Ronald
Sharon	11. Richard
12. Catherine	Steven
13. Kathy	13. Gary
Susan	14. Donald
15. Elizabeth	15. Dennis
Pamela	Kenneth
17. Cynthia	17. Joseph
Donna	18. Carl
Janet	Edward
Sandra	George
Vicki(e)	

California

1. Susan	1. John
2. Deborah	2. Robert
3. Patricia	3. James
4. Karen	4. Michael
Mary	5. Richard
6. Catherine	6. David
7. Barbara	7. Steven
8. Nancy	8. William
9. Linda	9. Gary
10. Kathleen	10. Thomas
11. Dian(n)e	11. Kenneth
12. Ann(e)	12. Donald
13. Janice	Paul
Sandra	14. Mark
15. Cheryl	Ronald
Janet	16. Charles
17. Cynthia	17. Jeffrey
Elizabeth	18. Dennis
Gail	19. Gregory
Joan	20. Al(l)an
Laurie	
Pamela	

Connecticut

1. Susan	1. John
2. Deborah	2. David
3. Barbara	3. Robert
4. Patricia	4. Richard
5. Mary	5. William
6. Linda	6. James
7. Nancy	7. Michael
8. Karen	Thomas
9. Carol(e)	9. Steven
Elizabeth	10. Paul
11. Janet	11. Charles
12. Catherine	12. Joseph
13. Dian(n)e	13. Mark
14. Cynthia	14. Peter
15. Joanne	15. Daniel
Margaret	16. Bruce
Pamela	Donald
18. Ellen	Jeffrey
19. Ann(e)	19. Edward
20. Judith	Gary

Florida

1. Susan	1. Robert	
2. Deborah	2. John	
Mary	3. James	
4. Barbara	4. Steven	
Karen	5. David	
Nancy	6. Michael	
7. Maria	7. Richard	
Sandra	8. Jeffrey	
9. Carol(e)	9. Paul	
Linda	Thomas	
11. Lynn(e)	11. Gary	
Catherine	Joseph	
Michelle	William	
Pamela	14. Daniel	
15. Sharon	Kenneth	
Elizabeth	16. George	
17. Janet	Mark	
Janice	Ronald	
Wendy	19. Charles	
20. Ann(e)	20. Al(l)an	
Cynthia	Jose	
Gail		
Patricia		

Georgia

1. Mary	1. James
2. Susan	2. Robert
3. Deborah	3. William
4. Patricia	4. John
5. Catherine	5. Steven
6. Barbara	6. David
Carol(e)	7. Michael
Linda	8. Charles
9. Nancy	9. Richard
10. Carolyn	10. Thomas
Donna	11. Gary
Janet	12. Joseph
Pamela	13. Ronald
14. Gail	14. George
Martha	15. Donald
16. Beverly	Mark
17. Cynthia	17. Paul
18. Sandra	18. Daniel
Sharon	19. Al(l)an
20. Kathy	Kenneth
Elizabeth	

Illinois

1. Deborah	1. Robert
2. Susan	2. James
3. Mary	3. John
4. Linda	4. Michael
5. Nancy	5. Mark
6. Barbara	6. Steven
Margaret	7. Thomas
8. Elizabeth	8. David
Karen	William
10. Catherine	10. Jeffrey
11. Ann(e)	Richard
Carol(e)	12. Philip
Christine	13. Donald
Pamela	Joseph
15. Cynthia	15. Kenneth
Janet	Paul
Judith	17. Peter
Patricia	18. Edward
19. Ellen	Ronald
Gail	20. Gary

Indiana

1. Mary	1. John
2. Susan	2. Michael
3. Barbara	3. Thomas
4. Deborah	4. James
5. Linda	5. William
6. Janet	6. Robert
7. Karen	7. Joseph
Nancy	8. David
Patricia	9. Mark
10. Marilyn	10. Richard
11. Cynthia	11. Kevin
12. Janice	Paul
13. Jane	13. Steven
Kathleen	14. Charles
Kathy	15. Daniel
16. Rebecca	Edward
17. Carol(e)	17. Timothy
Elizabeth	18. Dennis
Sandra	Patrick
20. Margaret	20. Gregory

Iowa

1. Mary	1. David
2. Deborah	Steven
3. Barbara	3. John
4. Susan	4. James
5. Ann(e)	Michael
6. Patricia	Richard
7. Carol(e)	7. Gary
8. Linda	8. Mark
9. Nancy	Robert
10. Kathleen	10. William
11. Catherine	11. Thomas
Cynthia	12. Dennis
Jane	13. Daniel
14. Dian(n)e	Jeffrey
Janet	Timothy
Marcia	16. Kenneth
Margaret	Roger
Pamela	18. Al(l)an
19. Janice	Joseph
Jean	Paul
Karen	
Rebecca	

Kansas

1. Deborah	1. John
2. Mary	2. Michael
3. Susan	3. David
4. Linda	4. Robert
5. Patricia	5. James
6. Catherine	6. Steven
7. Barbara	7. Richard
8. Karen	8. William
9. Nancy	9. Mark
10. Elizabeth	Thomas
11. Ann(e)	11. Charles
Cynthia	12. Gary
13. Jane	13. Dennis
14. Pamela	Jeffrey
15. Kathleen	15. Daniel
16. Kathy	Gregory
Janet	17. Bruce
18. Carol(e)	Donald
Dian(n)e	19. Paul
20. Margaret	Ronald
Marilyn	Timothy

Kentucky

1. Mary	1. John
2. Deborah	2. James
3. Nancy	3. David
4. Susan	4. William
5. Linda	5. Robert
6. Patricia	6. Steven
7. Pamela	7. Michael
8. Catherine	8. Charles
9. Elizabeth	9. Richard
10. Janet	10. Thomas
11. Ann(e)	11. Joseph
Carol(e)	12. Gary
Jane	13. Mark
Karen	14. Donald
15. Barbara	Larry
Sharon	16. Ronald
17. Margaret	17. Paul
Rebecca	18. George
19. Donna	19. Kenneth
Vicki(e)	20. Timothy

Louisiana

1. Deborah	1. James
2. Mary	2. William
3. Patricia	3. Robert
Susan	4. John
5. Nancy	5. Charles
6. Margaret	6. Richard
7. Karen	7. David
Rebecca	8. Michael
9. Donna	9. Steven
Kathy	10. Thomas
11. Carol(e)	11. George
Martha	12. Larry
Pamela	13. Gary
Sharon	14. Mark
15. Catherine	Paul
Jane	16. Dennis
Janice	Joseph
Judith	Kenneth
19. Linda	19. Daniel
20. Ann(e)	20. Philip
Barbara	
Brenda	
Kathleen	

Maryland

1. Deborah	1. John
Mary	2. Robert
3. Patricia	3. James
4. Barbara	4. Michael
5. Susan	5. Steven
Nancy	6. Richard
7. Linda	7. William
8. Carol(e)	8. Thomas
Karen	9. David
10. Margaret	10. Mark
11. Catherine	11. Joseph
12. Ann(e)	12. Al(l)an
13. Janet	13. Jeffrey
Kathleen	14. Edward
15. Dian(n)e	Paul
Elizabeth	16. Charles
17. Joan	17. Donald
Sharon	18. Gary
19. Cynthia	Ronald
Pamela	20. Dennis

Massachusetts

1. Deborah	1. David
2. Mary	2. Robert
3. Susan	3. John
Ann(e)	4. Michael
5. Carol(e)	Richard
6. Barbara	6. Steven
Ellen	7. James
8. Margaret	8. Mark
Nancy	9. Jeffrey
10. Karen	Paul
Linda	11. Peter
Patricia	Joseph
13. Cynthia	13. Lawrence
Dian(n)e	14. William
15. Elizabeth	15. Al(l)an
Janice	Bruce
17. Catherine	17. Edward
Gail	18. Ronald
Judith	19. Brian
Kathleen	Christopher
Pamela	Daniel

Michigan

1. Mary	1. Michael
2. Barbara	2. Robert
Susan	3. John
4. Linda	4. James
Nancy	5. Thomas
6. Deborah	6. Richard
Patricia	7. David
8. Karen	William
9. Carol(e)	9. Kenneth
10. Dian(n)e	10. Mark
Sharon	Dennis
12. Sandra	12. Gary
13. Janet	Paul
14. Elizabeth	Ronald
Gail	15. Charles
16. Ann(e)	Joseph
17. Judith	17. Gerald
Kathleen	Steven
19. Catherine	19. Daniel
20. Beverly	George

Minnesota

1. Mary	1. John
2. Nancy	2. James
3. Susan	3. David
4. Deborah	4. Robert
5. Linda	5. Thomas
6. Barbara	6. Michael
7. Patricia	7. Mark
8. Catherine	Richard
9. Cynthia	Steven
10. Elizabeth	10. Jeffrey
Karen	Scott
Lynn(e)	12. Al(l)an
Sharon	David
14. Janet	Dennis
Kathleen	Paul
Margaret	16. William
17. Ann(e)	17. Charles
Carol(e)	Gary
Christine	Kevin
20. Sandra	Philip

Mississippi

1. Deborah	1. James
2. Mary	2. William
3. Susan	3. Robert
4. Barbara	4. John
5. Donna	5. David
Margaret	6. Charles
Patricia	7. Richard
8. Pamela	8. Michael
9. Nancy	9. Thomas
10. Betty	10. Paul
Elizabeth	11. Joseph
12. Brenda	12. Gary
Karen	George
Linda	Mark
15. Carol(e)	Steven
Jane	16. Samuel
Sandra	17. Kenneth
18. Cynthia	Larry
Janice	19. Daniel
Sharon	Donald
	Edward
	Jack

Missouri

1. Mary	1. James
2. Deborah	2. John
3. Susan	Michael
4. Linda	4. William
Nancy	5. Robert
6. Patricia	6. Steven
7. Barbara	7. David
8. Catherine	8. Richard
9. Carol(e)	9. Thomas
10. Karen	10. Mark
11. Janet	11. Gary
12. Kathleen	12. Charles
13. Cynthia	13. Donald
Elizabeth	14. Daniel
15. Pamela	Dennis
16. Martha	Gregory
17. Janice	Paul
18. Dian(n)e	18. Joseph
19. Jill	19. Al(l)an
Margaret	Jeffrey
Marcia	
Vicki(e)	

Nevada

1. Linda	1. Robert
2. Patricia	2. John
3. Susan	3. James
4. Deborah	4. Steven
5. Mary	5. William
6. Nancy	6. David
7. Catherine	7. Thomas
Karen	8. Michael
9. Carol(e)	9. Richard
10. Cynthia	10. Charles
11. Pamela	Gary
12. Barbara	12. Joseph
Elizabeth	Kenneth
Kathleen	Mark
16. Ann(e)	Paul
Janet	16. Donald
18. Jane	17. Ronald
T(h)eresa	18. George
20. Cheryl	19. Douglas
Dian(n)e	20. Christopher
Joanne	Dennis
Kathy	
Sandra	
Sharon	

New Mexico

1. Mary	1. James
2. Patricia	2. John
3. Linda	3. Robert
4. Deborah	4. Richard
5. Barbara	5. William
6. Nancy	6. Michael
Susan	7. David
8. Karen	8. Gary
9. Janet	9. Thomas
Catherine	10. Steven
11. Rebecca	11. Charles
Sandra	12. Mark
13. Elizabeth	13. Larry
Kathleen	14. Donald
Maria	George
16. Brenda	16. Dennis
Donna	17. Daniel
Judy	Joseph
Pamela	Paul
T(h)eresa	20. Roger

New York

1. Susan	1. Robert
2. Barbara	2. Michael
3. Patricia	3. Steven
4. Deborah	4. Richard
5. Mary	5. John
6. Linda	6. David
7. Karen	7. James
8. Carol(e)	William
9. Kathleen	9. Paul
10. Judith	10. Joseph
11. Dian(n)e	11. Jeffrey
12. Margaret	12. Mark
13. Ellen	13. Peter
14. Janet	14. Charles
15. Pamela	15. Al(l)an
16. Ann(e)	Edward
17. Catherine	17. Andrew
18. Gail	18. Daniel
Robin	19. Bruce
20. Donna	20. George

North Carolina

1. Catherine	1. John
2. Susan	2. James
3. Mary	3. David
4. Deborah	Robert
5. Elizabeth	William
6. Karen	6. Steven
7. Ann(e)	7. Richard
Linda	8. Michael
9. Barbara	9. Charles
Cynthia	10. Thomas
Patricia	11. Mark
12. Margaret	12. George
Sarah	13. Bruce
14. Lynn(e)	Jeffrey
15. Carol(e)	15. Daniel
Ellen	Donald
Marcia	Douglas
18. Carolyn	Paul
Kathleen	19. Joseph
20. Dian(n)e	Peter
Julia	
Laura	
Marilyn	
Martha	
Pamela	
T(h)eresa	

North Dakota

1. Mary	1. John
2. Deborah	2. Michael
3. Dian(n)e	3. Robert
Karen	4. David
5. Barbara	5. James
6. Carol(e)	Richard
Patricia	7. Steven
Susan	8. Thomas
9. Nancy	9. Roger
10. Linda	10. Jeffrey
11. Cynthia	Mark
Sandra	Timothy
13. Catherine	13. Donald
Margaret	Ronald
15. Julie	15. Larry
Rebecca	William
Vicki(e)	17. Douglas
18. Colleen	Kenneth
Gail	Paul
Judith	20. Dennis
Marilyn	Gregory
	Keith
	Rodney

Ohio

1. Deborah	1. Robert
2. Mary	2. James
3. Susan	3. John
4. Barbara	4. David
5. Linda	5. Richard
6. Patricia	6. Michael
7. Nancy	7. Thomas
8. Carol(e)	8. Steven
9. Karen	9. William
10. Cynthia	10. Mark
Kathleen	11. Gary
12. Ann(e)	Jeffrey
13. Judith	13. Charles
Kathy	14. Ronald
15. Catherine	15. Daniel
16. Pamela	Joseph
17. Jane	Paul
Janet	18. Timothy
19. Margaret	19. Kenneth
Sandra	20. Donald
Sharon	

Oklahoma

1. Mary	1. John
2. Patricia	2. Robert
3. Susan	3. Michael
4. Dian(n)e	4. William
5. Deborah	5. James
6. Barbara	6. Charles
Catherine	7. David
Sandra	8. Richard
9. Nancy	Steven
Sarah	10. Gary
11. Ann(e)	11. Joseph
Karen	Mark
Linda	Paul
Marilyn	Ronald
15. Carol(e)	15. Donald
Kathleen	16. George
Marcia	17. Gregory
18. Donna	18. Thomas
Janice	19. Larry
20. Rebecca	Peter
	Timothy

Oregon

1. Mary	1. Robert
2. Deborah	2. John
Nancy	3. Steven
4. Susan	4. James
5. Barbara	5. Michael
Catherine	6. David
7. Linda	7. Richard
8. Karen	8. Thomas
9. Janet	9. Gary
Kathleen	10. William
11. Ann(e)	11. Mark
12. Margaret	12. Daniel
13. Patricia	Jeffrey
Sandra	14. Charles
15. Carol(e)	15. Gregory
16. Cynthia	16. Paul
Laura	17. Joseph
Marcia	18. Bruce
19. Elizabeth	Donald
Jane	Kenneth

Pennsylvania

1. Mary	1. James
2. Patricia	2. John
3. Kathleen	3. Michael
4. Linda	4. Richard
5. Susan	5. Thomas
6. Barbara	6. William
Deborah	7. David
Karen	Joseph
9. Carol(e)	9. Robert
Margaret	10. Edward
11. Catherine	11. Steven
12. Joanne	12. Daniel
13. Dian(n)e	13. Dennis
Nancy	George
15. Elizabeth	Lawrence
Janice	Mark
Michel(l)e	Paul
T(h)eresa	18. Ant(h)ony
19. Ann(e)	Charles
Donna	Jeffrey
Joan	Ronald

Tennessee

1. Mary	1. James
2. Deborah	2. William
3. Linda	3. John
4. Susan	4. David
5. Patricia	5. Robert
6. Nancy	6. Michael
7. Elizabeth	7. Steven
8. Janet	8. Thomas
Karen	9. Charles
10. Carol(e)	10. Richard
Kathy	11. Gary
12. Catherine	12. Donald
13. Barbara	13. Joseph
Rebecca	14. Mark
15. Margaret	15. Ronald
Sandra	16. Philip
17. Martha	17. Edward
Pamela	George
19. Ann(e)	Kenneth
20. Jane	20. Larry

Texas

1. Deborah	1. John
2. Mary	2. William
3. Patricia	3. Robert
4. Cynthia	4. David
Nancy	5. Michael
6. Rebecca	6. James
7. Barbara	7. Charles
Catherine	Steven
Janet	9. Richard
Linda	10. Thomas
11. Carol(e)	11. Gary
12. Karen	12. Larry
13. Carolyn	13. Donald
Elizabeth	Kenneth
Kathy	15. Ronald
16. Marcia	Paul
Sandra	17. Mark
Sarah	18. Daniel
19. Beverly	19. Douglas
Judy	20. Jerry
Laura	
Lynn(e)	
Susan	

Utah

1. Susan	1. John
2. Kathleen	2. David
Linda	Steven
4. Patricia	4. Robert
5. Catherine	5. Richard
6. Christine	6. James
Karen	7. Michael
Nancy	8. William
9. Barbara	9. Thomas
Mary	10. Mark
11. Carolyn	11. Paul
Deborah	12. Douglas
13. Ann(e)	13. Gary
Dian(n)e	14. Ronald
15. Carol(e)	15. Al(l)an
16. Margaret	16. Craig
17. Sharon	17. Jeffrey
18. Jane	18. Gregory
Lynn(e)	19. George
Marilyn	Scott
Michel(l)e	

Vermont

1. Susan	1. John
2. Mary	2. James
3. Deborah	3. Robert
4. Barbara	4. Michael
5. Linda	5. William
6. Patricia	6. David
7. Nancy	Steven
8. Ann(e)	8. Peter
Elizabeth	Thomas
10. Catherine	10. Mark
11. Kathleen	11. Charles
12. Carol(e)	Gary
Margaret	Richard
14. Cynthia	14. Donald
Jane	15. Paul
Karen	16. Bruce
17. Dian(n)e	Christopher
Ellen	Timothy
Gail	19. Andrew
Janet	Philip

Virginia

1. Mary	1. James
2. Linda	2. William
3. Elizabeth	3. John
Patricia	Robert
5. Deborah	5. Michael
6. Carol(e)	6. David
Nancy	7. Thomas
Susan	8. Steven
9. Ann(e)	9. Richard
Catherine	10. Charles
11. Judith	Mark
12. Jane	12. Donald
13. Cheryl	13. Al(l)an
14. Sharon	Gary
Sheila	George
16. Alice	16. Daniel
Brenda	Kenneth
Dian(n)e	Larry
Donna	Paul
Kathy	Ronald
Margaret	

Washington

1. Mary	1. Robert
2. Deborah	2. Michael
Susan	3. John
4. Nancy	Steven
5. Barbara	5. David
6. Linda	6. James
7. Catherine	7. Richard
8. Patricia	8. William
9. Kathleen	9. Thomas
10. Dian(n)e	10. Mark
11. Carol(e)	11. Ronald
12. Karen	12. Donald
13. Janet	13. Gary
Pamela	14. Paul
15. Ann(e)	15. Douglas
Gail	16. Patrick
17. Christine	17. Gregory
18. Cynthia	Larry
19. Sandra	19. Jeffrey
20. Lynn(e)	20. Al(l)an
Marcia	Daniel
Rebecca	

West Virginia

1. Deborah	1. John
2. Mary	2. Robert
3. Linda	3. James
Patricia	4. Michael
5. Susan	5. David
6. Karen	6. Richard
7. Kathleen	7. Charles
8. Barbara	William
9. Nancy	9. Thomas
Pamela	10. Gary
11. Catherine	Paul
Donna	12. Donald
13. Carol(e)	13. George
14. Janet	Steven
Sandra	15. Joseph
16. Beverly	16. Dennis
17. Dian(n)e	17. Ronald
18. Bonnie	18. Bruce
Jean	Edward
Margaret	Mark
Sharon	
Vicki(e)	

Wisconsin

1. Mary	1. James
2. Susan	2. John
3. Barbara	Michael
4. Deborah	4. Thomas
Linda	5. Robert
6. Nancy	6. Steven
7. Patricia	7. David
8. Ann(e)	8. William
9. Christine	9. Mark
10. Jane	10. Richard
11. Catherine	11. Jeffrey
12. Karen	12. Daniel
Margaret	13. Charles
14. Judith	14. Gary
15. Carol(e)	Paul
16. Dian(n)e	16. Dennis
Sandra	Peter
18. Jean	Timothy
Lynn(e)	19. Bruce
20. Joan	Gregory
	Joseph
	Scott

Wyoming

1. Mary	1. John
2. Deborah	2. James
3. Susan	Robert
4. Linda	4. Michael
5. Barbara	5. David
Sandra	6. Richard
7. Kathleen	Steven
Patricia	8. William
9. Catherine	9. Thomas
Janet	10. George
11. Pamela	11. Douglas
12. Ann(e)	Kenneth
Dian(n)e	Ronald
Margaret	14. Charles
15. Carol(e)	Daniel
Karen	Jack
Nancy	Jeffrey
18. Cynthia	Mark
Janice	19. Dennis
20. Jane	Donald
Joan	
Marilyn	
Peggy	
Sharon	
T(h)eresa	

13 Names Freely Given

The first names of black Americans

The naming habits of black Americans differ in some ways from those of the whites. It is not that black Americans use one set of names while whites use another: most Americans use the same names, but in ways that nevertheless reflect their own taste and cultural heritage. In what follows I shall concentrate on the characteristics of black American naming habits and some of the historical reasons for them.

I must acknowledge before I begin a special debt to the late Professor Newbell N. Puckett. He made a collection of some 340,000 names borne by blacks in America from 1619 onwards. A further 160,000 white American names were also collected for the purposes of comparison. The names were arranged and edited by Murray Heller and published in 1975 as *Black Names in America: Origins and Usage*. This work should obviously be consulted by those with a specialized interest; meanwhile I propose to make extensive use of the lists of names. The interpretation of what the names tell us, however, is my own.

Slave names

The names of American blacks begin with the arrival in America of the first slaves. All of those who came undoubtedly had tribal names of their own already, but they often came from cultures where it would not have been the custom to reveal one's true name to strangers. We saw some of the reasons for this in the chapter on Name Magic. Most slaves were probably not invited to reveal their names in any case. They were regarded as property, and owners of property always consider that they have a right to bestow a name if one is required. Even the slave-owners who adopted a more humane attitude would have found the African names difficult to pronounce and remember, and they would have sounded alien to American ears. For all these reasons, slaves were usually given new names at the time of purchase.

The traders did little naming, for they probably thought of their cargoes in the way they would have thought of cattle. Evidence of this comes in various records which show, for example, that when traders offered slaves for sale, or described in the ship's log-book a death during the voyage, they used phrases such as a 'man slave' or 'negro man'. No further identification was felt to be necessary.

The occasional naming that did take place on board the slave ships was merely an opportunity to exercise humour. One seaman described in 1860 how favourite slaves on board might be dubbed **'Main-Stay, Bull's-Eye, Rope-Yarn,** and various other sea-phrases'. The surgeon on board an English slaver, *The Ruby*, had earlier written: 'The first slave that was traded for . . . was a girl of about fifteen who was promptly named Eve, for it was usual on slave ships to give the names of Adam and Eve to the first man and woman brought aboard.' These names may sometimes have stuck, for **Adam** and **Eve** are both to be found amongst black slaves of the eighteenth century. They are just as likely, however, to have been names bestowed by the plantation owners or overseers.

A small number of African names did occasionally survive amongst the slaves. A group recently arrived might be strongly influenced by the social hierarchy they had known at home. J. B. Cobb reports on men whose facial tattooing caused them to be treated with great respect by other slaves, and it is significant that these men retained their African names in their own community. Such names were rarely passed on to descendants, however. The usual names amongst the slaves very quickly became those of the whites.

Slave names were chosen for simplicity and convenience. Heller makes a comparison between the names of mules in Mississippi and names that were common amongst the slaves. Shoutable names such as **Jack, Tom, Ned,**

Some slaves may have been given the names of the ships on which they travelled to America. The ships in turn often bore first names: 'The popularity of particular feminine names for ships correlates with fashion in names among the general population. By way of illustration, Sukey, a diminutive for Susan or Susanna, had a brief two-continent popularity. Sukey *appeared seven times in* Lloyd's *edition of 1776 as the name for ships, mostly brigs, built between 1759 and 1773.* Sukey *appeared in American registers between 1789 and 1795 but not thereafter.'*
D. H. Kennedy, Ship Names: Origins and Usages During 45 Centuries

The wives and daughters of the plantation-owners seem to have suggested names for slaves culled from their reading of literature. *The Complete Works of Shakespeare* in itself offered as many suggestions for names as any modern *Naming the Baby* book. Those listed below all occur in his plays and poems.

Women

Adriana	Cytherea	Hippolyta	Lychorida	Regan
Aemilia	Desdemona	Imogen	Margaret	Rosalind
Alice	Diana	Iras	Margery	Rosaline
Andromache	Dionyza	Isabel	Maria	Silvia
Anne	Doll	Isabella	Mariana	Tamora
Audrey	Dorcas	Jaquenetta	Marina	Thaisa
Beatrice	Eleanor	Jessica	Miranda	Timandra
Bianca	Elinor	Joan	Mopsa	Titania
Blanche	Elizabeth	Julia	Nerissa	Ursula
Bona	Emilia	Juliet	Octavia	Valeria
Calphurnia	Francisca	Katharine	Olivia	Viola
Cassandra	Gertrude	Katherina	Ophelia	Violenta
Celia	Goneril	Katherine	Patience	Virgilia
Charmian	Helen	Lavinia	Paulina	Volumnia
Cleopatra	Helena	Luce	Perdita	
Constance	Hermia	Lucetta	Phoebe	
Cordelia	Hermione	Luciana	Phrynia	
Cressida	Hero	Lucretia	Portia	

Men

Aaron	Charles	Hubert	Nathaniel	Quintus
Abraham	Christopher	Hugh	Nestor	Ralph
Achilles	Cicero	Humphrey	Nicholas	Richard
Adam	Claudius	Iago	Oberon	Robert
Adrian	Clitus	Jack	Octavius	Roderigo
Agamemnon	Cornelius	James	Oliver	Roger
Agrippa	Curtis	John	Orlando	Romeo
Ajax	Demetrius	Julius	Orsino	Ross
Alexander	Dennis	Junius	Osric	Sampson
Alonso	Diomedes	Launcelot	Oswald	Saunder
Andrew	Duncan	Lawrence	Othello	Sebastian
Angus	Edgar	Lear	Owen	Sextus
Anthony	Edmund	Leontes	Pandarus	Simon
Antonio	Edward	Lewis	Paris	Stephen
Archibald	Eros	Lorenzo	Percy	Tarquin
Arthur	Fabian	Lucius	Pericles	Theseus
Banquo	Ferdinand	Lysander	Peter	Thomas
Benedict	Francis	Macbeth	Philip	Timon
Bernado	Frederick	Malcolm	Pierce	Titus
Bertram	George	Marcus	Pindarus	Toby
Brutus	Gregory	Mark	Polonius	Troilus
Caesar	Hamlet	Matthew	Pompey	Ulysses
Cassio	Hector	Menelaus	Priam	Valentine
Cassius	Henry	Michael	Prospero	Walter
Cato	Horatio	Moth	Proteus	William

Bill and the like were used for both, but one cannot necessarily attach too much significance to the point. These names were also common amongst the whites. Surnames were not felt to be necessary for the slaves, though the custom later arose of distinguishing between those of the same name by adding the surname of their owner. These surnames were often retained by slaves who gained their freedom.

Shakespearian names

Apart from simple forms of white first names, slaves were frequently given names like **Caesar, Cato, Pompey, Jupiter, Scipio, Nero, Cicero** and **Ulysses**. The women in their turn became **Diana, Dido, Phoebe** and **Venus**. This seems to indicate that some owners had a grim sense of humour or wished to display their own education.

Some of these names were not necessarily taken directly from classical sources. A slave-owner could have opened any *Complete Works of Shakespeare* and found most of them. Pompey looks especially Shakespearian, in fact, since a character of that name is clown and servant to Mistress Overdone in *Measure for Measure*. As Mistress Overdone's name suggests, the humour in this play is often bawdy. Shakespeare again amused himself with the name in *Love's Labours Lost*. If it really was bestowed on black slaves as a joke, it seems to me to have been one that misfired. The plantation owner's wife became, by implication, a Mistress Overdone.

An alternative source for these classical-looking names in the eighteenth century was the best-selling novel, *Tristram Shandy*. The famous passage from the book I quoted earlier (page 41) about the significance of names mentions both Caesar and Pompey.

Place names

Enough British place names occur as male slave names in the eighteenth century to suggest that slave-owners operated a definite system. Some white

---

Escalus: Come you hither to me, Master Tapster; what's your name, Master Tapster?
Pompey: Pompey.
Escalus: What else?
Pompey: Bum, sir.
Escalus: Troth, and your bum is the greatest thing about you; so that, in the beastliest sense, you are Pompey the Great.
William Shakespeare, Measure for Measure, *Act 2*

settlers may have felt that names should be used for slaves which were familiar and therefore easy to remember, but that white first names were not appropriate. Slaves therefore found themselves bearing names such as **Bristol, York, London, Cambridge, Essex, Limehouse, Salisbury** and **Warwick**. Some of these could also have been given on board the slave ships, for they could have been the sailors' home towns. In this connection it is interesting to remember that Pompey, discussed above, has long been the slang name amongst British sailors for Portsmouth.

Whatever the reasons for their bestowal, it is unlikely that the slaves given these names would have objected to them. They would not have been able to distinguish between place and personal names, and one name would have seemed as good as another. An indication that they were accepted by their bearers is that those slaves who became free often retained names of this type. One man, for instance, was quite happy to remain **Isle of Wight**.

Other names borne by eighteenth-century slaves are obvious nicknames by origin. **Smart, Lemon, Mink, Orange, Scrub, Tomboy, Floor, Chat, Cherry** and **Punch** are amongst those found in the lists. These normally occur, however, as single examples, whereas **Peter, John, James: Mary, Sarah, Hannah** and the like are very frequent. Floor occurs four times in the lists and may just possibly have been, as Heller suggests, the name given to a female slave whose job was to keep the floors clean. But **Flora** was a frequent name among the slaves, and Floor is probably a form of it. **Easter** is another name classed by Heller as a nickname, but in early British registers this is sometimes the written form of **Esther**.

Prince was early established as a slave name and occurs as often as a name like James. It looks a highly flattering name, but it could as easily have been an ironical nickname bestowed on a man who was the opposite of princely. Naming a short man **Lofty** or a bald man **Curly**, after all, is a long-established custom. To me, there is something highly suspicious about the name Prince, in spite of its apparent suggestion of nobility, but this may be because in modern times the name more readily suggests a pet dog or a horse than a person.

Sambo

Sambo, the name that was later to become a generic nickname for a black person, was already to be found as a personal name in the eighteenth century. The origin of the name is obscure. A number of African languages seem to offer possible explanations for it, but so does Spanish. There is a term in that language meaning 'bandy-legged' which many etymologists believe led to Sambo. Whatever its origin, in terms of frequency the name seems at no point to have been all that typical for a black male. Caesar was far more so, and even Prince occurs twice as often as Sambo in the early sources.

> *British newspapers reported in 1974 the case of a West Indian factory worker who was addressed as **Sambo** by one of his white colleagues. Use of the name led to a fight and hospital treatment for the white worker. At the subsequent trial, the judge was of the opinion that the West Indian worker had been in the wrong to react so violently. He considered that Sambo was no more than a playful name of the type that British workmen frequently used to one another.*

Nineteenth-century names

Slavery continued into the nineteenth century, though many more black Americans had by now become free. Professor Puckett's lists are more extensive for the period between 1800–1860, but what does not emerge from them is which names were given at birth by parents and which were nicknames. It is not even clear whether parents were always responsible for names like John and Mary, for these could have been re-namings by slave owners.

As they stand, the Puckett lists show a large number of biblical names in use before 1860, just as there were for the whites. Classical names such as **Caesar**, whether in that form or as **Caezar, Cesar, Seasar** or **Sezar**, remained common amongst both free blacks and slaves, but were not used by whites. Place names as first names continued to indicate that their bearers were black, a few such names now being borne by women as well as men. Favourite male names of this type were now **York, Essex, Richmond, London, Aberdeen, Holland, Glasgow, Scotland, Boston, Dublin, Paris** and **Troy**. All these clearly reveal their place name origins, but with the many girls called **Charlotte** it is impossible to know whether the white first name was being used or whether the places of this name in Virginia and North Carolina provided the source. These had themselves been named in honour of Charlotte Sophia, wife of George III. No doubt the fact that an important person and place *could* bear the same name made the use of names like **Virginia** and **Georgia** acceptable first names at all social levels from this time on.

Poetic names

A girl's name that suddenly appears amongst female slaves in the early century is **Malinda** or **Melinda**. Murray Heller refers to this as 'an African

A famous personal name in literature that derives from a place name is that of **Romeo**. *The name means 'one who comes from Rome' or 'one who made a pilgrimage to Rome'. Romeo's rival in the play is Count* **Paris**, *but this does not necessarily derive from the city of the same name. The name could have been borrowed from the Paris of the Greek myths, who carried off Helen. As a child he had been exposed on Mount Ida, but his life was saved by a she-bear, who suckled him. Agelaus found him and brought him home in a 'paris', a kind of traveller's bag, or wallet.*

place name' and includes it with rarely used names like **Venice, India** and **Tennessee** which undoubtedly did derive from places. Ernest Weekley, however, hints at the true origin in his *Jack and Jill*: 'The later Stuarts had rather a craze for names in -inda, such as **Clarinda, Dorinda, Florinda, Melinda** . . . ' The latter form of the name occurs in a poem by Mrs Aphra Behn (1640–1689) which begins:

> Melinda, who had never been
> Esteemed a beauty at fifteen,
> Always amorous was, and kind.

The poem goes on to describe Melinda as a flirt. It is more than likely that Mrs Behn, like most poets of the time, invented the name herself.

Heller himself rightly remarks that 'Southern mistresses seem to have had a great affection for British novels.' It seems obvious that the wives and daughters of the plantation owners must often have suggested 'pretty' names to their servants, culled from their reading of both poetry and fiction. I have not the slightest doubt that Melinda came from this source. If further proof were needed, **Belinda, Celinda** and **Clarinda** are other names that occur in the slave name lists, the latter again wrongly classed by Heller as a place name but probably invented by Robert Burns. **Lucinda**, with fifty-four occurrences, is well among the most popular names. There are even two examples of **Ellender**, which probably derive from a poem by Lovelace, *Ellinda's Grove*.

Apart from the names in -inda, female names of the time that suggest literary sources include **Celia, Chloe, Cynthia, Eugenia, Flora, Iris, Julia, Laura, Myra, Phyllis, Sally** and **Sophia**. Samuel Richardson's two heroines, **Clarissa** and **Pamela**, were also to be found, Clarissa being especially popular. Pamela, as the name of the most famous literary servant girl of the time, might have seemed more appropriate, but she ended up by marrying her employer after resisting his advances. Perhaps this did not recommend her to the plantation owners. Clarissa, on the other hand, had merely wasted away after being raped.

Titles

Amongst the men, it was possibly the continued use of **Prince** as a first name that had given rise to a number of similar title-names. There were now slaves called **Major, Squire, King, Judge, Duke, General, Captain** and **Governor**. Most of these were probably nicknames, conferred humorously in adulthood. **Doctor** and **Lawyer** could have acknowledged particular skills or ways of speaking, and a **Bishop** was no doubt noticeably religious. Women do not seem to have borne such names, which strengthens the view that they were nicknames rather than official names.

One new development during the first part of the nineteenth century was the borrowing of famous surnames as first names. **Washington** was the clear favourite, and those that did not use the surname used **George**, which rose to third position in the frequency table. **Madison** and **Jefferson** had their followers, and the practice was extended to include **Napoleon, Lafayette, Columbus** and **Van Buren**. This habit was not confined to blacks, however. Many whites were naming their children in a similar way.

Most usual names

In fact, although it may not appear from what has been said so far, most male American blacks in the years before the Civil War, whether they were slaves or free, bore the same names as whites. It is not just the names themselves that have to be considered, but the relative frequency of their use. For every male slave named **Liverpool** there were at least three hundred others called **John**. For every girl who was a **Savory**, another three hundred were **Mary**.

Among the free blacks, normal white names were especially prevalent. The top twenty names at this time were **John, William, James, Thomas, George, Henry, Samuel, David, Charles, Peter, Joseph, Isaac, Daniel, Richard, Robert, Benjamin, Jesse, Jacob, Moses** and **Stephen**. Only Moses among these would seem to give the slightest hint that these were the names of blacks, but Puckett's own account of white names in Georgia, 1790–1818, shows that Moses was almost equally popular with the whites.

> *Like Paris,* **Moses** *received his name from the circumstances in which he was found. He had been left in an ark amongst bulrushes and was saved by the daughter of Pharaoh. The princess called him Moses 'because I drew him out of the water'. Mo = 'water', ushe, 'saved'. An explanation often given in reference books, however, is that the name derives from* mesu, *'child'.*

Similarly, the unusual names for blacks which were to be found early in the nineteenth century were easily matched by odd names amongst the whites. Puckett's list of white names for this period is based on Tax Digests and the names must have been recorded carefully by educated clerks. We can therefore believe it when we are told that there were white males at this time named **Brazil, Britain, Cloudless, Dial, Honour, Land, Mountain, Noble, Precious, Royalbud, Savage, Sion** and **Spire**. White women included a **Lovey** and **Welcome**. Once again, however, it must be stressed that for every man or woman with a name of this type there were hundreds of Johns and Marys.

If the most popular names at one end of the scale and the odd names at the other give little indication of whether they were borne by blacks or whites, a few other names in consistent use did carry racial overtones in the early nineteenth century. Male black names as a matter of preference were **Anthony, Ephraim** and **Miles**. Amongst the girls, a Southern **Nancy** at this time was far more likely to be black than white, as were a **Sally, Polly, Lucy, Jane, Milly, Peggy, Judy, Kitty, Charity, Patience** and **Keziah**. **Mourning** and **Grief**, while not amongst the more popular names for black girls, were nevertheless to be found as frequently as names like **Celia** and **Julia**. They were rareties amongst white girls.

The differences in usage are not difficult to understand. In many cases it must have happened that a name popular with the whites was taken up by the blacks, and this helped to make the name go out of fashion with the whites. This is something that would particularly have affected girls' names, for they would have been named by mothers sensitive to such matters. Boys continued to be named for their fathers and male relations, and this essential question of continuity would have delayed any turning away from names that had become 'black'.

The twentieth century

A more precise picture of the differences between the names of American blacks and whites can be drawn as we move on into the present century. In the mid-1930s Professor Puckett made extensive counts of names amongst college students in the southern states. Some 20,000 names of black students were analysed and compared with the names of 27,000 white students. The names concerned would have been mostly those being given by the urban middle classes, black and white, around 1915.

The first general difference between the two communities is revealed by the overall distribution of names. Black Americans used more names than white parents to name comparable numbers of children. The extra names used by the black parents were not necessarily unusual or odd; they might simply be names which whites considered old-fashioned and had therefore temporarily left aside. They could also be 'new' names, usually surnames of religious and other leaders used as first names for boys. It was mainly black students, for instance, who bore names like **Booker, Luther, Curtis, Calvin, Floyd, Wesley, Irvin, Wallace, Alton, Willis, Harrison, Anderson** and **Henderson**.

Relative frequency of names

Once again one must keep such names in perspective. Amongst 9064 black students only twenty-seven were called Booker, and only six Henderson. Over 600 students in the same student population were called **James**. There were also 522 **Williams**, 445 **Johns**, 248 **Charles**, 248 **Roberts** and 238 **Georges**. **Edward, Thomas, Joseph, Henry, Samuel** and **Willie** each scored more than a hundred. All of these names, except the last, were equally popular amongst white students. The differences in usage really began with the names that were less popular.

Willie however, was one name that was much favoured at this time by black parents, so much so that they had made it to all intents and purposes their exclusive property. They used it to name girls as well as boys, though in the case of girls they often extended it to **Willie Mae**. Their liking for the name seems to have faded rapidly as the century wore on, though there were still a few black students named Willie to be found amongst 1975 graduates.

Other black male names being given around 1915 were **Nathaniel, Johnnie, Eddie, Isaac, Oliver, Matthew, Alonzo, Solomon, Aaron, Isaiah, Reginald, Moses, Ulysses, Cecil, Clifford, Roscoe, Reuben** and **Abraham**. Many of these are obvious survivals—names that had been white favourites a short time previously. One or two have come back into fashion with white Americans in recent times. Aaron and Matthew, for instance, are now becoming popular again.

Fairly popular for black girls, but apparently little favoured by white southern parents who were naming children in 1915, were names like **Carrie**, bestowed in that form instead of the **Caroline** or **Carolyn** that was now preferred by the whites; **Rosa**, which was **Rose** for whites, and **Hattie, Inez** and **Fanny**, which tended to be **Harriet, Agnes** and **Frances** when given by white parents. Apart from bearing pet names or Spanish forms of names, black girls were also more likely to be called **Mamie, Cora, Daisy, Naomi, Viola, Alberta, Geneva, Irma, Beulah** and **Ernestine**, all of which were rare at this time amongst their southern white counterparts. In less frequent use, but also decidedly black rather than white, were names like **Cornelia, Gwendolyn, Leola, Lena, Eunice, Nanny** (as a form of Nancy), **Cleo, Estelle, Lydia, Silvia, Tommie, Flora, Lelia, Ophelia, Clarissa, Lavinia**.

According to counts based on the names of students in all-black universities in 1975, the most popular names used by black American parents in the early 1950s were as shown below. Variant spellings are shown under the main spelling.

Girls

1. Deborah	12. Janice
2. Sandra	13. Carolyn
3. Patricia	Linda
4. Beverly	Marsha
5. Cynthia	16. Gail
6. Barbara	Joyce
Mary	18. Brenda
8. Denise	Gwendolyn
Jacqueline	20. Constance
10. Catherine	Karen
11. Betty	Marilyn

Men

1. James	12. Francis
2. Michael	13. Paul
3. Robert	14. Raymond
4. Charles	Samuel
5. William	16. Donald
6. Edward	Joseph
7. John	Victor
8. Richard	19. Ernest
9. Ronald	Thomas
10. Gregory	
Kenneth	

Apart from the names that were used frequently, a wide range of other names were borne by the black American students. The examples listed below show some of the more individual names in use.

Girls

Aldith	Blyss	Delinda	Ermajean
Almeater	Bonita	Delisa	Evangeline
Alnita	Burlette	Delma	Everleana
Alvicia	Camilla	Delois	Evon
Angie	Carlene	Demetra	Fern
Antoinette	Catherlean	Deverne	Fleet
Applice	Ceola	Diretta	Frankie
Arcadia	Charlezetta	Dorcus	Freda
Arneathia	Charmane	Dortah	Geraldean
Arnita	Cherita	Drucilla	Gilda
Arthetta	Cheyenne	Dyane	Gilla
Artra	Clover	Earleen	Glinda
Arvella	Corliss	Eartha	Hattierene
Augusta	Corrinne	Ebbie	Hilda
Belita	Cozetta	Edwenia	Hyacinth
Benita	Dalinda	Ellana	Jeanarta
Berley	Davida	Elmira	Jenita
Bernetta	Dawana	Elnora	Jewel
Birdia	Dedra	Elsonia	Johnette

The Names of Black Americans

Juanita	Luevonnia	Nesta	Shirl
Kahlita	Lunnette	Noida	Shirlene
Katrinka	Luvenia	Obsie	Sigma
Kusella	Lynnerose	Ora	Sophronia
Lablanche	Malinda	Ouida	Sylvonia
Laveeda	Marquette	Pearl	Tawatha
Lazette	Marva	Percilla	Tenea
Le Ethel	Maryllynne	Peregrina	Theda
Lelia	Maurita	Pinnie	Thomasine
Lemae	Melendia	Princell	Thurma
Leneta	Melinda	Queenie	Tuleda
Lenettc	Melissa	Regina	Velma
Leticia	Melissia	Retta	Verity
Lila	Merthia	Romona	Verna
Lilia	Millicent	Ronie	Voneil
Lillette	Minnette	Ruby	Wilma
Livian	Montanette	Runia	Winona
Lonice	Moravia	Ruthena	Yolanda
Lottie	Moretta	Salona	Zanette
Louetta	Myrlin	Saundra	Zenobia
Louveller	Myrtle	Scherri	Zinna
Loverine	Nannie	Sherrie	

Men

Algernon	Early	Jonah	Myrtis
Alonzo	Egbert	Joshua	Nestor
Andra	Elbert	Jule	Oliver
Arphelius	Elijah	Junius	Porter
August	Elton	Knollie	Roddy
Austin	Emanuel	Lancelot	Roland
Avon	Ephraim	Leander	Roosevelt
Beaufus	Errol	Legustus	Roscoe
Berry	Ervin	Leister	Rudolph
Boyd	Everett	Leland	Salone
Byron	Floristine	Lemarr	Selwyn
Cleophus	Gabriel	Leverne	Sherman
Cliffie	Garfield	Levonne	Stacy
Clyde	Harlee	Linwood	Sylvester
Cornelius	Hobart	Lloyd	Tamba
Craddock	Hubert	Luther	Vernal
Dante	Ichabod	Milloyd	Wilbert
Devon	Ivory	Monroe	Windsor
Dionysius	Jake	Montez	Winston
Dorsey	Joel	Mortimer	

> *For some reason the pet names from **Ann**, usually **Nancy** but sometimes **Nanny**, have taken on a variety of unpleasant meanings. A 'Nancy boy', 'nance' in the U.S.A., is an insulting name for an effeminate man. A 'nanny' in the eighteenth century was a prostitute, and a 'nanny-house', or 'nanny-shop', a brothel. The female goat became a 'nanny' at about the same time. 'Nanny' was given new respectability in the nineteenth century when it became the term, in Britain, at least, for an upper-class nursemaid. It is also used as a term of address to a grandmother.*

The names just mentioned were not only black names. All were available to white parents, and many had already been well used by them. The basis for saying that **Cora**, for example, was a name popular with the black middle classes in 1915 but not with the white lies in the occurrence of the names amongst students some twenty years later. Of 11,148 black female students counted by Professor Puckett in 1935–36, forty-seven were named Cora. In my own similar count of white students in colleges all over the country at this time the name hardly occurred at all. As it happens, the name has an impeccable Greek origin (*kore*, 'maiden'), and had been used in James Fenimore Cooper's famous story, *The Last of The Mohicans*.

A few Coras were still to be found amongst black university students who graduated in 1975. Other names occur amongst the 1975 graduates which recall the still more distant past. There was at least one **Prince**, for example, at Howard University, and **Malinda/Melinda** still flourished, recalling those days when well-read young ladies suggested names for their servants' children. The names would have been chosen, of course, because of personal links with the past. They no doubt kept alive the memory of much-loved parents and grandparents, or had other family associations which made them especially meaningful.

Range of names in use

I give on pages 156–7 a list of some of the first names that were to be found in all-black universities in 1975. I have also quoted the top twenties, just to show how similar the latter are to similar lists of the most popular names for white students. But whereas roughly one black American family in two falls in completely with white American ways, favouring the same names as the whites at any particular time, the remaining black families will tend to choose names for a child that are unusual for the year.

'Unusual' in this context means little used at the time; it does not necessarily mean odd. Black parents, in their diligent search for the right name, are prepared to consider a wide range of sources, to go back into the past, to invent new names or adapt existing ones. One might say that they are also more prepared to have confidence in their own taste and that they do not feel obliged to conform to the latest fashions. The names of a group of black Americans are therefore always less predictable than a group of whites of the same age.

White reactions to black names

One result of this is that white Americans are not always sure how they should respond to the names of their black colleagues. By their own conventions they are used to the majority of people they meet having 'normal' names, those which were popular when they were being named themselves or which they know to have been popular at an earlier time. An unusual name does not send out the right signals, giving the immediate assurance that is implicit in a common name. The latter says, in effect, that its bearer was brought up in the same kind of home, and with the same kind of parents, as everyone else.

White Americans are rather wary of fellow whites who have names that seem at all strange. As I have said before, a name that is unusual instinctively suggests to them that the person who bears it is unusual. This is a shaky enough way of thinking at any time, but when applied to black Americans, who go about the business of naming a child in quite a different way, using different criteria, it is obviously totally misleading.

There are, after all, sound historical reasons for the pride in individuality which black American names reveal. It is completely understandable that black parents should wish to exercise to the full the freedom they have in choosing names for their children. It was not so very long ago that an alien naming system was imposed upon them forcefully. These days, then, it is black Americans who give names freely: white Americans tend to remain slaves to their own naming conventions.

14 Provincial Names

First names in Canada

I now want to move northwards from the U.S.A. and consider the use of first names in Canada. As I hope to show, the names drawn by Canadians from the common pool have their distinct characteristics. I shall also take the opportunity, in this chapter, of allowing some Canadian parents who have had the happy task of choosing a name for a child in the last few years to tell us the stories behind the names—what kind of motives prompted their choice.

French-Canadian names

It will be obvious that I am going to talk primarily about the first names used by English, rather than French-speaking, Canadians. French Canadians use French names generally speaking, though inter-marriage between the two communities sometimes interferes with that basic premise. There are also some Canadians, of both linguistic groups, who consciously choose names that are the same in both languages, names like **Richard, Robert, Joseph**; **Louise, Madeleine, Catherine**. But a glance at the names of students in French-speaking universities reveals that they often have names that make no concessions at all to speakers of English, who might well find them difficult to pronounce. They are names like **Jean-Pierre, Laurent, Yves, Normand, Luc, Yvon, Gilles, Jean-Fernand, Benoit; Marie-Claire, Françoise, Monique, Pierrette, Jocelyne, Chantal, Celine**. As if to emphasize their French origins, some Canadian girls are also called **France, Marie-France** or **Francine**.

English-speaking Canadians likewise seem to make little effort to choose names that would be easy for a French-speaker to pronounce. **Heather**, for example, has been popular recently, and it would be unusual to hear a French-speaker cope effectively with that. The borrowing of French feminine names that occurs is probably due more to the search for novelty than thoughts about bilingual convenience.

The only male French names that seem to have been adopted in recent times by English-speaking Canadians are **Michel** and **Pierre**. It will be interesting to see whether use of these names spreads to other English-speaking countries.

French names are sometimes adapted in Canada, as they are elsewhere, to suit the English language. **Sherri,** for instance, is a phonetic rendering of *chérie*, a name substitute in French equivalent to our 'darling'. **Bernice,** on the other hand, is an established alternative form of **Berenice**, not an anglicization of it.

The insistence by most English and French Canadians on using their own set of first names reflects their wish to retain separate national identities. If parents in Britain or the U.S.A. name their son **Marc** instead of **Mark**, the spelling will be interpreted as a variation made for novelty's sake. In Canada the conversion of the English Mark into French Marc could be far more significant, suggesting that the boy concerned comes from a completely different cultural background. This is so, at least, for English-speaking Canadians who happen to live in the province of Quebec, or in nearby cities such as Ottawa. In faraway Vancouver, perhaps, the French consideration would hardly cross the minds of parents choosing a name. There they might well be more influenced by American naming habits.

American influence

This is hardly surprising, for American ways and habits in all spheres of life have had an impact all over the world. The first names used by Americans have certainly spread far afield, though in many cases, as we saw, after a time-lag. Given the physical situation of Canada and the U.S.A., the constant movement of people between the two countries, the common exposure to social influences such as television programmes, books and magazines, it would be strange indeed if Canadian first names did not mirror those of the U.S.A. to a certain extent. But as the comparative figures which I quote in a later chapter will show, Canadians by no means simply do as the Americans do when they name their children. There are American favourite

---

*Sherri sometimes appears as **Sherry**, making it look like a first name derived from a favourite drink. A name with a similar appearance which is occasionally found is **Brandy**. **Perry** and **Porter** also look like 'drink names', though by accident, and at least one instance of **Shandy** as a first name has been recorded.*

Variant spellings are grouped under most frequent forms.

Women		Men	
1950	1975	1950	1975
1. Linda	1. Jennifer	1. Robert	1. Michael
2. Mary	2. Sarah	2. John	2. Scott
3. Susan	3. Tania	3. David	3. Christopher
4. Catherine	4. Alison	4. William	4. Daniel
5. Patricia	5. Heather	5. Michael	5. Mark
6. Barbara	6. Kathleen	6. James	6. Sean
Margaret	7. Amy	7. Brian	7. Matthew
8. Deborah	8. Jodi	8. Richard	8. James
9. Elizabeth	9. Catherine	9. Donald	9. Robert
10. Nancy	10. Mandy	10. Peter	10. Jason
11. Janet	11. Christine	11. Kenneth	11. Stephen
12. Carol(e)	12. Kimberly	12. Ronald	12. Jeffrey
13. Ann(e)	13. Lisa	13. Douglas	13. Jonathan
14. Donna	14. Stephanie	14. Alan	Kevin
15. Karen	15. Erin	15. Paul	15. Thomas
16. Sharon	16. Laura	16. Stephen	16. Brent
17. Judith	17. Cindy	17. Gary	Paul
18. Joanne	Tracey	Gordon	Peter
Marilyn	19. Samantha	19. George	19. John
20. Sandra	20. Andrea	20. Thomas	20. Patrick
21. Diane	Danielle	21. Bruce	21. Andrew
22. Heather	Christina	22. Gerald	22. Charles
23. Cheryl	23. Elizabeth	23. Joseph	23. David
Janice	24. Paula	24. Charles	24. Joseph
Joan	25. Ann(e)	25. Mark	25. Benjamin
26. Christine	26. Megan	26. Barry	26. Brian
Gail	27. Shannon	27. Dennis	Chris
28. Brenda	Theresa	28. Edward	28. Joshua
29. Beverly	29. Chantal	29. Christopher	Ryan
30. Dorothy	Melanie	Daniel	30. Trevor
31. Marie	Tamara	31. Lawrence	31. Todd
Marion	32. Natasha	32. Raymond	32. Adam
33. Carolyn	Patricia	33. Ian	33. Timothy
Helen	34. Marie	34. Glenn	34. Nicholas
Sheila	35. Victoria	35. Eric	35. Anthony
36. Maria	36. Lyndsay	36. Frederick	Edward
37. Kathleen	37. Kelly	37. Larry	Jamie
Shirley	38. Ellen	Wayne	38. Alexander
Wendy	39. Holly	39. Gregory	Kenneth
40. Jean	40. Tara	Philip	40. Cameron
41. Audrey	41. Cynthia	41. Andrew	Gregory
Jacqueline	42. Celine	Patrick	42. Darryl
Valerie	Lynn(e)	Terrence	Donovan
44. Bonnie	44. Shelley	44. Arthur	George
45. Ruth	45. Diana	Carl	Shane
46. Leslie	Jessica	46. Murray	46. Jeremy
Maureen	Linda	Neil	Philip
Pamela	Nicola	Timothy	48. Aaron
49. Diana	Ruth	49. Frank	Michel
50. Lynn(e)	50. April	Jeffrey	Richard
		Keith	

names which Canadians accept less enthusiastically or of which they have grown tired—and *vice versa*.

Canadian preferences

In the remarks that follow I base my comments on two important counts of Canadian first names. One was of university students who graduated at various universities in 1975, and who would have been born in the early 1950s. The second count, carried out with the invaluable aid of many Canadian friends and correspondents, was based on birth announcements in Canadian newspapers during 1975–76.

To begin then, with a few American–Canadian name differences, Canadians were in agreement with the rest of the English-speaking world about the name **Charles** in the early 1950s. They used it modestly compared to Americans, for in the U.S.A. Charles was still one of the star names at that time. **Daniel, Jeffrey** and **Jerry** were also used significantly more frequently in the U.S.A. **Stephen,** or **Steven,** and **Timothy** were treated with caution by Canadians if one thinks about the warm welcome being given to the names across the border. Three Americans to every one Canadian received the name **Thomas** in the early 1950s, but in this case American influence was later to be reflected in the name's return to popularity in Canada.

Among the girls' names being given at this time **Cynthia** failed to appeal to Canadians in spite of American fondness for it, and the pet name **Cindy** was a rarity in Canada. Newspaper birth announcements in 1975, however, tell a somewhat different story. Cynthia has gained little ground in Canada, but Cindy is now making its presence strongly felt.

Jane was still fairly popular in the 1950s, not only in the U.S.A. but in Britain and Australia. Canadian parents had already begun to treat Jane coolly. The name had been in use for centuries and had a certain simple charm, but an indefinable feeling in the air, soon to be reflected in the other English-speaking countries, was beginning to act against it. This feeling affected other feminine forms of John, such as **Jean** and **Joan**. Even **John** itself was soon due to be dislodged after centuries of leadership in the English-speaking world. Canadian parents seem to have sensed this as well in the 1950s, for their use of John was already less than that of anyone else.

The modest use in Canada of **Kathleen, Martha** and **Pamela** provides further examples of Canadian resistance to American name usage. Pamela is a particularly interesting example, for although almost equally popular in the 1950s in the U.S.A., England and Australia, the name was far less favoured by both Canadians and Scots. This negative agreement between Canada and Scotland is matched by many more examples of shared preferences, leaving one in little doubt of the ancestry of many Canadians.

Scottish influence

Cameron, for example, the Scottish clan-name meaning 'hook nose', was being used as a first name in the 1950s only in Scotland, Canada, and that other Scottish outpost, Australia. It may have been used in the first place by those who had some connection with the clan, but its use quickly spread to those who simply liked its sound as a first name. Other primarily Scottish names more usual in Canada than the U.S.A. at this time included **Blair, Donald, Douglas, Duncan, Gordon, Grant, Hugh, Ian** and **Murray**.

Of these, Donald, Gordon, Ian and Murray are especially interesting because of the marked difference in Canadian and other usage. Donald, for instance, was used twice as much in Canada as Scotland in the 1950s, and far more than in the U.S.A. Roughly eight Canadians to one American were being named Gordon during the same period, and only in Scotland itself was the name being used in a comparable way. Ian was then, as it still is, virtually unknown in America but was certainly not so in Canada. As for Murray, it is entitled to be called one of the most distinctively Canadian first names. Its use possibly honours General James Murray, first Governor of British Canada, or may have been suggested by the town in Ontario that was named for him. Whatever the reason, the name has become decidedly Canadian by its usage.

It seems to be in the naming of boys that Canadians wish to remember their Scottish ancestry. Favourite Scottish girls' names, such as **Margaret** and **Agnes**, have been largely set aside in Canada. **Heather** and **Noreen** are perhaps the only names used in recent times that show definite Scottish influence, and both are far more recent in origin than the male names.

Close links between England and Canada are also revealed by the use of certain first names. The popularity in England and Wales of **Barry, Clive, Kelvin, Norman** and **Peter**—revealed by a count of births in 1955—is reflected in a use of those names at the same time in Canada. This usage considerably exceeds that in the U.S.A. Taken together with the Scottish–Canadian links, this further evidence reminds us strongly of the close contacts between Canada and Britain, though that is not to imply that Canadian name usage is British usage. A British visitor to Canada, in fact,

Murray, as a surname, derived from the place name Moray, in Scotland. An inhabitant of Moray can be described as a Moravian, but the Protestant sect known as Moravians were not Scottish by origin. They came from Moravia, in Czechoslovakia, which took its name from the river Morava.

would think the names he heard being used around him were far more American than the names he was used to at home. An American visitor would almost certainly find them more British. Both would be acknowledging the existence of an independent Canadian first name system.

This blending of American and British ways to produce a Canadian way is seen in the spelling of the names as well as the names themselves. We saw in an earlier chapter that American **Beverly** was British **Beverley**. In Canada the two spellings are almost equally used. Again, when the Americans and English were favouring the spelling **Ann** instead of **Anne** in recent years, Canadians joined with the Scots in preferring Anne.

Eva and Shelley

In the comparative lists of name usage which are given in a later chapter, two more names spring out which seem to me to add further chapters in themselves to the Canadian names story. The first of these is **Eva**, the Central and Northern European form of **Eve**. I was remarking earlier that the name is more popular in several European countries than it has ever been in America or Britain. Nevertheless it seems to be frequently used in Canada. It fits in smoothly with the Canadian name stock, but for many new Canadians it must be a reminder of family members in other lands.

The second name that stands out in the lists is **Shelley**. This, like Murray, was a truly Canadian name in the 1950s. It makes no difference that it began as an English place name, or that it became a surname which was made famous by an English poet. Its use as a first name probably owes more to **Shirley** than either of these sources, for Mencken tells us that the two names were interchangeable in some regions. I note too that the actress Shelley Winters, who no doubt helped to make this name known, actually began life as Shirley Schrift.

Shelley may not have taken on its existence as a first name in Canada, but it seems to have been more enthusiastically welcomed there in that role. Since its use in Canada in the 1950s the name has spread widely, but Canadian parents seem to have been the first to spot Shelley's potential as a modern first name.

Comments from Canadian parents

That reference to Canadian parents can perhaps serve as a cue for some of their own comments on naming. On a visit to Canada at the beginning of 1976 I appealed through the media for information from parents who had named a child in recent years. I asked them to tell me the main reasons for choosing the names they did. The letters that flowed in have more than just a Canadian interest. In the representative selection of comments which I give

The lists below give some indication of regional preference in Canada in the 1950s. The Quebec list refers to the English-speaking community. Variant spelling forms are once again grouped under the main spellings.

British Columbia

WOMEN		MEN	
1.	Susan	1.	John
2.	Linda		Robert
3.	Catherine	3.	David
	Margaret	4.	James
5.	Mary	5.	William
6.	Patricia	6.	Michael
7.	Marilyn	7.	Brian
8.	Janet	8.	Richard
	Karen	9.	Peter
10.	Barbara	10.	Donald
11.	Elizabeth	11.	Douglas
12.	Ann(e)		Kenneth
13.	Janice	13.	Gordon
14.	Carol(e)	14.	George
	Donna		Ronald
16.	Deborah	16.	Alan
	Heather	17.	Thomas
18.	Christine	18.	Bruce
	Sharon	19.	Gary
	Wendy		Stephen

Ontario

WOMEN		MEN	
1.	Catherine	1.	Robert
2.	Susan	2.	John
3.	Barbara	3.	Michael
4.	Patricia	4.	David
5.	Margaret	5.	William
6.	Linda	6.	James
7.	Nancy	7.	Stephen
8.	Janet	8.	Brian
9.	Ann(e)	9.	Peter
10.	Deborah	10.	Richard
	Donna	11.	Donald
	Judith	12.	Christopher
13.	Carol(e)	13.	Paul
	Karen	14.	Douglas
	Marilyn	15.	Thomas
	Mary	16.	George
17.	Elizabeth		Kenneth
	Kathleen		Ronald
	Marion	19.	Bruce
	Sharon		Eric
			Gary
			Joseph

Quebec

WOMEN		MEN	
1.	Linda	1.	Robert
2.	Mary	2.	John
3.	Susan	3.	David
4.	Carol(e)	4.	Michael
5.	Elizabeth	5.	Paul
	Maria		Richard
7.	Ann(e)	7.	Alan
	Patricia	8.	Mark
9.	Nancy	9.	Peter
10.	Barbara	10.	William
	Margaret	11.	Joseph
12.	Deborah	12.	Brian
13.	Marie		James
14.	Catherine	14.	Ronald
15.	Donna	15.	Douglas
16.	Joanne		Gerald
	Judith	17.	Charles
	Karen		Gary
	Sandra	19.	Donald
	Sharon		Jeffrey
			Kevin
			Lawrence
			Stephen

Saskatchewan

WOMEN		MEN	
1.	Linda	1.	Robert
2.	Catherine	2.	David
3.	Deborah	3.	William
4.	Mary	4.	Donald
	Patricia	5.	James
6.	Margaret	6.	John
7.	Joan	7.	Kenneth
	Joanne	8.	Brian
	Shirley	9.	Ronald
10.	Donna	10.	Richard
	Sandra	11.	Douglas
12.	Barbara	12.	Dennis
	Beverly		Gordon
14.	Audrey	14.	Gerald
	Diane	15.	Larry
	Dorothy		Peter
	Elizabeth		Raymond
18.	Bonnie		Wayne
	Elaine	19.	Gary
	Janet		George
	Judith		Glen
	Karen		
	Sharon		
	Valerie		

below the authentic voice of young parents of today can be heard. Many of the topics already discussed in this book are mentioned in passing. There are indications of a belief in name magic, though 'name magic' as such is not what the writers call it. There is a constant concern with whether a name is popular or not—parents usually being concerned to avoid a name that is being used too frequently. The various other points mentioned will strike a chord, I feel sure, in anyone who has ever named a child.

Here, then, are the extracts from parental letters:

'Our daughter, **Heather Marie**, was born in 1972. She was called Heather because my husband and I were both reading Hugh MacLennan's book *Two Solitudes* at the time and we both liked the name (and the character). Marie was chosen because my mother is French-Canadian and we wanted to represent both cultures in our daughter's names.'

Louise McDiarmid

'Born May, 1970, **John Christopher** (called Christopher): John chosen because it is his father's name. Christopher because with a one-syllable surname we felt the first name should be two or more syllables.

Born November, 1971, **Michael Thomas** (called Michael): Michael chosen because it fulfilled syllable requirements and was maternal grandfather's name. Thomas was initial choice for first name but we thought **Tom** or **Tommy** Tapp would be a little trite.

Born January, 1975, **Jessica Jeanette** (called Jessica): Jessica seemed slightly more refined in comparison with all the faddish **Tracey, Stacey, Tammy, Tara, Vikki, Jodie, Julie** names of today. Also a widely used family name with great sentimental meaning. Jeanette chosen in honour of paternal grandmother who had recently passed away.'

M. L. Macneil-Tapp

P.S. You can tell I'm a late forties baby. My names are **Mary Linda**. My husband is a mid-forties **John Paul**.

'1971 **Kathryn Elizabeth**. Living in Montreal we wanted names which were easily "converted" to French.

1972 **Philip Charles**. Same reasons as above, plus both names being somewhere in my husband's family. We definitely did *not* choose them because of the Royal Family.

1974 **Joanne Kelly**. Our daughter chose Joanne, and Kelly was my mother's maiden name. (Joanne was born on my late mother's birthday.) We rejected my mother's christian name **Minnie** in favour of Kelly!

My choice of names was also very much influenced by the fact that having taught for a number of years I had good or bad impressions of certain names, and the children who fit them. This ruled out **Stephen**,

Christopher, James and **Robert**. I also wanted names which would fit into a French sentence easily as mine—**Cynthia**—is somewhat difficult for a French-speaking person to spell and pronounce.'

Paul and Cynthia Greer

'We named our son D. **Keelan** Green. The "D" stands for **David**. One might say that David was to satisfy my ego. David came first because my wife felt the names sounded best in that order.

Keelan was chosen only after exploring books containing thousands of names. I wanted a name which was unusual and had not previously been used, to my knowledge, in the Green clan. Keelan is Irish Gaelic meaning "little slender one". I believe the Gaelic spelling is actually **Caolan**.'

David Green

'First son born June, 1970—**Erich**. He was a large baby with blond-red complexion. Hopefully he will be a traveller and discoverer like the Viking Eric the Red.

Second son born October, 1972—**Jason**. He was of slight build, dark brown curly hair and a very determined little lad. Hopefully a leader of men like Jason of the Golden Fleece.'

Helen Fischer

'Our daughter was born in October, 1974, and we named her **Sairin**. People ask: "Is that Celtic or Gaelic?" In fact, my husband made up the name— for several reasons. Most important was the fact that we couldn't agree on a name. We are both teachers, and each of us has positive or negative associations with most popular names.

We liked the name **Sarah**, but it seemed it was being used frequently. We didn't want our daughter to be one of four Sarahs in her class at school. Basically, we wanted a different name, for we believe from our experience as teachers that a different name usually belongs to an unusual person.

If we'd had a boy it would have been a different matter. We would probably have chosen an uncommon name, like **Spencer**, **Tyler** or **Ryan**, rather than make one up.'

Becci Hayes

The authority on the origins of Irish names is Dr Edward MacLysaght. In The Surnames of Ireland *he mentions the theory that Keelan derives from O Caolain (which would make it a diminutive of caol, 'slender,') but goes on to suggest that it is in fact an abbreviation of Keelahan, from O Ceileachain, 'the name of an Oriel family formerly chiefs of Ui Breasail.'*

'**Bruce Alvin**. I named him Bruce after his uncle, Alvin after his grandfather.

    Steven Bruno. There I was looking at this little fellow with no name. Would it be **Derek**, **Boyd**, or **Tony**? He didn't look like any of these. The name Steven came to mind. Yes, he did look like a Steven, and there was my problem solved. His middle name Bruno was for his proud Dad.

    Angelina Eva. Our angel arrived at last and that she is. Her grandmother's name is **Lina** so we called her Angelina. Eva is the name of her other grandmother.'

Karen Boschetti

'**Fraser Karl Sydney**, born November, 1974. Fraser was chosen primarily because it was the maiden surname of the child's paternal great grandmother. She is still alive and Fraser is her first great grandchild. We also wanted something that couldn't be shortened, but already I have heard our son called Frase. Also, with a common surname, we wanted something different but not so unusual that no-one could pronounce or spell it. Wrong again—it is often spelled Frazer.'

Vicki Robinson

'**Jocelyn LoAnn**, born 1971. Jocelyn for its meaning of "joy and light". Middle name used to honour paternal and maternal grandmothers, **Anne** and **Lola**.

    Valerie Shawndelle, born 1975. Valerie for its meaning of "strength". Shawndelle was our feminization of Shawn and we liked its French sound, though our French-speaking friends think we've mispronounced Chantal.'

Mr and Mrs J. H. Hanna

'I had a daughter six years ago and named her **Cynthia Lynn**, Cynthia because it was pretty and not terribly common, but also not so unusual that people had never heard of it.

    Ten and eleven years ago, when I had my first children, names like **Tracey**, **Tammy**, **Kelly**, **Kim**, **Lisa** and **Corey** were amazingly common, most of them being quite "cutesie". Cynthia's friends now have names like **Meaghan**, **Jessica**, **Tanya**, **Erin**, **Sarah**; **Mark**, **Jason**, **Patrick**, **Shannon**.'

Margaret Rayburn

'In 1974 we named our daughter **Sarah Elizabeth**. Both names had been in the family. I tend to steer away from the popular names, as does my husband.'

Virginia Hodgins

'Daughter born May, 1973—**Elissa Sierra**. Elissa chosen because it was a very feminine sounding yet fairly unique name. It was chosen by my husband, who believed he had invented the name. Months later we discovered several Elissas amongst Letters To The Editor and authors. Then we discovered it was not only a form of **Elizabeth** but the given name of Queen (Elissa) Dido of Carthage, the lover of Aeneas. There appears to have been a small rash of similar sounding names shortly after Elissa's birth, including Alyssa, Alissa, Melissa.

Sierra was chosen as a reminder of the mountains of the same name.'

Ottawa parent

'My son was born in June, 1970. His name is **George Nicholas** and he gets called either **Nicky** or **Nick**.

George was chosen because there is a tradition in my husband's family to name the firstborn son after his antecedents. Rather than burden our son with his father's name and both his grandfathers' names, we used only his father's name.

Nicholas was chosen because I felt it to be a strong, proud name and I thought our son would benefit from having such a name. It was a choice between Nicholas and Alexander, both of which were chosen from kings. I preferred the diminutive Nick to Al (although I like Alex) and therefore chose Nicholas.'

Marilyn Olmstead

'We chose our children's names because they ran smoothly with our surname. Given another surname we would have chosen other names. All three children were born in the last six years. Their names are: **Felix Adrian**; **Jayne Averill**; **Juliet Irene**. We were anxious to have first names which could not easily be shortened. We like names such as **David** and **Peter**, but we don't like **Dave** or **Pete**.

The "y" in Jayne was on my insistence as I really prefer longer, more unusual names and wanted her to share her name with fewer little girls. My husband likes plain one-syllabled names and **Jane** is the only plain girl's name I like.

In the case of the second names, these are all family names which happened to blend in well.

I had wanted **Juliette** instead of Juliet, but my husband felt it was too French for our surname.'

Angela and Gerald Irwin

'Our youngest child was three on March 17th. We named him **William George**. My husband felt that to name him after my father would please my aged mother.

Personally I like a name that is easily shouted. Here a two-syllable name has an advantage over a name like **Kim**, which does not shout well.'

Florence M. Collison

'Four years ago our first son was born and we named him **Ryan**. We chose this name because it was different and not popular. Unfortunately, since then several have named their sons Ryan.

Our second son was born ten months ago. We named him **Wylie**. Again we liked it because it was not a common first name. We have discovered that both Ryan and Wylie are popular surnames.'

Mrs B. Kentfield

'My son is named **Sean Patrick**, after his father, who was born in Ireland. There are six boys with that name in this area, all within two years of each other. Needless to say, I did not know how popular the name would be.

My daughter is **Caroline Margaret Elizabeth**. Caroline after her paternal grandmother and her aunt, Margaret after her paternal step-grandmother, and Elizabeth after her maternal great-grandmother.'

Pat Morrison

Valid reasons?

The above letters show why the namers think they chose the names they did, but one suspects, often, that the name comes first and the reasons afterwards. For some quite indefinable reason a name seems 'right' when it is mentioned, and a search then begins for logical justification. One family will say: the name is already in the family, so we're carrying on a tradition.

'*That wasn't so bad for you, after all,*' he says.
'*It was—oh Skinner—*'
'*Hey, could you call me by my real name, eh?*'
As though it were now necessary to do this. By right . . .
'*Okay. I will. Jules.*'
He laughs.
'*You say it kind of funny.* Jewels.'
'*How, then?*'
'*Jules.*'
'*Jewels.*'
'*You better learn French, kid.*'

Margaret Laurence, The Diviners

Another family will say of the same name that they chose it because it *wasn't* already in the family, and that the child concerned would therefore be clearly identified.

Most of us react very personally to names, and we are sometimes disconcerted when we later discover that our own seemingly individual reasons for choosing a name have somehow led us to one that many other people have also selected. The normal reaction is to think that they have copied one's own example. I meet or hear from quite a few people each year who believe that they personally began the fashion for a particular name. All they have done is to sense the spirit of the times.

We can return to such topics later. For the moment, after this brief look at the first names of Canada and the welcome comments from some Canadian parents, it is time to cross the Atlantic to Britain. There was a time when names were taken from Britain to the New World, providing the basis of a naming system. With that firm base established Americans and Canadians showed their flair for invention and adaptation, adding many new names to the stock. As we return now to Britain, many of those new names will come with us.

15 Classy Names

First names in England and Wales

We have seen that the use of first names can be affected by national or racial preferences. Within a particular country, regional fashions can also influence the names that are chosen at a particular time. Another factor that helps to determine which names parents will choose for their children is the social or professional class to which the parents belong.

The evidence to support this statement is found most easily in England. To begin with, it is relatively easy to see which names were being used in the country as a whole at any one time. Since 1838 the names of all children born each year have been entered in Indexes of Births, which are freely available for consultation in the office of the Registrar General. A great many counts for different years based on those indexes have been made by my colleague, C. V. Appleton, and these show in detail how names have gained or lost favour.

Comparative name studies

The Indexes of Births cover the whole of England and Wales and cut across all social classes. For purposes of comparison we also have available counts of the names used by a special section of the community, readers of *The Times* newspaper. These counts are based on the names which appear in the 'Births' column every day, and they have been made annually since 1949. They were begun by Mr John Leaver and are being continued by Mrs Margaret Brown.

The Times has a rather special readership, difficult to pin down in a few words. It is read by professional people, but also by the modern equivalent of what used to be called the 'upper-class'. It is possibly the latter who announce the births of their children in the newspaper, and it is interesting to see how the names they choose differ from those popular in the country as a whole.

Upper class male names

In recent years, for instance, **James, Edward, Thomas, Alexander, William, Benjamin** and **Daniel** have all been used significantly more by readers of *The Times* than by the population as a whole. In the use of James, Edward, Thomas and William we see signs of resistance to change, for the names have been consistently used for centuries. Perhaps it is the tradition of naming a son after his male relations which is surviving, carrying such names along with it. If this is so, however, the custom is not managing to preserve all the popular names of previous generations. John, for example, is slipping into a lower position in the frequency lists each year.

In an earlier chapter (*Pet Names*) I mentioned another reason which could make names like James and William more acceptable at a higher social level in England than at a lower. In educated circles they retain their full forms and no-one finds them strange. Elsewhere convention demands their permanent conversion into **Jim** or **Bill**. It would also be extremely unusual to hear two workmen, for example, addressing each other as Edward and Thomas. They would only depart from the more usual **Ted** and **Tom** if they were deliberately mocking upper-class usage.

That remark applies to certain other names, such as **Richard, Charles** and **Robert**, where the full forms would sound 'posh' to many English ears. It does not apply to a name like **Peter,** for although someone of this name would be called **Pete** by his workmates, they would not react as strongly to hearing him called Peter as they would to hearing **Charlie** addressed as Charles.

The male names that have been nationally popular in England and Wales recently avoid these class associations on the whole. **Stephen, Andrew** and **Michael** are like Peter in being acceptable in those forms or as **Steve, Andy** and **Mike. Mark** and **Paul** avoid the issue by having no obvious pet forms.

Leaders of fashion

The use of Benjamin and Daniel by readers of *The Times* hints at another aspect of class distinction in names. In 1971 Benjamin was the fourteenth

> '*Laura* was *Lor* or *Low*, and *Edmund* was *Ned* or *Ted*. *Laura's mother disliked this cheapening of names and named her third child* **May**, *thinking it would not lend itself to a diminutive. However, while still in her cradle, the child became* **Mayie** *among the neighbours.*'
> Flora Thomson, Lark Rise to Candleford

most popular name used by readers of the newspaper. That year it did not get into the top fifty for England and Wales as a whole. Daniel was in twentieth place in *The Times* for 1971, but only forty-first in the national list. Four years later Daniel had become the eighth most frequently used name throughout the country and Benjamin was twenty-ninth. One can only conclude that *Times* readers were proving to be leaders of fashion.

For more examples of *Times* readers apparently leading the way we can turn to the girls. **Emma** was third in *The Times* list for 1971 but twenty places lower for the whole country. **Rebecca** was seventh in *The Times* that year, but twentieth in the list compiled from the Indexes of Births. In 1975 the latter source shows **Emma** having risen to fourth place and **Rebecca** to twelfth.

These names were not mere survivals amongst readers of *The Times*, they were being brought back into use after a length period in the attic. Those near the top of the social hierarchy seem to have an instinct which tells them which names can be restored to favour. In 1971, again, many of them were naming their daughters **Charlotte**, though the name had been out of general use in England and Wales for over a century. Four years later Charlotte is there in the national top fifty, in thirty-seventh place and rising.

Following the top names in *The Times* each year is something of a national pastime in Britain, for after the lists have been printed there they are usually reproduced in many other newspapers and quoted on radio and television. There must therefore be some cases where parents are influenced in their decision by learning that a certain name is acceptable to this special social group. But this cannot always apply, for Charlotte, to give just one example, was not mentioned in the list that was actually published in *The Times* in 1971. The lists there give only the first ten names and Charlotte was sixteenth at the time. I personally extended the *Times* list to a top fifty when my late friend, John Leaver, generously gave me access to his records. But it is not published lists which mainly affect such matters. More important is social interaction, as young mothers-to-be notice who is calling Benjamin and Emma over to her side, and who is calling **Jason**, say, or **Karen**.

Jane Austen's Emma *has been required reading for a great many students in England and Wales in recent years. The book is included in the syllabuses of several examining boards. The re-introduction of Emma may well have been sparked off by the literary character. She is described as follows in the opening sentence of the novel: 'Emma Woodhouse, handsome, clever, and rich, with a comfortable home and happy disposition, seemed to unite some of the best blessings of existence; and had lived nearly twenty-one years in the world with very little to distress or vex her.'*

The Top Fifty Names For Girls – England & Wales

Variant spellings grouped under the main spelling forms.

1900
1. Florence
2. Mary
3. Alice
4. Annie
5. Elsie
6. Edith
7. Elizabeth
8. Doris
9. Dorothy
   Ethel
11. Gladys
12. Lilian
13. Hilda
14. Margaret
15. Winifred
16. Lily
17. Ellen
18. Ada
19. Emily
20. Violet
21. Rose
    Sarah
23. Nellie
24. May
25. Beatrice
26. Gertrude
    Ivy
28. Mabel
29. Jessie
30. Maud
31. Eva
32. Agnes
    Jane
34. Evelyn
35. Frances
    Kathleen
37. Clara
38. Olive
39. Amy
40. Catherine
41. Grace
42. Emma
43. Nora
44. Louisa
    Minnie
46. Lucy
47. Daisy
    Eliza
49. Phyllis
50. Ann(e)

1925
1. Joan
2. Mary
3. Joyce
4. Margaret
5. Dorothy
6. Doris
7. Kathleen
8. Irene
9. Betty
10. Eileen
11. Doreen
12. Lilian
    Vera
14. Jean
15. Marjorie
16. Barbara
17. Edna
18. Gladys
19. Audrey
20. Elsie
21. Florence
    Hilda
    Winifred
24. Olive
25. Violet
26. Elizabeth
27. Edith
28. Ivy
29. Peggy
    Phyllis
31. Evelyn
32. Iris
33. Annie
    Rose
35. Beryl
    Lily
    Muriel
    Sheila
39. Ethel
40. Alice
41. Constance
    Ellen
43. Gwendoline
    Patricia
45. Sylvia
46. Nora
    Pamela
48. Grace
49. Jessie
50. Mabel

1950
1. Susan
2. Linda
3. Christine
4. Margaret
5. Carol
6. Jennifer
7. Janet
8. Patricia
9. Barbara
10. Ann(e)
11. Sandra
12. Pamela
    Pauline
14. Jean
15. Jacqueline
16. Kathleen
17. Sheila
18. Valerie
19. Maureen
20. Gillian
21. Marilyn
    Mary
23. Elizabeth
24. Lesley
25. Catherine
26. Brenda
27. Wendy
28. Angela
29. Rosemary
30. Shirley
31. Diane
    Joan
33. Jane
    Lynne
35. Irene
36. Janice
37. Elaine
    Heather
    Marion
40. June
41. Eileen
42. Denise
    Doreen
    Judith
    Sylvia
46. Helen
    Yvonne
48. Hilary
49. Dorothy
    Joyce
    Julia
    Theresa

1975
1. Claire
2. Sarah
3. Nicola
4. Emma
5. Joanne
6. Helen
7. Rachel
8. Lisa
9. Rebecca
10. Karen
    Michelle
12. Victoria
13. Catherine
14. Amanda
15. Tracy
16. Samantha
17. Kelly
18 Deborah
19. Julie
    Louise
21. Sharon
22. Donna
23. Kerry
24. Zoe
25. Melanie
26. Alison
27. Caroline
28. Lynsey
29. Jennifer
30. Angela
31. Susan
32. Hayley
33. Dawn
    Joanna
    Lucy
36. Natalie
37. Charlotte
38. Andrea
    Laura
40. Paula
41. Marie
42. Teresa
43. Elizabeth
    Suzanne
45. Kirsty
    Sally
    Tina
48. Jane
49. Ann(e)
    Jacqueline

Imitative naming

Naturally, I am not suggesting that there is a situation where two social classes of people exist, one of which imitates the behaviour of the other. It is not as simple as that. But I do claim that countless people are affected by the behaviour of those whose social standing is slightly better than their own, and which they themselves would like to attain. An important aspect of social behaviour concerns the names given to children, and the naming habits of the social élite have been imitated in England since the Norman Conquest. The second social layer copies the top layer, the third layer copies the second layer, and so on down through the ranks.

According to this theory, the many little English girls who have been named Lucy in the last few years represent the second or third stage of the imitation process. Lucy is another name that was very popular with readers of *The Times* in 1971, but was then little used throughout the country. The 1975 figures drawn from the Indexes of Births show that it is now well into the top fifty and is rising rapidly. In my view the increase in the use of the name is strongly influenced by social aspirations, but I shall not be surprised if a flood of indignant letters arrive to tell me I am wrong.

Working-class names

Let me turn now to names used at the other end of the social scale. Some names are noticeably absent from the birth announcement columns of *The Times* though they can be shown to be popular nationally. What seems to characterize these names is that they are new to the English first name system.

A good example is **Darren**, a name unknown in Britain before the American television series *Bewitched* was first shown in 1960. Something about this name made an almost instant appeal to the English public and Darrens immediately began to appear on the scene. By 1971 Darren was the seventh most popular name bestowed on boys, and in 1975 it was still in tenth position. This popularity was not reflected amongst readers of *The Times*. They seem to have stood back from the name, as if they wanted to know more about its background before forming an opinion.

As it happens, the origin of the name is extremely obscure. I have an excellent collection of surname dictionaries and Darren is not in any of them. Neither does it appear to be a place name. Most books on first names seem to be unaware of its existence, though *Name Your Baby*, by Lareina Rule, does include it. This author states confidently that the name is Irish and originally meant 'little great one', but none of the scholarly Irish sources I have consulted gives this statement any support. Miss Rule may have been

Variant spellings grouped under the main spelling forms.

	1900	1925	1950	1975
1.	William	John	David	Stephen
2.	John	William	John	Mark
3.	George	George	Peter	Paul
4.	Thomas	James	Michael	Andrew
5.	Charles	Ronald	Alan	David
6.	Frederick	Robert	Robert	Richard
7.	Arthur	Kenneth	Stephen	Matthew
8.	James	Frederick	Paul	Daniel
9.	Albert	Thomas	Brian	Christopher
10.	Ernest	Albert	Graham	Darren
11.	Robert	Eric	Philip	Michael
12.	Henry	Edward	Anthony	James
13.	Alfred	Arthur	Colin	Robert
14.	Sidney	Charles	Christopher	Simon
15.	Joseph	Leslie	Geoffrey	Jason
16.	Harold	Sidney	William	Stuart
	Harry			
17.		Frank	James	Neil
18.	Frank	Peter	Keith	Lee
			Terence	
19.	Walter	Dennis		Jonathan
20.	Herbert	Joseph	Barry	Ian
			Malcolm	Nicholas
21.	Edward	Alan	Richard	
22.	Percy	Stanley		Gary
23.	Richard	Ernest	Ian	Craig
24.	Samuel	Harold	Derek	Martin
25.	Leonard	Norman	Roger	John
26.	Stanley	Raymond	Raymond	Carl
27.	Reginald	Leonard	Kenneth	Philip
28.	Francis	Alfred	Andrew	Kevin
		Harry		
29.	Fred		Trevor	Benjamin
30.	Cecil	Donald	Martin	Peter
31.	Wilfred	Reginald	Kevin	Wayne
32.	Horace	Roy	Ronald	Adam
33.	Cyril	Derek	Leslie	Anthony
34.	David	Henry	Charles	Alan
	Norman		George	
35.		Geoffrey		Graham
36.	Eric	David	Thomas	Adrian
37.	Victor	Gordon	Nigel	Colin
38.	Edgar	Herbert	Stuart	Scott
39.	Leslie	Walter	Edward	Timothy
40.	Bertie	Cyril	Gordon	Barry
41.	Edwin	Jack	Roy	William
42.	Donald	Richard	Dennis	Dean
43.	Benjamin	Douglas	Neil	Jamie
44.	Hector	Maurice	Lawrence	Nathan
45.	Jack	Bernard	Clive	Justin
	Percival	Gerald	Eric	Damian
46.			Robin	Thomas
47.	Clifford	Brian		
48.	Alexander	Victor	Frederick	Alexander
	Baden	Wilfred	Patrick	Alistair
49.				Nigel
50.	Bernard	Francis	Donald	Shaun
	Redvers		Joseph	

influenced by the fact that the first bearer of the name to achieve any kind of prominence was someone with a Gaelic-looking surname, Darren McGavin, an American actor born in 1925. In the 1950s he was to be seen in films like *Summer Madness* and *The Man With The Golden Arm*.

The New Age Baby Name Book, by Sue Browder, mentions **Daren**, which does sometimes occur in England as a form of Darren. The explanation given by Miss Browder is that Daren is a Hausa name used in Nigeria for a boy 'born at night'. Its resemblance to Darren is almost certainly a pure coincidence.

A great many English parents were obviously willing to take Darren on trust, not bothering about its pedigree. It may well be that the name was thought to be generally popular in the U.S.A. because it was used to name a main character in a series. This was not the case at the time, for amongst the thousands of American students who were born in the 1950s, and whose names I analysed in 1975, I could find only one Darren. He came from Illinois.

Samantha

The mere use of a name in a television series was not recommendation enough for most upper middle-class parents in England, it seems, and Darren is currently a name that strongly hints at working-class parents. This is less true of **Samantha**, the girl's name that somewhat parallels Darren, for it was given an enormous impetus by the same television series. It had also occurred earlier, however, in the popular film *High Society*, and the young actress Samantha Eggar was helping to make it known. In Samantha's case middle-class parents acted less suspiciously, using the new name as much as old favourites such as **Laura** and **Jennifer**. Perhaps it was because it was a girl's name that they worried less about its past, and for that matter, about its future. After all, pleasant though the name is, it could easily prove to be a passing fancy, fashionable for a few years but then virtually disappearing from sight. It is too soon to say whether this is what will happen.

Samantha is as much a mystery as Darren when its origin is investigated. I suspect that it is a new formation based on **Sam**, and it may emanate from the American South. In *Black Names of America* the name is included in a list of female slave names before 1864, and in another list of 'unusual black given names found amongst white females'. **Samella** is found beside it, as a shortened form of **Samuella**. The latter listing shows the name to have been in restricted use by 1910 for both black and white girls.

If the name was an individual's invention, it has done remarkably well. Many thousands of new names are invented each year, but the vast majority of them are doomed to remain unknown to all but a small group. Samantha is now accepted throughout the English-speaking world. I note that it is currently holding its place in the Australian top fifty, for instance, as well as in England.

But if Samantha has been accepted at all social levels, many other names have not. **Tracey, Sharon, Joanne, Lisa, Julie, Karen, Deborah, Angela, Kelly** and **Kerry** have all been used very much less by readers of *The Times* in recent years than by English and Welsh parents generally. Their caution may have been justified, for some of these names are already beginning to suffer a reversal. It is interesting to note, by the way, the closeness in sound between names like **Sharon, Karen** and **Darren**. Perhaps linguists should investigate this area of fashionable sounds.

Other boys' names which seem to carry a social stigma in England in the 1970s are **Stephen, Jason, Gary, Kevin, Lee, Craig, Carl, Wayne, Scott, Shane, Barry** and **Dean**. The name of one of my own sons, Stephen, appears in this list, so I am clearly unable to say which criteria a name must fulfil in order to earn its place in high society.

Acceptable names

Boys' names that now seem to be acceptable at all social levels include **Mark, Paul, Andrew, David, Christopher, Richard, Matthew, Michael, Robert, Simon, Jonathan, Nicholas, Philip** and **Peter**. English girls who will later find that their names are acceptable everywhere include those who have received the following names in the last few years: **Catherine, Sarah, Emma, Helen, Rachel, Rebecca, Amanda, Louise, Alison, Caroline, Jennifer**.

I do not want to give the impression that English parents are obsessed with the question of social class when they name their children. I believe that an awareness of such matters is at the back of many parents' minds, but that is probably equally true of parents throughout the English-speaking world. It just happens to be in England that we have the most concrete evidence of how social-class considerations affect the choice of names.

National preferences—boys' names

Let us move on now to consider some of the names that have been more used in England and Wales this century than in the other English-speaking countries. Men's names that fit this description include **Barry, Graham, Keith, Kevin, Malcolm, Martin, Nigel, Roy, Simon, Terence** and **Trevor**.

One suspects that the first of these, Barry, is often used by Welsh parents who connect it with the name of a place in Glamorgan. There is another place of the same name in Scotland, but in spite of that, the first name is probably of Irish origin. It derives in Ireland from the word *beara*, meaning a 'spear' or 'javelin'. This caused a commentator on the life of the Irish saint **Bearach** to explain the name fancifully as that of one 'who takes a direct aim at an object, or reaches it, as it were, with the point of a sword'.

A different explanation is given in *A Book Of Welsh Names*, by Trefor Rendall Davies. He derives it from 'son of **Harry**', making it the same as the surname Parry (Welsh *ap Harri*). Mr Davies's theory is repeated by other writers on first names, but the scholarly authorities do not agree with him. Other writers, incidentally, have linked Barry to the French surname made famous by Madame du Barry. That derives from a word meaning 'rampart' and was applied originally to someone who lived outside the town's fortifications.

None of this explains why Barry began to appeal to English and Welsh parents around 1930, reaching the peak of its popularity in 1950. The Irish actor Barry Fitzgerald may have had something to do with it, for his name was appearing very regularly in film credits at that time.

Kevin and Trevor

Kevin is Irish, from **Caoimhghin**, 'handsome at birth'. Until the 1940s one would have been fairly safe to assume that any man bearing the name was Irish by birth, but it then began to spread. In England the name reached its peak in 1960, but it has slowly been fading away since then. More recently it has been taken up in the U.S.A.

Trevor is essentially a Welsh name, as **Trefor**, and names several Welsh places. Its original meaning was either 'big village' or 'village by the sea'. It became a surname, and its first name use presumably derives from that. The actor Trevor Howard has undoubtedly made many parents aware of the name in recent years, and it has been well used, especially in the 1950s.

Scottish influence on the naming of children is shown by the use in the 1950s of Graham, Keith, Malcolm and Roy, though the last of these could equally well have come from the U.S.A. Purely Scottish in origin, all four were more used in England and Wales at that time than in Scotland itself. Graham and Keith began as place names, then became surnames. They probably passed through the middle name stage before becoming first names, for the Scots have long had the habit of using maiden surnames in the middle name position. Malcolm and Roy were once descriptive personal names, the first indicating a 'follower of Saint Columba', the second telling us that the original bearer of the name was 'red' of hair or complexion. All four names are now retreating into the background after a spell in the limelight, but Scottish interests will not be forgotten. **Stuart** and **Ian** are steadily becoming more popular with English parents.

Reasons for use

I have allowed myself to talk of the origins of some of these names, yet I am quite sure that the original meanings had nothing whatever to do with the use of the names in modern times. **Simon** is another name that has been climbing in England in recent years, and it is more relevant to talk of the Saint, the fictional creation of Leslie Charteris, than to delve into Hebrew or Greek to try to establish the name's original meaning.

What it does 'mean' to many young parents is the suave and handsome figure of Simon Templar, a regular visitor to their television screens in the form of Roger Moore. Similarly, with **Nigel**, we need not bother with the complicated etymological arguments that trace the name from Gaelic to Latin. We should be more concerned with the public exposure given to the name since 1945 by such men as the writer Nigel Baldwin, and the actors Nigel Bruce, Nigel Davenport and Nigel Patrick.

National preferences—girls' names

As with the men, a few names tend to label girls as English or Welsh rather than American, say, or Australian. Sometimes it is the name spelling that marks the nationality. **Carole**, for instance, is likely to be English or Welsh, though a **Carol** could be from any English-speaking country. A girl called **Lesley** will probably spell it in that way in England instead of **Leslie** as it normally is in North America.

Dawn has appealed to the English imagination recently, though the signs are that it will not take the country by storm. In a sense the name translates **Lucy**, which could originally have been used for girls born at daybreak. Some girls called Dawn may bear a genuine incident name, commemorating the exact time of their birth, but the name has undoubtedly been given just as often because of its poetic associations.

Denise is similar to Dawn in the way it has recently had ten or fifteen years of popular use in England. Prior to that the name had lain in the background for hundreds of years, though it continued in popular use in France. Its re-emergence may have been due to French usage, though only

---

Carol, or Carole, is often thought to be a suitable name for a girl born at Christmas, when carols are being sung. The name is not connected with the word, as it happens. The girl's name is a shortening of Caroline, which derives directly from Charles. The Christmas carol began as a round dance, the word deriving from Latin corolla, 'garland.'

Denise Darcel comes to mind as a public figure bearing the name. Miss Darcel was seen in films like *Tarzan and the Slave Girl* and *Vera Cruz*, both of which appeared in the 1950s as the name was gaining popularity. It has since lost ground again.

Gillian

Gillian has also lost its place in the English top fifty, but it has had a remarkable run in England this century. The name is used to playing an important role. It was once so common that its pet form **Jill** took its place alongside **Jack** as the typical girl's name. Jill is still used, but the spelling **Jillian** is much less common than Gillian.

In the seventeenth century a Gill-flirt was the usual description of a flighty young lady, someone whom the Scots came to call a Jillet. The latter word is more familiar to use as 'jilt', so that a Gillian has this nasty accusation of fickleness associated with her name. This does not seem to have deterred parents in England and Wales, who suddenly began to re-use the name around 1930. More and more parents used it each year until 1955, when it levelled out. Soon after 1960 it began to disappear from the Indexes of Births, and it now seems destined for another period of obscurity. Nevertheless, I estimate that between 1950 and 1960 alone, some 67,000 girls born in England and Wales received the name. Apart from in Scotland, where the name was used to a certain extent, the name hardly occurred during that period in the rest of the English-speaking world. It is only in the 1970s that Jill has become popular in the U.S.A.

Nicola

Nicola appeared later than Gillian, and is very much a name of the 1970s in England and Wales. It is the Italian form of **Nicholas**, the feminine form in Italian being **Nicoletta**. The -a ending of Nicola, however, has convinced most English people that it is a girl's name. Elsewhere in the English-speaking world the French feminine form **Nicole** is preferred. Not surprisingly, the spelling **Nichola** occurs fairly frequently. Nicholas itself has steadily become more popular in England since the 1920s, so that it is now the twentieth most used male name.

It may be that parents who had decided on Nicholas for a son began to switch to Nicola for a daughter, setting the name on its way in the 1950s. I know from personal experience that parents can have a linked pair of names in mind before their child is born. My youngest son **Laurence** would have become a **Laura**, for instance, had things turned out differently. But if Nicola did begin as a secondary choice for Nicholas, it has now reversed the roles. Two girls are named Nicola each year in England and Wales for every

> '*Gladys Bertha. Those were the names given to me when I was young and helpless. I have always pretended to dislike Gladys more than in actual fact I do; it was in fashion as a pretty name when Mother picked it out for me; her own name was Elizabeth, and I still slightly resent that blindness of vision which made her discard Elizabeth as old-fashioned, along with Anne and Sophia and Harriet and Susan. All that group have now (1953) swung round into fashion again, whereas from about 1910 onwards, Gladys was frequently disowned as the type of name associated with that slightly giggling girl of fiction, fond of cheap scent, high heels and whispering in corners.*'
>
> G. B. Stern (*born 1890*), A Name To Conjure With

boy who becomes Nicholas. That is not to say that the situation will remain stable. It is highly likely that the rapid and striking success of Nicola will prove to be the name's downfall. I expect it to fade away in the 1980s.

Valerie and **Hilary**, finally, are two names that are more likely to be borne by English girls than by their cousins from other English-speaking countries. Both names have enjoyed modestly successful periods of use since the 1930s, though both have since fallen away again.

'*Dated*' *female names*

This continuing process, by which names come and go, particularly affects girls' names. It is therefore possible to 'date' many of them by referring to the lists I give on pages 186–192. A few examples of dated names are mentioned below, but I stress the fact that I am now referring only to women born in England and Wales.

Born before 1920: **Bertha, Clara, Eliza, Fanny, Flora, Gertrude, Gladys, Hannah, Harriet, Isabella, Jessie, Louisa, Martha, Matilda, Millicent, Minnie.** Some other names which would have belonged here, such as **Emma** and **Sarah**, have been given a completely new image recently by being re-introduced in great numbers. Clara and Louisa are very much younger in the forms **Claire** and **Louise.**

Born before 1930: **Ada, Agnes, Amelia, Annie, Beatrice, Constance, Daisy, Dora, Esther, Ethel, Eunice, Eva, Florence, Grace, Ida, Mabel, May, Nellie, Nora, Rose, Ruby, Vera, Violet, Winifred.** **Emily** would have belonged to this group, but there are signs that it is being revived.

Born before 1940: **Alice, Alma, Audrey, Beryl, Betty, Cecilia, Daphne, Doris, Edith, Edna, Ellen, Elsie, Enid, Evelyn, Gwendoline, Iris, Ivy, Joan, Joyce, Lilian, Maisie, Margery, Marina, Muriel,**

Olive, Peggy, Phyllis, Sylvia. Many of these names could be rejuvenated fairly easily: e.g., Joan could become **Joanne**, Alice should change to **Alison**, Betty to **Bettina**.

Many more girls' names are clearly doomed to become dated although their present image is still young. Since 1960, for instance, the majority of English and Welsh parents have been turning away from the following names: **Avril, Barbara, Bernadette, Beverley** or **Beverly, Brenda, Carol** or **Carole, Carolyn, Christine, Cynthia, Deborah** or **Debra, Denise, Diana, Doreen, Dorothy, Eileen, Elaine, Frances, Gail, Gillian, Glenda, Glenys, Gloria, Heather, Hilary, Irene, Jacqueline, Janet, Janice, Jean, Jeanne, Judith, June, Kathleen, Kay, Kim, Lesley, Linda** or **Lynda, Margaret, Marilyn, Mary, Maureen, Norma, Pamela, Patricia, Pauline, Penelope, Rita, Rosemary, Sandra, Sheila, Shirley, Valerie, Veronica, Wendy** and **Yvonne**.

This may seem to dismiss a great many names but there are plenty of others which are healthily flourishing. These include traditional names which are being re-introduced and new names of various kinds. The signs to look for in the frequency lists quoted in this chapter are increasing usage in the 1970s, but preferably not enough usage to put a name into the top twenty or thirty. In all cases, a name that is being considered for a child should be checked to see if and when it has been popular.

Boys' names can also be checked against the lists, and it will quickly become obvious that certain names have disadvantages because of the way they have been used. If I were naming a boy in England or Wales in the late 1970s, for example, I would avoid the following names: **Alan** or **Allan, Albert, Alfred, Anthony** or **Antony, Arthur, Barry, Bernard, Brian** or **Bryan, Charles, Clifford, Clive, Colin, Cyril, Denis** or **Dennis, Derek, Donald, Eric, Ernest, Francis, Frank, Frederick, Geoffrey** or **Jeffrey, George, Gerald, Gordon, Graham, Harold, Harry, Henry, Herbert, Jack, John, Keith, Kenneth, Leslie, Leonard, Malcolm, Maurice, Nigel, Norman, Patrick, Peter, Philip, Raymond, Reginald, Roger, Ronald, Roy, Samuel, Sidney, Stanley, Terence, Thomas, Trevor, Victor, Walter, Wilfred** and **William**.

I shall be devoting a complete chapter a little later to the names that *are* being used at the moment, and making more positive suggestions about the way to choose a name for a baby. I know how complicated the process can be. If I am right, then on top of everything else parents are likely to class their children for life by the names they choose.

The figures given below show the detailed use of first names in England and Wales since 1850. They are based on the Indexes of Births which are available to the public at St Catherine's House, London, W.C.2. The numbers against the names relate to 10,000 births of the same sex in that year. E.g., '50' would indicate that one girl or boy of every 200 born that year received the name; '250' would mean that one girl or boy in every forty received the name. In other words the higher the number the more popular the name.

Girls

	1850	1875	1900	1925	1950	1960	1970	1975
Abigail	5	8	4					24
Ada	12	249	166	26			2	
Adele					2	5	14	7
Agnes	46	89	94	34				
Alexandra				2	6	4	9	29
Alexis					2	2	4	5
Alice	166	389	361	80	4	4	7	2
Alison	2				28	100	149	100
Allison					4	4	30	7
Amanda		3			12	84	181	167
Amelia	83	54	18	2			2	
Amy	15	75	73	14	2	4	5	17
Andrea					14	23	88	71
Angela				4	92	168	123	90
Anita			1		28	36	37	14
Ann	573	202	34	4	128	63	30	24
Anna	54	25	1	2	10	5	21	24
Anne	68	39	4	4	84	57	26	26
Annette	2		1		18	29	21	7
Annie	27	402	357	88	2			
April					4	2	2	14
Audrey			9	152	24	14	4	2
Barbara	5	3	13	162	216	71	11	2
Beatrice		51	119	36	8			
Belinda						18	9	7
Bernadette					4	14	5	
Bertha		46	36	10		2		
Beryl			7	82	20	5		
Bessie		20	22	22				
Betsy	39	20	1	4	4	2	2	
Betty	10	2	1	214	16	4		
Beverley					8	129	25	40
Beverly					6	20	4	
Blanche		8	13	8		2		
Brenda				42	88	18	2	2
Cara								14
Carla					2	2	7	19
Carol					244	204	25	29
Carole					68	105	7	7
Caroline	120	79	24	8	38	120	100	107
Carolyn					28	64	16	7
Carrie		7	3	4			4	10

First Name Profiles – England & Wales

	1850	1875	1900	1925	1950	1960	1970	1975
Catherine	54	59	60	44	40	70	82	81
Cecilia		11	13	20				5
Celia	2	7	3		18	5	4	2
Charlotte	115	100	28	14	14	7	39	74
Charmaine					6	2	5	12
Cheryl					14	39	35	29
Chloe							4	10
Christine		3	4	12	352	209	23	26
Clair							11	14
Claire					2	13	123	310
Clara	71	166	76	16	2			
Clare		5		4	2	20	49	110
Claudia			1		2		2	5
Colette						9	7	10
Constance	5	8	46	78	2	2		
Coral				4	2	2	4	
Daisy		5	58	28				
Danielle						2	4	10
Daphne				38	12	7		
Dawn					14	4	77	81
Debbie						9	23	14
Deborah	2				20	279	170	119
Debra						86	23	14
Denise				4	56	102	25	14
Diana	4	2		8	28	21	4	7
Diane					72	100	56	14
Dianne					10	13	9	7
Donna					2	25	91	124
Dora		8	36	34				
Doreen			1	190	60	7	7	
Doris			266	278	10	2	2	
Dorothy	4	3	246	350	48	7		
Edith	12	277	337	120	8	4		
Edna	2	5	40	160	10		2	
Eileen			10	192	62	16	2	
Elaine				8	68	109	54	24
Eleanor	56	74	34	14	4	4	4	10
Eliza	437	221	60	4		2		
Elizabeth	1002	652	296	128	124	105	84	52
Ellen	290	275	176	78	14	11	7	10
Elsie		10	339	148	8			
Emily	232	282	157	34	4	7	11	33
Emma	393	239	67	8	2		114	283
Erica					8	4	5	2
Estelle						2	9	5
Esther	71	54	40	20	2	2	5	5
Ethel		97	246	82				
Eva		18	97	28		4	2	
Eveline		7	25	10		2		2
Evelyn		7	63	96	20	9	4	
Fanny	124	80	24	2		2		
Fay				4	2	2	4	7

	1850	1875	1900	1925	1950	1960	1970	1975
Faye							4	12
Fiona					4	32	46	21
Flora	7	26	15	4			2	
Florence	2	307	394	142	10		4	
Frances	93	103	79	44	46	23	19	7
Freda				52	18	2		
Gail					12	36	28	10
Gaynor					8	13	19	7
Gemma							7	19
Georgina	4	16	13	6	22	14	12	36
Geraldine				4	34	13	5	2
Gertrude	2	69	112	26				
Gillian					132	170	42	17
Gladys			222	156	4			
Glenda					10	7		
Gloria				2	16	11		
Glynis					14	7	2	
Grace	17	15	70	64			2	
Gwendoline			15	72	8	2		
Hannah	310	133	49	18			4	33
Harriet	176	115	37	8	2		2	
Hayley							51	79
Hazel		3		38	44	36	16	24
Heather				6	68	66	26	15
Heidi							19	21
Helen	15	25	27	26	58	109	140	226
Helena	10	13	12	8	4	2	4	10
Henrietta	17	36	9	6	2			2
Hilary				4	48	20	12	4
Hilda		10	231	142	6	2		
Holly			1	2				7
Ida		7	31	30				
Irene		2	31	238	74	16	4	
Iris			7	94	4	5		
Isabel	10	34	12	2	8		2	5
Isabella	63	67	36	10	2		2	
Ivy		2	112	120	8	4	2	
Jacqueline				2	160	205	98	45
Jane	429	234	96	148	76	127	95	38
Janet	2	8	12	18	262	157	30	19
Janice					64	46	12	7
Janine						9	21	7
Jayne				2		39	32	10
Jean				180	176	46	5	
Jeanette					12	38	9	12
Jennie			13	8			2	12
Jennifer				2	278	95	65	98
Jenny	2	2	9	2	2	7	4	19
Jessie	10	72	97	62	2			
Joan				510	82	21	2	
Joanna	2				16	27	32	79
Joanne					2	39	309	271

	1850	1875	1900	1925	1950	1960	1970	1975
Johanna	2	3	6	2		4	2	10
Josephine		5	6	24	36	21	19	10
Joy				8	20	7	5	4
Joyce			3	390	48	5	2	2
Judith	4		1		60	57	19	7
Julia	37	23	15	10	48	59	44	33
Julie					44	159	239	133
Juliet	4					7	12	2
June				38	66	36	4	7
Justine					2		49	12
Kara								10
Karen					18	439	239	186
Kate	29	118	51	6		5	19	21
Katharine	2		3		6	4	14	7
Katherine		7	9	10	6	11	44	40
Kathleen		3	79	240	164	54	21	14
Kathryn					42	55	56	26
Katrina					2	9	16	21
Kay					8	32	12	14
Keeley						2	7	24
Kellie							11	14
Kelly						2	67	131
Kerry						21	98	107
Kim					2	84	23	19
Kirsten							11	10
Kirsty							19	45
Laura	15	56	27	16	8	5	28	71
Leah		11		6			5	5
Leanne							12	36
Lesley			3	2	118	145	30	33
Lilian		52	200	178	8	2	4	
Lilly		51	4				2	
Lily		39	166	82	6	2		
Linda			7	6	486	170	46	38
Lindsay			1	4	2	5	7	12
Lindsey						13	11	21
Lisa						5	249	224
Lois	5	10	6	2	4	2	2	2
Lorna			3	20	14	13	21	14
Lorraine					24	64	67	29
Louisa	137	200	63	16	4	4	7	12
Louise		8	3	2	6	34	121	133
Lucy	78	95	61	22	4	4	19	71
Lydia	27	34	13	4		5	2	2
Lynda				2	74	32	16	5
Lyndsey						5	2	17
Lynette					2	9	4	4
Lynn					30	54	11	17
Lynne					48	39	11	
Mabel		34	106	58				
Madeleine					4	5	2	7
Mandy						55	49	24

	1850	1875	1900	1925	1950	1960	1970	1975
Margaret	151	243	194	352	326	105	28	24
Margery	4	2	9	30	4			
Maria	139	70	25	6	20	18	21	24
Marian	2	11	9	24	16	5	2	
Marianne	4				4	4	2	
Marie		5	6	28	18	20	39	62
Marilyn					128	7	4	
Marion		15	33	16	52	16	9	
Marjorie			21	146	24	2	2	
Marlene					16			
Martha	259	146	48	12				
Martina						2	4	5
Mary	1505	1013	391	408	132	52	25	14
Matilda	63	28	19	4		2		5
Maud	2	52	22	12				
Maureen				12	142	34	11	
Mavis			1	34	4			
Maxine					4	29	32	21
May		16	130	46			2	
Melanie					8	21	81	112
Melinda							4	5
Melissa							12	21
Melody					2		5	5
Michaela							18	12
Michelle					2	18	205	188
Mildred		7	22	14		2		
Millicent		3	15	10				
Minnie		87	63	20	2		2	
Miranda	2			2		7	2	7
Miriam	7	8	9	12	2	4		
Moira				4	18		4	
Molly			1	14			2	
Monica				6	18	9		
Muriel		2	18	84	8	4		
Myra		5	3	4	8			
Myrtle			3	6				
Nadine						4	11	5
Nancy	29	8	7	36	6	4	11	7
Naomi	7	5	1		2	7	16	12
Natalie					2		37	69
Natasha							19	40
Nellie		16	124	56				
Nichola							25	26
Nicola					10	45	247	340
Nicole						5	5	14
Nora		3	37	40	2			
Norah			28	26				
Norma			1	18	28	5	4	
Olive	2	11	73	140	6	2		
Olivia		2	1	2	2			7
Pamela	2	2	1	66	186	154	18	21
Patience	2	3	1	4	4	2	2	

	1850	1875	1900	1925	1950	1960	1970	1975
Patricia				76	258	136	35	24
Paula					12	18	95	67
Pauline			1	22	186	93	23	10
Pearl			3	22	10	4	4	
Peggy				110	10			2
Penelope	2		1		34	41	12	10
Penny					2	4	7	12
Philippa	2	2	1	2	6	7	14	33
Phoebe	22	23	16	6				
Phyllis		2	37	112	12	2		
Priscilla	24	18	3	6	2	4		
Rachael	4			2			33	45
Rachel	46	21	13	4	8	21	160	179
Rebecca	49	34	12	4	4	13	121	174
Rebekah	2	2					2	17
Rhoda	8	18	16	8	2		4	
Rhonda						5		2
Rita				32	44	7	4	
Roberta			1	2	2	2	2	2
Robyn					2		5	2
Rosa	10	33	16	2				
Rosalind		2	3	4	26	16	11	
Rose	37	95	152	88	14	14	4	2
Rosemarie					12	2	5	
Rosemary				14	78	38	14	2
Rosetta	4	10	4	6	2		2	
Rosie			7	10				4
Rosina	4	31	12	20	12	5		
Rowena						2	2	4
Ruby		5	21	32		4	2	
Ruth	27	25	22	38	16	11	14	26
Sadie						4		7
Sally	4			2	46	71	42	55
Sallyann					2		5	10
Samantha							168	152
Sandra					192	120	18	17
Sara					6	5	32	24
Sarah	893	541	152	30	18	57	282	371
Selina	29	28	7	6	4		5	2
Sharon					20	161	286	119
Sharron					2	4	19	4
Sheena					8	5	4	4
Sheila				78	150	41	9	7
Sheryl						5	4	5
Shirley				8	84	46	14	5
Shona							5	10
Sonia				4	6	7	19	14
Sophia	63	21	10	2			2	2
Sophie				2		2	9	10
Stacey						2	16	21
Stella		3	1	20	12	5	7	7
Stephanie				2	28	27	35	43

	1850	1875	1900	1925	1950	1960	1970	1975
Susan	63	15	19	8	654	446	102	86
Susannah	95	41	18	2		2	2	12
Susanne					2	2	21	12
Suzanne				2	14	25	32	45
Sylvia	2	3	7	68	60	27	7	7
Tamara	2						4	5
Tammy							7	31
Tamsin						2	2	10
Tania						4	7	5
Tanya						2	21	21
Tara							21	17
Teresa	2	5		12	32	27	46	43
Thelma			1	26	6			
Theresa	2	8	3	6	16	23	18	7
Tina					2	80	74	55
Tracey						38	184	74
Tracy						50	198	88
Ursula		2	3	8	2		4	2
Valerie			1	6	150	50	7	5
Vanessa					18	7	26	26
Vera			28	190	12	5	5	
Veronica			3	24	26			
Vicki							12	12
Vicky					4	11	11	19
Victoria		2	12	2	22	20	181	176
Vikki							4	5
Violet		15	155	136	12	3	2	2
Virginia					6	9	4	2
Wendy				2	96	177	84	50
Winifred		21	191	142	8	2		
Yvonne				6	58	52	18	19
Zara							5	7
Zoe	2		1		2	2	30	107
Boys								
Aaron	7	5		4			7	26
Adam	10	7	7	6		7	77	110
Adrian			1		40	68	96	81
Alan			12	126	324	182	82	71
Albert	63	325	333	238	34	4	9	
Alexander	32	41	27	24	16	9	35	48
Alfred	224	302	260	132	18	4		2
Alistair					8	14	12	21
Allan		5	4	24	52	27	9	10
Andrew	15	20	13	16	124	338	428	421
Anthony		5	3	46	214	200	130	83
Antony		2		2	2	73	33	21
Arthur	105	420	367	224	32	13		
Ashley			3	2	6	9	26	24
Barry				4	132	82	35	60
Benjamin	90	36	31	22	8		30	119

	1850	1875	1900	1925	1950	1960	1970	1975
Bernard		8	25	60	32	7	5	
Bertie		8	60	16	2			
Brendan					2	4	5	10
Brian				36	240	95	53	29
Bryan				20	26	23	7	7
Calvin						4	4	7
Carl				6	16	20	56	86
Cecil		10	76	40			2	
Charles	444	418	390	206	88	25	11	17
Christian			1	2		2	23	31
Christopher	15	16	7	24	200	196	230	276
Clifford	2		30	44	20	25	4	
Clive				2	46	54	12	21
Colin			9	36	204	209	88	76
Craig					2	29	118	162
Cyril		3	57	104	10	7		
Dale					2	14	11	17
Damian					4	2	23	38
Damien							2	14
Daniel	49	34	6	10	10	21	61	286
Darren						7	309	269
David	80	67	52	106	832	625	386	369
Dean				2		16	82	64
Denis		2	3	60	20	2	2	
Dennis		3		128	38	23	2	12
Derek				60	122	64	25	14
Derrick				46	14	7	2	5
Desmond			1	42	4	9	7	5
Dominic							14	33
Donald	2	3	34	128	42	13		12
Douglas		3	22	94	32	32	9	7
Duane							4	10
Duncan		2	1	6	18	30	28	26
Dylan							4	12
Edgar	7	25	42	12	2		2	
Edward	254	233	166	228	70	43	49	43
Edwin	78	52	39	46	20	4	7	
Eric		3	48	232	46	9	14	7
Ernest	10	198	269	154	16	4		
Francis	56	85	87	52	32	5	9	12
Frank	32	136	206	196	34	14	7	10
Fred	7	89	82	42	4	4		
Frederick	207	384	376	256	44	13	12	2
Garry					8	43	35	33
Gary				4	20	250	161	129
Gavin				2	2	13	42	21
Geoffrey			10	98	122	79	40	17
George	788	762	609	442	88	55	18	21
Gerald		3	6	60	32	13	4	
Giles	5		1				9	12
Glen			1				22	21
Glenn					6	21	7	14

	1850	1875	1900	1925	1950	1960	1970	1975
Glyn				2	12	4	9	7
Gordon	2		16	106	64	30	23	14
Graeme					2	16	12	17
Graham	2		1	12	246	173	104	67
Grant					4	4	11	12
Gregory		2			12	21	16	43
Guy			3	2		9	9	12
Harold		36	213	152	12	5	2	
Harry	41	251	213	132	16	5	4	
Hector		2	31					
Henry	563	421	261	114	38	16		
Herbert	34	166	175	106	10	2		
Horace	12	15	66	30	4			2
Howard	2	5	12	12	26	29	9	10
Hugh	20	10	12	16	6	4	2	10
Ian			6	8	152	270	196	150
Isaac	37	34	10	12				2
Ivan			1	14	4	5	7	5
Ivor			10	20	2	2		
Jack		2	31	100	12	7	2	2
James	712	490	355	320	176	89	163	248
Jamie						2	58	64
Jason						7	454	207
Jeffrey			1	8	54	55	30	17
Jeremy					20	48	35	29
John	1241	1003	776	728	646	305	168	150
Jonathan	22	10	7		38	66	112	164
Joseph	420	366	221	174	42	32	30	50
Julian				4	12	18	39	17
Justin						2	72	57
Karl					2	11	26	45
Keith				10	164	75	32	36
Kenneth			22	280	126	63	12	7
Kevin				4	98	279	137	126
Laurence		2	1	16	22	13	11	5
Lawrence		8	15	18	26	5	5	2
Lee	2		1		2	30	158	193
Leon				4	4	4	4	36
Leonard	7	15	103	134	36	9	4	7
Leslie		2	40	204	94	50	5	10
Luke	2	7	1			4	16	24
Malcolm		2	1	2	158	77	26	7
Marc							16	24
Marcus		2	1	2	2	2	35	29
Mark	10	8	6	6	12	398	467	426
Martin	10	10	3	2	96	234	142	145
Martyn					10	38	18	12
Matthew	32	25	22	6	6	27	211	288
Maurice	2	5	15	66	28	5		5
Michael	12	8	12	36	460	421	240	255
Nathan	2	3				2	19	57
Neil					48	107	114	195

	1850	1875	1900	1925	1950	1960	1970	1975
Nicholas	10		1	2	36	118	165	167
Nigel			1	4	76	143	49	48
Norman		5	52	150	36	5	4	2
Oliver	5	16	9	2	4		5	24
Owen	5	7	6	2	4	7	5	14
Patrick	7	7	10	16	44	25	12	7
Paul	5			18	278	445	465	424
Percival	2	5	31	14	2			
Percy	5	61	131	34				
Peter	34	39	24	194	534	343	135	119
Philip	27	25	22	40	174	200	130	107
Phillip	15			4	44	32	39	21
Ralph	17	15	21	44	12	4	4	2
Raymond		2	12	138	136	68	21	26
Reginald	5	13	91	128	14	2		5
Richard	188	128	112	96	158	161	256	314
Robert	290	231	267	284	356	161	239	231
Robin					44	32	35	19
Roger		8	1	8	134	63	19	26
Roland		3	9	30	6	11	2	10
Ronald			21	308	96	27	11	2
Roy			3	122	62	29	11	12
Russell			3	8	10	66	42	40
Ryan							7	21
Samuel	256	141	106	38	2	11	5	24
Scott					2	2	42	79
Sean					4	9	47	17
Shane						11	23	38
Shaun						23	67	31
Sidney	34	79	155	110	10	4	2	
Simon	2		1		10	98	239	219
Spencer	2	2	3			2	14	21
Stanley		8	93	158	12	5	2	5
Stephen	27	23	22	10	268	454	282	233
Steven	2				32	202	195	219
Stewart			4	6	18	32	21	21
Stuart		2	4	6	58	52	125	181
Sydney	15	72	99	88	6			
Terence			1	30	154	88	9	14
Terry				2	20	29	16	29
Thomas	788	595	452	254	82	39	44	52
Timothy		2	1	2	38	84	70	76
Tom	29	39	16	8	2			2
Tony					22	29	26	29
Trevor			1	22	114	107	39	19
Victor		3	43	54	10	11	4	2
Vincent	2	2	12	24	16	7	14	10
Walter	112	266	187	106	12	5	4	
Warren					2	9	19	19
Wayne					2	25	93	114
Wilfred		13	49	50	2			
William	1449	1133	897	590	178	127	33	67

16 Jock and Jill

First names in Scotland

The use of first names in Scotland over the last hundred years is well documented. The Scottish Registrar General has on three occasions issued an official report showing how names were used. A comparison between the 1935 and 1958 reports is especially interesting. It shows at a glance the effects of name fashions in recent times on a people who do not easily change their habits. A further comparison between the names used in Scotland in the 1950s and those used at the same time in other English-speaking countries reveals which names are particularly Scottish in character.

Changing fashions—boys' names

On the first of these two points, there is a striking difference between the way fashion affects the girls' names rather than those of the boys. In 1935 **John, James** and **William** headed the boys' list, followed by **Robert, Alexander, George, Thomas, David, Andrew** and **Ian**. A generation later John, James and William again led the way, followed by David, Robert, Ian, Thomas, **Alan**, Alexander and **Brian**. The two newcomers, Alan and Brian, had managed to knock George and Andrew into eleventh and fourteenth places respectively—hardly a complete defeat. Nor were the 'new' names completely new. Both had been present in the top fifty for 1935 but in lower positions.

Only a handful of other male names had improved their position in a noticeable way. **Michael, Stephen, Colin, Graham, Derek** and **Paul** were amongst those which managed to do so, displacing **Charles, Ronald, Joseph, Hugh, Francis, Henry** and **Archibald**. The latter was less used in 1958, but by no means completely abandoned. There were still 175 Scottish boys who received the name Archibald that year, though the name had long been considered something of an embarrassment in other English-

> '*What do you think they are going to name the baby? **Anne**; after her and her mamma. So very ugly a name!*'
>
> '*I do not think so,*' said Mr Carlyle. '*It is simple and unpretending. I like it much. Look at the long, pretentious names in our family—Archibald! Cornelia! And yours, too—Barbara! What a mouthful they all are!*'
>
> *Mrs Henry Wood*, East Lynne

speaking countries. George Robey may have been partly responsible for that with his comic music-hall song, 'Archibald, Certainly Not.'

Changing fashions—girls' names

Fluctuations in the use of girls' names over the same period are far more noticeable. Though **Margaret, Elizabeth** and **Mary** remained highly placed, **Ann(e), Linda, Susan, Fiona, Carol, Jacqueline, Christine, Elaine, Sandra, Caroline, Janice, Alison, Lorraine, Lesley, Karen, Heather, Yvonne, Angela, Lorna, Valerie, Diane** and **Jennifer** had all made dramatic improvements by 1958. In most cases the use of these names showed an awareness, sometimes belatedly, of name fashions affecting the rest of the English-speaking world. Fiona, however, was very much a homegrown product.

This name is now slowly spreading to the other English-speaking countries. Its use in Scotland originally was entirely due to the romantic novels that appeared in the 1890s under the name of Fiona Macleod. For a long time it was a well-kept secret that Fiona was really William Sharp. It is possible that he invented this name himself by translating **Blanche** or **Candida** into the Gaelic *fionn*, 'fair, white'. But **Fionn** and **Fionnan** were already thoroughly established as male names in Ireland. The latter name was borne by several saints. Similar names were **Fionnbharr** and **Fionntan**, usually anglicized as **Finbar** and **Fintan**. If Mark Twain's Huckleberry Finn had Irish ancestors, then his surname meant that he was a descendant of a Fionn. William Sharp, in other words, had plenty of clues to point him towards Fiona, but he seems to have been the first to use the name in that form.

The 'new' girls' names accepted by the Scots meant the displacement of others. **Jane, Joan** and **Jean** were victims, as were **Agnes, Sheila, Christina, Isabella, Barbara, Dorothy, Sarah** and **Annie**, though the last of these was simply replaced by Ann and Anne. Sarah's eclipse may well have been only a temporary one. The name has returned in force in all the English-speaking countries.

Scottish names

Many first names, borne by men or women of any age, hint very strongly at Scottish parentage. Some of these, like Fiona, show the influence of Gaelic; others are imported names which the Scots have made their own. Often the English form of a name is used alongside its Gaelic adaptation—**John** with **Ian**, **Alexander** with **Alistair**, etc.

I said 'adaptation', but it would have been nearer the truth to speak of 'adaptations'. The Scots seem to be in some doubt as to whether the Gaelic version of Alexander, for example, should be written as **Alistair, Alasdair, Alaister, Alisdair, Alastair, Alister, Allistair** or **Allister**. All of these were used in 1958. Some of the confusion may be caused by names taking a vocative form in Gaelic. Perhaps Scotsmen would do better to stick to Alexander, used since the thirteenth century when three kings of Scotland bore the name. It had been borrowed, of course, from Alexander the Great, and derived from Greek words meaning 'defender of men'.

Any name that has been in long and frequent use in a country will take on a variety of pet forms, and Alexander is no exception. **Alec, Alick, Alex** and **Sandy** were all given as independent names in Scotland in 1958. So too were the feminine forms **Alexa, Alexanderia, Alexanderina, Alexandra, Alexandria, Alexandrina, Alexandrine, Alexina** and **Alexis**, the latter having been converted from an independent male name. By far the commonest female version of the name used at the time was **Sandra**, which seems to have passed through the intermediate stage of Italian **Alessandra**.

The use of various name forms, all deriving from a single source, provides a good example of how to make the fullest use of a name. The Scots seem to be masters of name-husbandry. **John**, to take another example, becomes not only the usual **Joan, Jean** and **Jane**, but **Jeanette, Jeanie, Jeanne, Jan, Janet, Janetta, Janette, Janey, Janice, Janie, Janine** and **Janis** for

---

By the seventeenth century Joan had acquired rather a poor image. Shakespeare clearly thought of a Joan as a country simpleton. There is his famous reference to 'greasy Joan' who 'doth keel the pot', where 'keel' refers to cooling by stirring. In the same play, Love's Labour's Lost, *there is the remark: 'Some men must love my lady, and some Joan.' In* King John *the Bastard, who has just been knighted, says: 'Now I can make any Joan a lady.'*

Joan was linked with Darby in an eighteenth century ballad, The Happy Old Couple. *The originals were said to be John Darby, a printer, and his wife Joan.*

Scottish parents. They add **Johan, Johanna, Johanne, Johnann, Joh-nanna, Seona, Shauna, Sheona, Shiona, Shona, Shonagh** and **Shonah** to the list for girls, and name their sons **Ian, Iain, Ivan, Euan, Evan, Ewan, Ewen, Hans, Sean, Shane** and **Shaun**, as well as **John** and **Johnnie**.

James leads to the feminine form **Jamesina**, but more frequently to Gaelic adaptations for boys in the forms **Hamish** or **Seamus**. **Jamie** is used for boys in Scotland, though it is often a girl's name in North America. Hamish, incidentally, earned the severe disapproval of Miss E. G. Withycombe some years ago in her *Oxford Dictionary of English Christian Names*. In spite of the name's use by Scottish novelists of high repute, Miss Withycombe was of the opinion that 'the use of this pseudo-Gaelic form is to be discouraged'.

Hamish is one of those names which fairly reliably indicates Scottish parenthood. Many parents use such names in an effort to make the children concerned especially aware of their national heritage. With such Scottish names I would once have classed **Graham**, especially when written as **Graeme**. This was the form established by George Buchanan in the sixteenth century and used by several aristocratic Scottish families. As we have seen, however, Graham was adopted in large numbers by English parents. **Duncan** would also have indicated Scottish parentage at one time, but this name too was being taken up in England in the 1950s.

Angus is usually Scottish, and inevitably a female form is found, usually Angusina. I say 'inevitably' because the Scots have long had the habit of making simple conversions of almost any male name. In 1958, for instance, there were Scottish girls who were given the names **Andrewina, Andreana, Andreena, Andrena, Andrene, Andriene, Andrina** and **Andrine** by parents who were presumably fond of the name **Andrew**.

Lindsay, Lindsey

Until recently the name **Lindsay** might have been another indicator of Scottish nationality, but the name is making very rapid progress in England and Wales. This is in spite of the problems the name presents. As a first name that derives from a surname which was formerly a place name, it obviously gives no clear indication as to which sex it belongs to. The Scots themselves give little guidance in the matter. In 1958 sixty-three boys in Scotland received the name, but so did thirty-seven girls. Other girls were named **Lindsey, Linsay, Lyndsay, Lyndsey** and **Lynsay**. English and Welsh parents, who seem to have decided that the name properly belongs to girls, used all those spellings in 1975 but added **Lynsey** and **Lindsie** for good measure.

Eight spellings of a name and indeterminate sex might seem to be

Most Frequently Used First Names in Scotland

These lists are based on surveys by the Scottish Registrar General's Office. Variant name-spellings are counted as one name.

Girls		Boys	
1935	1958	1935	1958
1. Margaret	1. Margaret	1. John	1. John
2. Mary	2. Ann(e)	2. James	2. James
3. Elizabeth	3. Elizabeth	3. William	3. William
4. Catherine	4. Linda	4. Robert	4. David
5. Annie	5. Mary	5. Alexander	5. Robert
6. Isabella	6. Catherine	6. George	6. Ian
7. Agnes	7. Carol(e)	7. Thomas	7. Thomas
8. Jean	8. Susan	8. David	8. Alan
9. Helen	9. Helen	9. Andrew	9. Alexander
10. Janet	10. Fiona	10. Ian	10. Brian
11. Christina	11. Jacqueline	11. Charles	11. George
12. Sarah	12. Patricia	12. Peter	12. Stephen
13. Jane	13. Christine	13. Joseph	13. Michael
14. Jessie	14. Elaine	14. Ronald	14. Andrew
15. Sheila	15. Jane	15. Hugh	15. Peter
16. Marion	16. Alison	16. Francis	16. Kenneth
17. Patricia	17. Maureen	17. Henry	17. Gordon
18. Irene	18. Sandra	18. Edward	18. Colin
19. Dorothy	19. Janice	19. Donald	19. Graham
20. Joan	20. Janet	20. Archibald	20. Alistair
21. Kathleen	21. Caroline	21. Allan	21. Stuart
22. Grace	22. Jean	22. Daniel	22. Charles
23. Barbara	23. Agnes	23. Patrick	23. Derek
24. Alice	24. Irene	24. Alistair	24. Douglas
25. Maureen	25. Lorraine	25. Gordon	25. Ronald
26. Williamina	26. Kathleen	26. Douglas	26. Joseph
27. Rose	27. Eileen	27. Kenneth	27. Donald
28. Evelyn	28. Marion	28. Michael	28. Paul
29. Ellen	29. Lesley	29. Norman	29. Hugh
30. Frances	30. Lynn(e)	30. Richard	30. Neil
31. Georgina	31. Karen	31. Samuel	31. Edward
32. Marjorie	32. Sheila	32. Walter	32. Richard
33. Moira	33. June	33. Arthur	33. Francis
34. Martha	34. Moira	34. Duncan	34. Patrick
35. June	35. Joan	35. Angus	35. Martin
36. Susan	36. Heather	36. Eric	36. Gary
37. Joyce	37. Yvonne	37. Neil	37. Raymond
38. Doreen	38. Joyce	38. Matthew	38. Anthony
39. Euphemia	39. Isabel	39. Frederick	39. Christopher
40. Janette	40. Christina	40. Albert	40. Daniel
41. Eileen	41. Angela	41. Stewart	41. Keith
42. Edith	42. Diane	42. Malcolm	42. Malcolm
43. Shirley	Lorna	43. Stanley	43. Gerard
44. Audrey	44. Isabella	44. Colin	44. Henry
45. Theresa	45. Barbara	45. Denis	45. Norman
46. Violet	46. Marie	46. Adam	46. Duncan
47. Norma	47. Dorothy	47. Brian	47. Kevin
48. Robina	48. Frances	48. Alfred	48. Mark
49. Muriel	49. Theresa	49. Lawrence	49. Gerald
50. May	50. Valerie	50. Leslie	50. Leslie

drawbacks enough, but the situation is actually far more complicated than that. *Peerage of Scotland*, edited by Sir J. Balfour Paul, mentions that there have been nearly 200 variations in the spelling of the name. Lord Lindsay, in his *Family of Lindsay*, quotes eighty-four of them, but may seem to have solved the problem of which one to use by the title of his book.

Discussing the origins of the family, Andrew of Wyntoun, in rather less than inspired verse, pronounced:

> Off Inglande coyme the Lynddissay
> Mare of thaim I can noucht say.

If he was right, then the origin of the name is probably that of Lindsey, in Lincolnshire. There it means 'Lindon's isle', Lindon being the former name of Lincoln itself.

Having introduced so many complications, it would be unfair of me not to offer guidance about the use of the modern first name. I believe it will become firmly established as a girl's name, not a boy's, but the spelling is bound to present problems for a long time to come. In spite of the fact that Lindsay is the normal place name and surname spelling in Scotland, and Lindsey the normal spelling in England, I suspect that Lynsey is the spelling that will win through for the first name. Perhaps the male form of the name, incidentally, could be considered to be **Lyndon**.

Irish names in Scotland

A feature of some names used in Scotland in 1958 is their apparent Irishness. Sean and Seamus have already been mentioned, and other names one would tend to associate with Ireland include **Brendan, Cornelius, Dermot, Eamon** or **Eamonn, Kennedy, Kevin, Kieran, Neil** and **Niall, Patrick** and **Ryan**. Girls' names that belong to this group include **Aileen** or **Eileen, Bridget** or **Bridie, Doreen, Ena, Ina, Kathleen** and **Kaitrin, Marta, Mona, Monica, Oonagh, Sioban, Theresa** and **Teresa**. Some of these, it is true, have come into very general use throughout the English-speaking world, and others could easily do so.

Brendan is known to many because of the playwright Brendan Behan. In more recent times the name has also been much publicized in Britain by a popular athlete, Brendan Foster. Further afield, Brendan is already in the Australian top fifty and becoming more popular all the time. It looks all set, in fact, to make the kind of impact that **Brenda** made some time ago.

Brendan and Brenda

The two names are not necessarily connected, as it happens. Brendan came from Ireland originally, where it named several saints. Brenda is thought to have come from Scandinavia, via Shetland, as the feminine form of **Brand**. This fact inspired one writer on names to assume that Brenda meant 'firebrand' and talk eloquently about 'a dark beauty who kindled a flame of love in every heart'. Brand actually means 'sword'.

Brenda seems to have been a great stimulus to the imagination of various writers on names. In the *Harrap Book of Boys' and Girls' Names*, for instance, we find the following statement: 'The early Victorians, who had a great liking for names from the distant past with a pleasant ring to them, seized on Brenda, with the result that it steadily gained ground throughout the 1800s, and its popularity has been maintained during the present century.'

This could hardly be more misleading, for the name was virtually unknown in Britain before the present century. A check on the Indexes of Births reveals that the Smiths, for example, who were giving birth to some 5000 daughters a year when records began in 1838, did not name a single one of them Brenda until 1858. The name began to be used to some extent in the 1890s, though Brenda's real heyday was in the 1920s and 1930s.

Roma Thewes, in her *Name Your Daughter*, also says that Brenda 'was a popular name with the Victorians'. Perhaps she assumed this to be the case because Sir Walter Scott used the name in his novel *The Pirate*, published in 1821. Thackeray also used it in 1861 in *The Adventures of Philip*, making Brenda and Minna the schoolgirl daughters of the Hon. Mrs Boldero. Thackeray was playing a literary joke, for Minna was also one of Brenda's sisters in Scott's novel.

In spite of these literary mentions, neither Brenda or Minna aroused any general enthusiasm at the time. Around the turn of the century, however, the name seems to have been used as a pseudonym by Mrs Castle Smith, a writer of stories for children. This lady does not appear to have made a significant contribution to English literature, but her choice of a pseudonym may have provided the name with the public exposure it needed.

One more name that belongs to the Irish group of Scottish names is **Dougal**, or **Dugald** as it is often written. When it was first used in Ireland this was a generic nickname, something like **Paddy** and **Taffy** in modern times. The Irish applied it to Norwegians, who were 'black strangers'. The Scots have taken this name over, and it now manages to carry a suggestion of a kilted giant.

Traditional names

But Dougal or Dugald was by no means the typical male name in Scotland in 1958. Scottish parents at that time showed far more respect for traditional names, those common to the English-speaking world but perhaps out of fashion elsewhere. **George, James, John** and **William,** for example, were used in Scotland in 1958 far more than in any other English-speaking country, and in that respect deserve to be described as Scottish names. Their intensive use meant that the names evoked a more youthful and acceptable image than was the case outside Scotland. The English and Welsh, for instance, had virtually abandoned George by 1958, and six Scottish lads received the name that year for every young Englishman who was so named. James, as we have seen, was plagued to some extent by social-class problems in England. No such difficulty stood in the way of the Scots, who used it six times more frequently. William appealed to four Scottish families for every one who chose it in England, and John was used twice as often by the Scots.

Traditional girls' names

The names of Scottish girls show a similar instinct for preservation. **Agnes** may have fallen into a lower position in the top fifty for 1958, but at least it was still amongst the top names. This was certainly not the case anywhere else in the English-speaking world, and an Agnes born since 1940 is fifty times more likely to be Scottish than English, American, Canadian or Australian. One pet form of the name, incidentally, is **Nessie,** so it was doubly fitting to bestow this name on the Loch Ness monster.

The French formerly had a saying: elle fait l'Agnès, *'she's doing an Agnès'. It meant that the girl or woman concerned was pretending to be innocent and unsophisticated. The allusion was to the Agnès of Molière's play,* L'Ecole des Femmes, *1662. In the play Arnolphe tries to have her kept in ignorance of conventional social behaviour so that she will become a model wife. His plan rebounds on him.*

The fondness in Scotland for Agnes must surely have been responsible for the name **Senga**, given to thirty-six girls in 1958. That amount of use suggests a literary source for the name rather than an individual family hitting on the idea of reversing a name. Scotland is the last place where one would have expected a rather gimmicky name to take root, though the result of the reversal has a slightly exotic look about it and a not unpleasant sound.

Anne, or **Ann**, must also be considered a Scottish first name in modern times. Here it is necessary to emphasize 'first' name, for we have already seen that it is an outstandingly popular middle name in all the English-speaking countries. It occupies the latter position easily, blending with the sound of many other names.

At first glance, the lists showing comparative usage of first names in the 1950s (see the later chapter *Namers' Names*) seem to indicate a special Scottish fondness for **Catherine**. The preference is really one of spelling, however. Girls who would answer to the same name from elsewhere in the English-speaking world would be far more likely to write it down as **Katherine** or **Kathryn**. Some Scottish parents use a Gaelic diminutive based on the name—**Catriona** or **Caitriona**.

Elizabeth and **Caroline** have been 'preserved' in Scotland more than elsewhere, as have **Irene, Joyce, Rose** and above all, **Margaret**. Scottish loyalty to Margaret really has been amazing, and one girl in every eighteen born in Scotland in 1958 received the name. It certainly deserves to be called the outstanding Scottish name of modern times, in spite of its foreign origin, though many people, I know, will feel that **Moira**, say, or **Morag** *looks* more Scottish. Moira is a form of **Mary** that shows Gaelic influence, and Morag is a genuinely Gaelic name. Both have been in consistent use in Scotland over a very long period, but neither have been established in the country as long as Margaret, nor used as often at any time.

Leslie, Lesley

But if the Scots have imported names like Margaret, they have exported many other names to the rest of the English-speaking world. **Leslie** comes to mind and perhaps it may serve as an example. This began as a Scottish place name and appeared in early documents as Lesslyn, Lesellyn, Lescelye and Lechelyn. Gaelic scholars disagree as to the original meaning of the name, but all are agreed that it later became the surname of a prominent Scottish family. As a surname it was variously spelt as Leslie, Lesslie, Leslei, Lesli, Lesly, Lessely, Lesley and Leslyn. Eventually used as a first name, Leslie became the usual male form, Lesley the female. The latter spelling was established by Robert Burns in the eighteenth century.

It was the male first name which slowly established itself from the 1860s onwards. The actors Leslie Banks and Leslie Howard were both born in the

> *O, saw ye bonnie Lesley*
> *As she gaed o'er the border?*
> *She's gane, like Alexander,*
> *To spread her conquests farther.*
> *To see her is to love her,*
> *And love but her for ever;*
> *For Nature made her what she is,*
> *And never made anither.*
>
> *Robert Burns*

1890s, by which time the name was beginning to make a more general appeal to parents in both Scotland and England. It reached the peak of its popularity by 1925, some years before either of these two actors made any feature films. In spite of their subsequent success the name lost ground, but as Leslie for men faded away, so Lesley for girls became fashionable in both England and Scotland. This in turn reached its highest point in 1960 but has since faded away.

In the U.S.A. Leslie also began as a male name and is found from 1870 onwards, but Lesley at no time seems to have established itself for the girls. The French actress Leslie Caron appeared on the screen in 1951 as Gene Kelly's co-star in *An American In Paris*, and for Americans Leslie seems to have changed its sex from that time.

As I know from personal experience, there are some consolations to be had in bearing a name that can apply to both sexes. The female Lesleys or Leslies that I meet are invariably young and attractive, and I think of Robert Louis Stevenson's remark in his *Philosophy of Nomenclature*. He maintains that two people who find that they have the same name 'are friends from that moment forth'.

One other aspect of Scottish naming comes to mind when one looks at the carefully-chosen names given to Scottish children in 1958. The girls, if by now they are travelling to other English-speaking countries, will probably be safe. They will remain as Margaret or Elizabeth, Mary or Linda, Anne or Catherine, as their parents intended. Their brothers John or James, William, David or Robert may not fare so well. Many of them will have their own names ignored and will have to answer to **Jock**, the friendly generic nickname for all Scotsmen. This seemingly very Scottish name, needless to say, made not a single appearance in the Scottish Registrar General's report for 1958, so the Scots themselves made their opinion of the name quite clear. In spite of their views, Jock will continue to be heard frequently whenever a Scotsman is with a group of Englishmen. That, whether one likes it or not, is one way in which the names game is played.

17 Names Down Under

First names in Australia

By now I hope that it is clear that the first names used in a particular country at a particular time assume a kind of corporate identity. Given a set of names which were bestowed at roughly the same time and by parents of the same nationality it should be possible to identify both the period and country concerned. The group of names given below might help to prove this point. Let us imagine that we have no external evidence concerning the time and place to which they relate. What clues do the names themselves provide?

Men

Allan (2)	Duncan	George (3)	John (3)	Maurice	Urban
Charles	Eric	Harold	Kyrie	Noel	Victor
Cyril	Francis	Hugh	Leslie	Robert	Wilby
Donald	Frederick (2)	James	Martial	Roderick	William (2)

Women

Barbara	Edith	Florence	Jessie	Marcia	Phyllis
Carmen	Edna	Frances	Joan	Margaret	Sheelah
Catherine	Eileen	Gladys	Lucie	Marjorie	Stella
Dorothy (2)	Evelyn	Hannah	Lucy	Mollie	Veronica

Unusual names

Let us look first at the more unusual names in the list, mainly in order to eliminate them. A man named **Kyrie**, for instance, is going to be an odd man out at any period, in any of the English-speaking countries. The name may have been borrowed from the *Kyrie eleison* ('Lord, have mercy') of the Roman Catholic mass. The more usual form of the name which is based on the Greek word for 'lord' or 'master' is **Cyril**, which also occurs in the list.

Martial looks an unusual name, but I emphasize the word 'looks'. **Marshall** was used to a certain extent throughout the nineteenth century in all English-speaking countries. Martial would therefore not have *sounded* particularly unusual to our grandfathers, any more than it would today. In modern times, incidentally, Martial is regularly used as a first name in Switzerland.

Urban and **Wilby** are the other less usual names, the latter being a surname or place name transfer that gives no clues as to when or where it was borrowed as a first name. Urban will be familiar to Roman Catholics especially as the name of several popes, but even devoutly Catholic parents would be unlikely to use the name today. Its original meaning was exactly what it might seem to be, a 'town dweller' as opposed to **Pain(e)** or **Payn(e)**, 'country dweller'. It has never been much used by English speakers.

The Spanish girl's name **Carmen** has always been more used in the U.S.A. than Britain, so it might be thought to provide a clue. Also pointing in that direction is **Marcia**, definitely more American than British. **Sheelah** rather stops us in our tracks, however, for there is nothing of the American about it. Thomas Campbell places the name in his lines from *The Harper*:

> On the green banks of the Shannon, when Sheelah was nigh,
> No blithe Irish lad was so happy as I.

Eileen could also carry a suggestion of Ireland.

To confuse the issue still further, **Duncan** and **Roderick** seem to be decidedly Scottish, as is **Veronica** in a less obvious way. The latter name was introduced to Scotland in the seventeenth century, when the Earl of Kincardine married Veronica Sommalsdyck, of Holland. A descendant of the earl was James Boswell, who named one of his own daughters Veronica. The name only reached England and North America in any numbers in the present century.

Gladys

Until the latter part of the nineteenth century, **Gladys** would have been an indication in itself of a Welsh bearer, though it might well have been written as **Gwladys**. The name was then used by one or two romantic novelists who thought it would be suitably exotic for their heroines. They seemed to have judged well, for almost immediately the name took the English-speaking world by storm.

If a novelist or script-writer of today chose to name a character **Claudine**, say, no-one would think he had made a bad error. Ninety years ago, Gladys was the equivalent of Claudine. It suggested feminity, was interestingly 'foreign', and presumably had an inherent sex-appeal. Its image, in other words, was totally different to the one it has today, the dramatic change having taken place as the name grew older with all the ladies who bore it. Claudine, by the way, is not altogether unconnected with Gladys. The Welsh themselves have always considered the name to be a translation of the Latin **Claudia**, which leads to Claudine. Translating a name can sometimes do wonders for it!

A male name in the list is **Leslie**, which I referred to in the last chapter as being used outside Scotland from 1890 on. **Victor** hints at a similar date. The name probably began to be used then because of its association with **Victoria**. While the queen was still alive her own name remained sacrosanct, though **Albert** was a great favourite. It was after Prince Albert's death in 1861, when Victoria reigned alone, that Victor began slowly to appeal to English parents. Victor Hugo was by this time well-known to the educated classes, which may have helped the name along.

A moment ago I referred to the use of names 'outside Scotland'. A list of Scottish names from any period would almost certainly reveal its national background far more blatantly than does this one. There would be more than one **Margaret**, and at any time before 1935, an **Annie** and an **Isabella**. Amongst the boys one **David**, at least, would occur, and probably an **Alexander** and a **Thomas**. The Scots have always been so consistent in their naming habits, using few names with great intensity, that one can make these statements with some confidence. For negative reasons, then, this list is not from Scotland, though Scottish influence can be clearly seen.

Dating names

As for the dating of the names, amongst people born as late as the 1920s one would expect to find a **Betty** or **Jean**, **Kenneth** or **Frank**. On the other hand, **Dorothy**, **Edith**, **Florence**, **Gladys**, **Jessie**, **Mollie** and **Phyllis**, all of which do occur in the list, were much in use at the turn of the century, especially in England. That seems to put a date on the names, while the mixture of English, Irish, Scottish, Welsh and American names perhaps gives a clue to the country concerned. What we have, in fact, is a list of students who graduated from the University of Western Australia in 1925, and who were born in the early 1900s.

Had I genuinely been trying to identify the names myself I would have

> *She who comes to me and pleadeth*
> *In the lovely name of Edith*
> *Will not fail of what is wanted.*
>
> H. W. Longfellow

been most misled, I feel sure, by the occurence in the list of **Barbara** and **Joan**. In an American or English context both names would have been unusual at the turn of the century, but to anyone who had gone to Australia from Scotland during the nineteenth century they would have been completely familiar. Barbara was already the sixteenth most popular name in Scotland in 1858, with Joan twenty-ninth. Both names eventually became spectacular successes in the rest of the English-speaking world, but only in the 1920s.

Australian names of 1925

In the same university twenty-five years later there were still students to be found bearing most of the names in the early list, but they were now surrounded by students called **Anthony** and **Bruce**, **Brian** and **Keith**, **Hazel** and **Alison**, **Shirley** and **Ruth**. The whole names atmosphere had changed. One way in which it had done so was by becoming more distinctively Australian. This trend has continued, and Australian names given in the 1970s are far more easy to identify.

The names of the 1950 graduates offer some pleasing examples of individual names as well as evidence of general trends. A young lady called **Nona Bandy** was a graduate that year, for instance, together with an **Evert Dirk Drok**. I rather like, too, the resounding effect of **Noel Dora Nottle**, **Grecian Teresa Snooze**, **Zedekiah Hartstein**, **Paris Morton Drake-Brockman**, **Loisette Rutt**. Amongst the more unusual first names borne by the 1950 students were an **Athol**, **Isla**, **Aviva**, **Delys** and **Loris**.

When one consults other university lists Australian name preferences for those born around 1925 emerge clearly. **Peter, Alan, Brian, Keith, Kevin, Noel, Ross, Victor** and **Vincent** all show up strongly amongst the boys, alongside the normal names for the period such as **John, Robert, William** and **Albert**. Particularly noticeable amongst the girls is **Alison**, a name one thinks of as very modern. As with Barbara and Joan, this was another inheritance from Scotland, for the name had been in constant use there for a century.

Dulcie

Dulcie was an interesting name being given to Australian girls around 1925. Charlotte Yonge, writing in 1863, mentions **Dulcia** as a Spanish name, from a word meaning 'sweet'. She also reminds her readers of **Dulcinea**, Don Quixote's lady-love. The latter was described by Sancho Panza in rather lyrical terms—'her eyebrows two celestial arches, her eyes a pair of glorious suns, her cheeks two beds of roses, her lips two coral portals'—and some parents may have chosen Dulcie for their daughter in the hope that she

Most Frequent First Names in Australia-1925

The names listed below are drawn from those of 5000 university students who graduated in 1950. No rank order is assigned to the names, but all were clearly being frequently bestowed around 1925.

Girls

Alison	Judith		
Ann(e)	June		
Audrey	Kathleen		
Barbara	Laurel		
Beth	Marcia		
Betty	Margaret		
Catherine	Maria		
Doreen	Marie		
Doris	Marion		
Dulcie	Marjorie		
Edith	Mary		
Eileen	Nancy		
Elizabeth	Naomi		
Ellen	Norma		
Eva	Pamela		
Eve	Patricia		
Faye	Phyllis		
Frances	Rita		
Gwenda	Rosalie		
Helen	Rosemary		
Irene	Roslyn		
Jean	Ruth		
Jennifer	Sheila		
Joan	Shirley		
Jocelyn	Yvonne		

Boys

Alan	Keith
Albert	Kenneth
Alexander	Kevin
Alfred	Laurence
Anthony	Leonard
Arthur	Lloyd
Brian	Matthew
Bruce	Maxwell
Charles	Mervyn
Christopher	Michael
Colin	Nicholas
David	Noel
Donald	Norman
Douglas	Peter
Edward	Richard
Eric	Robert
Francis	Ronald
Frederick	Ross
George	Stanley
Harold	Stewart
Jack	Trevor
James	Victor
Jeffrey	Vincent
John	Walter
Joseph	William

would come to fit this description. This form of the name, Dulcie instead of Dulcia, had by now been given formal approval by Helena Swan, who wrote most entertainingly about girls' names in a book published in 1900.

Dulcibella was the earlier version of this name in English, though it became corrupted into **Dousabel** or **Dowsabel** and was used as a general term of address rather than as a first name. When **Doll**, in Ben Jonson's *The Alchemist*, is addressed as 'my Dousabel' she knows that the speaker means 'sweetheart'. This term became obsolete, and Dulcie must have been thought of as a new name when it was re-introduced in England at the end of the nineteenth century. Why it should suddenly have appeared then is a mystery, but it never became popular. In Australia it seems to have made a very definite appeal to middle-class parents a generation later.

Fay(e) is another name that was just coming into use in the 1920s. Various authors explain it as 'fairy', which I find very hard to accept. **May** had long been used as the pet form of **Mary**, and Fay could have come from a name like **Fanny**, itself a pet form of **Frances**. Another name of the period was **Gwenda**, imported from Wales. According to *Welsh Names for Children*, by Ruth Stephens, it means 'fair and good'.

Australian names of 1950

When we move on another twenty-five years and consider the names being given to children in 1950, the signs of Australia's 'name personality' become stronger. As an English-speaking country, names common to the English-speaking world were naturally in general use, but some new names were appearing and others were being made distinctly Australian by their usage. This was especially true of girls' names. The tradition of giving boys old-established and safe names did not begin to crumble in Australia until the 1960s, when it collapsed everywhere else.

Peter was the really fashionable boy's name around 1950, being used almost as often as **John**. The name was also very popular in England at the

---

*It is well known that **Peter** derives from the Greek petros or Latin petrus and means 'stone'. The Latin word has given us many other English words, including saltpetre, petrol and petrify. Saltpetre was sal petrae, 'salt of the rock or stone'; petrol was based on petrae oleum, 'oil of the rock', and petrify in its true sense means 'to turn into stone'. The phase 'to peter out' has been explained as a reference to goldmining in the U.S.A. Saltpetre was known popularly as 'peter', and when this was used to make gunpowder the powder itself became 'peter'. A seam from which all the gold had been removed by the use of explosive was said to 'have petered out'.*

time, otherwise the remarkably intensive usage in Australia would have made the name a symbol of Australian nationality. It was probably the affection for Peter which caused many young Australian ladies to become **Peta** around this time.

Other male names which appealed more to Australian parents than anyone else in the 1950s were **Gregory** and **Warwick**. Gregory Peck was by this time internationally known, though that is not to say that the movie-star necessarily inspired the use of the name. Historically it is associated with many popes and with the Eastern Church and has long been available as a first name. Warwick was modestly favoured in the 1950s but has become more popular since then. It occurred sporadically in England during the nineteenth century along with other place names turned first names that were associated with the aristocracy. The name's pronunciation (to rhyme with Yorick) must occasionally cause trouble to those who like to say names as they are spelt.

The Australian female equivalent of Peter around 1950, in terms of usage, was **Judith**. It has subsequently been eclipsed almost totally in the 1970s by its pet form **Jody** (or **Jodie, Jodi**). This gets the name away from **Judy**, which by the beginning of the nineteenth century had already become a slang term for any girl—a fate that was later to overtake **Sheila**. The extensive usage of Judith in Australia provides further proof that the original meaning of a name is rarely taken into account by parents. Originally Judith meant 'jewess', but there is not the slightest doubt that more Australian than Jewish girls born in the 1950s are bearers of the name.

Kerrie, Kerry

With **Kerrie (Kerry, Kerri)** we come to an Australian gift to the rest of the English-speaking world. The name has been known for some time as a first name, deriving from a county in Ireland. This in turn was called Kerry because it was occupied by '**Ciar**'s people', (*Ciarraidhe* in Irish), Ciar being a male personal name meaning 'black'. The original Irish name is actually more familiar in a diminutive form, **Kieran**, still used in Ireland and elsewhere.

Kerrie seems to have hit Australia in the 1940s, and by the 1950s it was the eleventh most frequently-used name for girls. Since it had begun as a male name, however, there was still some confusion about the name's sex. Some Australian boys were given the name in the 1950s, but the female take-over has subsequently been complete.

In terms of fashion, the name has suffered a set-back in Australia since 1965. But as the use of Kerrie, as it is usually spelt in Australia, declined there, so it rapidly rose elsewhere. In England and Wales, for example (now spelt as Kerry), the name reached a peak in 1970. It has since levelled out

Most Popular First Names – Australia

Spelling variants grouped under the main spelling.

Women		Men	
1950	1975	1950	1975
1. Susan	1. Michelle	1. John	1. Matthew
2. Margaret	2. Catherine	2. Peter	2. Andrew
3. Ann(e)	3. Kylie	3. Michael	3. David
4. Elizabeth	4. Nicole	4. David	4. Michael
5. Christine	5. Rebecca	5. Robert	5. Paul
6. Jennifer	6. Melissa	6. Stephen	6. Adam
7. Judith	7. Lisa	7. Paul	7. Christopher
8. Patricia	8. Belinda	8. Philip	8. Daniel
9. Catherine	9. Rachel	9. Christopher	9. Mark
10. Helen	10. Sarah	10. Ian	10. Scott
11. Kerry	11. Kellie	11. Gregory	11. Steven
12. Deborah	12. Jodie	12. Richard	12. Simon
Lynette	13. Emma	13. Anthony	13. Jason
14. Linda	14. Melanie	William	14. Benjamin
15. Pamela	15. Megan	15. Geoffrey	15. Bradley
Robyn	16. Fiona	16. Mark	16. Craig
17. Mary	17. Sally	17. James	17. Brett
18. Dianne	18. Amanda	18. Graham	18. Shane
19. Sandra	19. Kate	19. Andrew	19. Anthony
20. Janet	20. Natalie	20. Gary	20. Timothy
21. Julie	21. Danielle	21. Colin	Glenn
Suzanne	22. Tania	22. Alan	22. Darren
23. Carol(e)	23. Tracey	23. Bruce	23. Cameron
24. Barbara	24. Joanne	24. George	24. Damian
25. Jane	25. Karen	25. Ronald	25. Robert
Janice	26. Kim	26. Keith	26. Justin
25 Kathleen	27. Samantha	27. Terence	27. Dean
Marilyn	Jennifer	28. Thomas	28. Travis
Wendy	29. Narelle	29. Neil	29. James
30. Jillian	30. Renee	30. Patrick	Peter
31. Lynn(e)	31. Leanne	Stuart	31. Luke
32. Cheryl	32. Claire	32. Barry	Stuart
Heather	33. Elizabeth	Brian	Nicholas
Maria	Jacqueline	34. Dennis	34. Leigh
35. Frances	35. Jane	Raymond	Shaun
Jill	36. Simone	36. Arthur	36. Adrian
Marion	Julie	Joseph	37. Brendan
Maureen	Alison	Ross	Troy
Roslyn	39. Sharon	39. Kenneth	39. Richard
40. Gail	40. Melinda	40. Douglas	40. Gregory
41. Joan	41. Carly	41. Trevor	41. Ashley
Lesley	42. Deborah	42. Edward	42. John
Rosemary	43. Kristy	43. Adrian	43. Christian
Virginia	44. Kerrie	Bernard	44. Nathan
45. Michelle	Susan	Donald	45. Aaron
46. Beverley	46. Donna	Francis	46. Jeffrey
Lorraine	47. Christine	Malcolm	47. Gavin
Penelope	48. Vanessa	48. Alexander	48. Dale
49. Amanda	49. Angela	Frank	49. Wayne
Kay	50. Andrea	Russell	50. Kane
	Caroline	Wayne	
	Naomi		

but, nevertheless, it seems it will obviously continue to be used for many years.

Cleveland Evans, who studies name frequencies in Michigan, associated the name with **Carrie**. He is obviously right to remind us of possible phonetic confusion, and his case may be strengthened by the occurrence in Australia these days of **Kerryn**, an extension of Kerry that would bring it very close to **Karen** when pronounced by some speakers. In spite of this I believe the name that is currently being used more and more in the U.S.A. owes more to the importation of Kerry than to the restoration of Carrie.

A word 'kerrie' is to be found in the dictionary, incidentally. It refers to a knobbed stick used as a weapon by the Bushmen, and probably derives from a Hottentot word. This is one of those linguistic coincidences that sometimes occurs and is of little consequence, except that it may prevent Kerrie becoming a popular first name in South Africa.

Australian girls' names

Other names of the 1950s in Australia which had a marked national flavour about them were **Lynette** or **Lynnette, Narelle, Robyn, Roslyn, Vivien** and **Suzanne**. The last of these was an off-shoot of **Susan**, which was immensely popular at the time. The form **Susanne** was also used, and the parents of one young lady, at least, played safe by naming her **Suszanne**.

Lynette comes from the Tennysonian poem, *Gareth and Lynette*, published in 1872. Lynette asks the king for help in releasing her sister, **Lyonors**, who is besieged in her castle by four knights. Gareth, apparently a lowly worker in the royal kitchen, offers his services. The king agrees, much to Lynette's disgust, but after calling Gareth unkind names she is eventually won over by his bravery. He is a nobleman in disguise, in any case. Different writers dealing with this legend have disagreed as to its proper conclusion. The great problem has been whether Gareth should marry Lynette or her sister.

An Australian Lynette would stand a good chance of marrying a **Gary** (or **Garry**), but Gareths are thin on the ground there. The latter are to be found mainly in their native Wales, though interest in the name has recently been

---

Lynette
A damsel of high lineage, and a brow
May-blossom; and a cheek of apple blossom;
Hawk eyes; and lightly was her tender nose,
Tip-tilted like the petal of a flower.

Alfred Lord Tennyson

shown in England. Lynette can also be traced back to Wales if one pursues it far enough. Trefor Davies, in his *Book of Welsh Names*, lists the name **Eiluned**, from *eilun*, 'idol, icon'. He adds rather scathingly: 'This is the name which in the Arthurian legend has been Frenchified to Lynette.' Less French-looking is **Linnet**, a spelling of the name used by some Australian parents which immediately converts the name to 'song bird'.

Narelle looks Frenchified, but it is not a French word or name. Having looked at thousands of first names from all over the English-speaking world I can also safely say that for the moment the name is purely Australian. It has been very popular there in recent years, and may well spread eventually to other countries.

Sooner or later an Australian will write to tell me exactly how and when Narelle came into existence. My own collection of name books is unfortunately unable to do so. One or two of them mention a female name **Nara** (which I have never come across), and guess that this is from a Gaelic word meaning 'happy'. It is therefore vaguely possible that Nara came to Australia, was extended to Narelle, and has something to do with happiness. Those who bear the name may well prefer to regard it as an alternative form of **Narel**. This I find listed in Gustav Davidson's *Dictionary of Angels*, with the explanation that Narel is the angel of winter.

The other names I mentioned as being typically Australian were Robyn, Roselyn and Vivien. **Robyn,** by its spelling, firmly makes the name feminine, though it began life as a pet form of **Robert**. Soon, no doubt, there will be a television series based on the adventures of Robyn Hood and her merry men, giving an interesting new twist to the old story. **Roslyn**, or **Roslin**, is a Scottish place name by origin, similar to the Lesslyn that became Leslie. In Scotland we find the first name in many different forms: **Roslyn, Roslynn, Rosslyn, Roslyn, Roselynn, Roseleen, Roseline, Rosalyn, Rosaline.**

Vivien is theoretically the female version of **Vivian**, but the two spellings are often confused. The use of Vivien (sometimes **Vivienne**) in Australia, seems to link with Lynette, for a girl of this name appears in another Tennysonian poem. There she manages to get the better of Merlin. One must not forget the possible influence of Vivien Leigh, however, the much-admired actress whose films began to appear in the mid-1930s.

Present-day name counts in Australia

I must allow the other names in the list provided on page 213 to tell the rest of the story about Australian naming in the 1950s. On the same page I give the top fifties for 1975, based on birth announcements in the Melbourne *Sun*. These names are collected and analysed each year by Mrs Jodi Cassel. Mrs Cecily Dynes makes a similar yearly analysis of the names announced in

*Many Oriental students are reading for degrees at Australian universities. Their names add an extra touch of interest for the name-researcher. Two students I was especially glad to come across were **Wee Sock Chin**, and the truly enigmatic **May Be Eong Chua**.*

the 'Births' column of the Sydney *Morning Herald*, so that future researchers into the use of names in Australia will have their task much simplified.

I leave Australia and its names with one great regret, not having found a single instance of a young lady bearing the Australian name of names. No **Matilda** waltzed into view, not even a **Mattie**, a **Tillie** or a **Tilda**, as the pet forms used to be. Many names of the past are being used again now; surely Matilda is due for a revival? A magnificent name in itself, it carries with it the affection of all English-speaking people when associated with Australia. Surely there could be no better name for an Australian girl?

18 Namers' Names

First names in the 1950s

The use of first names in the English-speaking world now changes more rapidly than ever before. In this chapter I deal with the names that were being used in the 1950s, comparing usage in different countries. These are the names of today's young parents, who have become name-givers in their turn. The names that are being given now are discussed in the next chapter, and it will quickly be seen that the latter reflect a completely different image.

The figures quoted in this chapter refer to broad, national trends and obviously simplify complex situations. The countries concerned are multi-racial, are large enough to contain regions that have a local personality, have urban and rural areas, have social and professional hierarchies and allow their citizens to practise different religions. All these and many other factors can influence parents when they set about naming a child. It is therefore surprising, perhaps, that there should be national trends at all, but they do exist and on the whole are easy to identify.

The American figures that are given below are biased towards the white middle classes, living in cities. But black Americans, as I tried to make clear in an earlier chapter, do use the same names. They do not use them in such a concentrated fashion, and they extend the range of names considerably by using rather more exotic names, but the names they *mostly* use are the same as those of the whites.

American Indian names

Even special groups such as American Indians tend to conform to the normal naming habits of the English-speaking world. Here is the comment of a specialist in the field:

> The given names of the Yakima Indians today are Christian names such as Robert or Stanley, which are given to babies at birth without

ceremony, just as in the English-speaking community . . .

However, many of the Yakimas have been reluctant to give up many aspects of the Old Indian culture, and having a personal Indian name is one of the customs they cling to. They also continue to conduct their ancient ceremonies of formal name-giving.

Thelma E. Weeks, who published this article in *Names*, December 1971, gives some examples of Yakima names: **Kusinut** 'horseless', **Kiyiya** 'howling wolf', **Tiskayai** 'skunk', **Yumti-Bi** 'bitten by a grizzly bear', **Hwistaks** 'dress that swishes'. These are often new names given in adulthood, the equivalent of our nicknames but bestowed more formally.

Nearly every tribe has its own customs and names, and I recommend those interested to turn to specialized publications such as the *Handbook of Indians of Canada*. Meanwhile, the important point to note is in the first sentence quoted above. The Yakimas, whose reservation is in Washington, do recognize and conform to national naming habits.

Asian names in Britain

In Britain, on the other hand, the more recent immigrants from Asia seem to be continuing to name their children by their own conventions. The Indexes of Births for England and Wales do reveal that some Singh families in 1975 named their children **Steven** (or **Stephen**), **Mark** or **Paul**, thereby indicating complete integration with the native population, but far more families chose names like **Amardit, Ranjit, Rajinder, Guirdeep, Harjinder, Balbinder, Gurdip, Hardeep, Harjit, Jasvinder, Manjinder** and **Manjit**. The Patels, similarly, occasionally use names like **Sonia, Yasmin** or **Mark**, which blend with those of English children. More frequently they name their children **Hitesh, Sonal, Alpa, Amit, Bina, Chirag, Heena, Rajesh, Ashish, Manisha, Prakash, Rakesh** and **Reena**.

One naturally has complete sympathy with anyone's wish to preserve national or family customs, but when a family intends to remain permanently in an English-speaking environment some slight compromise may be needed if integration is to be achieved. Most of the names mentioned above are unfamiliar to an English-speaker's eyes and ears, but they present no real difficulties of pronunciation and there is no reason at all why English people should not learn to use them. Another name used by the Patels, however is **Shital**. This is clearly going to cause problems when the child concerned goes to an English-speaking school. It is in such cases that compromise is needed. The name could become the middle name, for instance. There is also a case to be made out for giving immigrant children both an Asian and English name for use in different situations.

Jewish names

Jewish names in all the English-speaking countries are likely to betray certain characteristics when seen as a group, but many popular Jewish names blend in completely with those in general use. At Jewish colleges in 1975, for instance, were students named **Adele, Anita, Barbara, Carolyn, Cheryl, Donna, Elaine, Jean, Joan, Karen, Laura, Marilyn** and **Sharon**. Even those girls with more traditionally Jewish names would pass almost unnoticed in a general list. I refer to those with names like **Sarah, Rebecca, Rachel, Leah, Miriam, Naomi, Abigail, Ruth, Esther** and **Judith**.

Jewish male names are likewise indistinguishable in many cases, though names like **Eli, Elihu, Herschel, Isaac, Ira, Isidore, Israel, Ivan, Joel, Lionel, Louis, Lyle, Maurice** or **Morris** and **Moshe** do suggest Jewish rather than Gentile parents.

Roman Catholic names

Roman Catholics do not seem to use names that in themselves indicate their religion. In Catholic colleges, however, the distribution of names shows certain characteristics. Traditional names are preferred to modern innovations, and fewer names are used in greater density. Amongst American Catholics in the 1950s **Mary** was still outstandingly popular, and names like **Kathleen** and **Maureen** were used more often than in the country as a whole. These seem to indicate Irish heritage rather than Catholicism as such, as does the use of names like **Joseph** and **Kevin**.

Amish names

I have been unable to find any variations in the name usage of other denominations that could be attributed to their religious beliefs, though extreme sects such as the Amish clearly go their own way more than most.

'*I have a passion for the name of Mary.*'

Lord Byron, Don Juan

'*What Mary is when she a little smiles
I cannot even tell, or call to mind,
It is a miracle so new, so rare.*'

Percy Bysshe Shelley

There are few Amish surnames because of the sect's strict rules about marrying within the group, but this does not lead to a wider range of first names being used in order to distinguish individuals. One study reported that there were forty Amish men living in one small Pennsylvanian locality who were all called Henry Stotzfus. Other common surnames amongst the sect, incidentally, are King, Beiler, Fisher, Lapp, Zook and Esh. There are also Amish families called Smucker, Smoker, Schwartzendruber, Blank, Schrock and Peachy.

With surnames such as these one might expect the sect members to bear foreign-looking first names. Amish men, however, tend to be called **John, Amos, Jacob, David, Samuel, Christian, Daniel, Benjamin, Levi, Aaron, Jonas, Elam, Stephen, Isaac, Henry, Jonathan, Eli, Gideon, Moses** and **Joseph**. Other names honour men like **Menno** Simmons, an early leader of the sect, or Jacob **Amman** himself, from whom the Amish take their name. Eighty per cent of Amish women, according to a survey made by Elmer L. Smith in 1968, are named **Mary, Sarah, Annie, Katie, Lizzie, Rebecca, Fannie, Barbara, Rachel, Lydia, Emma, Malinda, Susie, Sadie, Leah, Hannah, Naomi, Mattie, Lavina** or **Arie**.

Hawaiian names

A similar situation is frequently found in English-speaking countries. Surnames may strongly suggest other lands and other languages, but the first names that have been chosen to go with them are generally those of the English-speaking world. Further evidence of this is to be found in Hawaii. In the colleges there are students with surnames like Kamakana, Ala'imoana and Kamu. Occasionally such students have first names such as **Leva'ula** or **Leuga**. Far more often, however, names like **John, Alan, Cathy** and **Gail** are in front of them. The norm, once again, is being recognized. That norm, in the 1950s, is revealed in detail by the names and figures given below.

Comparative Use of First Names in the 1950s

The figures against the names relate to 10,000 births of the same sex. E.g. '50' indicates that, in that particular country, one boy or girl in 200 received the name; '250' indicates that one boy or girl in 40 received it. Absence of a figure indicates that less than one boy or girl in 10,000 received the name. In other words the higher the numbers the more popular the name.

Girls	U.S.A.	Canada	England and Wales	Scotland	Australia			U.S.A.	Canada	England and Wales	Scotland	Australia
Abigail	1						Bertha	2	2			
Ada	2	1		2			Beryl		6	6	1	2
Adele	4	4	2	3			Bessie				1	
Adrienne	3		6	4	6		Beth	20				3
Agnes	2	2		111	6		Bethany	2				
Aileen	4			47	10		Betsy	11	1	2	4	
Ailsa				5			Bettina					8
Alana			2	2			Betty	27	22	11	5	2
Alexandra	2	1	2	36	4		Beulah	2				1
Alexandrina				4			Beverley	1	27	51	5	44
Alexis	2			7			Beverly	50	36	11	1	10
Alice	34	21	9	26	8		Blanche	1	1	4		
Alicia	5			1	1		Bonita	5	1	2	1	
Alison	7	18	100	105	38		Bonnie	35	47			3
Allison	4	11	2	18	1		Brenda	40	67	53	41	11
Allyson			2	2			Bridget	2		9	11	
Alma	2	1	2	2			Camille	4			1	
Alyson			2	3	3		Candace	13	14			
Amanda	2	1	40	8	50		Candice	5				
Amelia	5		4	1			Candy	1				
Amy	25	16	2	1	6		Carla	17			1	
Andrea	24	18	21	12	9		Carmen	8	12			
Angela	10	16	98	63	19		Carol	158	96	226	106	88
Anita	24	13	21	5	5		Carole	17	25	94	35	25
Ann	84	40	123	195	106		Carolina	1			1	
Anna	17	1	6	18	37		Caroline	5	9	57	115	5
Annabel	1	1	1	1			Carolyn	56	45	38	28	44
Anne	67	85	106	260	212		Carrie	3				
Annette	8		45	26	31		Carroll	1		2		
Annie		12	4	37			Cary				7	
Antoinette	5	4		2	2		Cassandra	3				
Antonia	1			2	8		Catherine	71	122	62	251	150
April	5	1	2	1			Cathleen	4		2	2	2
Arlene	10	6	4	11			Cathy	28	12			
Audrey	12	49	11	51	2		Catriona			4	16	4
Ava	2						Cecile	1				1
Avril		1	6	24	6		Cecilia	6	11	2	9	19
Barbara	246	180	138	59	100		Cecily	1				4
Beatrice	6	16	2	4	19		Celia	5		4	1	3
Becky	5						Charlene	9	9			
Belinda	3	6	6	6	12		Charlotte	18	5	2	11	6
Benita	1						Charmaine	1		2		
Bernadette	6		13	43	16		Cheri	4				
Bernice	3	16					Cherry			6		

Name	U.S.A.	Canada	England and Wales	Scotland	Australia
Cheryl	60	55	26	3	75
Christina	14	25	38	64	2
Christine	71	69	306	158	294
Cindi	1				
Claire	9	6	11	9	10
Clara	5	1	2	1	1
Clare	2	1	13	7	3
Clarissa	1				
Claudette	1	1	2		
Claudia	22	1			
Colleen	16	27	9	2	31
Connie	17	6	2		2
Constance	24	20	4	7	
Cora	1				
Corinne	6	9	2		
Coralie	1				2
Crystal	1				
Cynthia	122	31	26	3	25
Dahlia			4		
Daisy	1				
Danielle	2	12			2
Daphne	1				1
Darlene	10	15			
Davina			2	5	
Dawn	11	14	32	12	
Deanna	5	7	2		
Debbie	9		2		
Deborah	212	140	64	24	137
Debra	110	31	15	4	21
Deirdre	3	1	9	7	9
Delia	1		6	2	
Della	1				1
Delores	3				
Denise	40	24	102	25	44
Devra	1				
Diana	29		15	16	32
Diane	102	67	94	54	62
Dianna	3	2			
Dianne	17	18	23	8	85
Dinah	1		2		
Dolores	8	2	4	1	
Dona	3				
Donna	80	124	4	15	2
Dora	1	1			
Doreen	5	20	15	27	4
Doris	15	6	2	4	6
Dorothea		1		3	
Dorothy	32	62	34	58	30
Edith	10	15	6	15	2
Edna	2	1	4	7	
Edwina		1	2	4	

Name	U.S.A.	Canada	England and Wales	Scotland	Australia
Eileen	22	7	42	53	22
Elaine	29	36	190	140	12
Eleanor	6	15	8	37	10
Elinor	1	2		2	
Elisa	2	2			
Elisabeth	4	9		1	17
Elise	3			1	
Elissa	2				
Eliza				1	
Elizabeth	133	145	134	409	295
Ellen	63	35	6	31	14
Ellyn	1				
Elsa	4	1		1	
Elsie	2	15	2	6	
Elspeth				10	
Elvira	1	1			
Emilie	1				
Emily	11	1		5	
Emma	5			2	
Enid			4		
Erica		1	4	2	
Erika	2	1			
Ernestine	3				
Esperanza	2				
Estelle			2		
Esther	8	20		10	
Ethel	5	1		3	
Eugenia	2				
Eunice		2	6	3	
Euphemia				7	
Eva	5	32		2	25
Eve				1	
Eveline				2	
Evelyn	20	13	6	36	23
Faith	3	1		1	
Faye	4	6	2	2	1
Fern	1	1			
Fiona		1	34	184	17
Flora		2		7	
Florence	8	24	4	4	3
Fran	3				
Frances	25	24	34	58	68
Francine	4	10			
Freda			6	5	
Frieda				2	
Gail	61	55	28	32	60
Galen	2				
Gay	4	1			
Gayle	19	15			4
Gaynor				8	
Geneva	1				

Name	U.S.A.	Canada	England and Wales	Scotland	Australia
Genevieve	3	1			17
Georgia	7		2	2	1
Georgina		2	11	24	5
Geraldine	13	18	28	18	3
Gertrude		2		2	
Gilda	1	1			
Gillian		10	204	44	19
Gina	3	1	6	2	
Gladys	2	1	4	5	
Glenda	8	1	10	5	14
Glenna	1	1			
Glenys		1	8		24
Gloria	22	20	10	5	16
Glynis	12	15	4		
Grace	7	16	6	39	
Gretchen	5				
Gwen	5	1	2	5	
Gwendoline			10	6	
Gwendolyn	11	12	2		
Gwyneth			2	2	
Hannah	2			6	
Harriet	8	6		3	
Hazel	3		21	36	
Heather	6	78	74	71	75
Heidi	6	1			
Helen	36	51	79	197	206
Helena		1	4	4	7
Helene	6	7			
Helga	1	1			
Henrietta				6	
Hilary		2	47	13	7
Hilda		1	6	6	
Hillary	1	2			
Hollis	3				
Holly	12	16			
Hope	4				
Ida	3				
Ilene	3			1	
Ilona	1				
Ina	1			1	
Ingrid	2			2	
Iona				2	
Irene	13	29	38	209	38
Iris	4	16	4	6	
Irma	3	16	4	6	
Isabel	2	1	6	24	
Isabella			2	59	
Isabelle				6	
Isobel			6	42	
Ivy	1			1	
Jacqueline	27	29	221	168	40
Jacquelyn	8	9	4	2	15
Jamesina				2	
Jana	3				
Jane	91	31	85	123	87
Janelle	2				
Janet	132	125	287	119	113
Janette	4	2	23	47	13
Janice	63	67	87	108	60
Janie	7	2	23	47	14
Janine	4	1	2	1	28
Janis	13	5	11	15	14
Jayne	3	2	13	8	4
Jean	54	44	81	114	25
Jeanette	9	6	26	22	37
Jeanie		1	2	12	
Jeanne	25	9	4	2	
Jeannie	2				
Jemima				5	
Jenifer	1	4	4		
Jennie	3				
Jennifer	34	60	102	51	275
Jenny	5	3	4	2	
Jeri	6				
Jessie			4	24	
Jill	35	10	26	16	67
Jillian			15	3	62
Jo	22				
Joan	69	75	45	74	63
Joann	5	2			
JoAnn	12	4			
Joanna	3	2	6	4	4
JoAnne	2	5			
Joanne	40	84	13	10	31
Jocelyn			6	1	27
Jodi	1				
Jody	6	2			
Johanna	4	1	4	3	8
Jolene	2				
Joni	3		2		
Josephine	5	2	15	29	19
Joy	12	10	23	6	22
Joyce	38	36	17	67	7
Juanita	5				
Judith	92	102	60	15	244
Judy	35	36	6	1	16
Julia	20	8	43	20	31
Juliann	2	1			
Julianne	4	3			2
Julie	32	10	117	28	125
Juliet			4	1	8
June	9	1	47	78	2

	U.S.A.	Canada	England and Wales	Scotland	Australia
Justine	2				
Karen	180	105	106	82	44
Karin	5	13	8	3	2
Karla	7				
Karyn			4		
Katharine	5	2	2	2	1
Katherine	48	58	6	14	10
Kathleen	146	55	85	100	88
Kathrine			2	1	
Kathryn	61	40	32	15	50
Kathy	45				4
Katrina	1	6	12		
Kay	13		19	13	50
Kelly	8	4			
Kerrie		2			81
Kerry	17	11		2	88
Kim	27	4	11	19	24
Kimberley	3		2	1	
Kimberly	10	6	2	1	
Kirsten				2	
Kirsty		1	2	2	
Kristen	3			2	
Kristi	6				
Kristin	7				
Kristina	3	2			5
Kristine	13	2			17
Kyle	4				
Lana	4				
Laraine		5		1	2
Lark	1				
Laura	62	27	4	24	6
Laurel	10	1			
Lauren	7				
Lauri	2	15			
Lavonne	1				
Leanne	1	1		1	
Leigh	2		2	1	14
Lena	1	1		2	
Lesley	3	13	151	88	63
Letitia				3	
Lila	2		2		
Lilian			11	9	
Lillian	8	16		7	
Lillie	3				
Lily		9	2	3	
Linda	258	225	363	331	119
Lindy					15
Linsay				4	
Lisa	33	4		2	
Lisbeth	2			1	
Lise	2	4			

	U.S.A.	Canada	England and Wales	Scotland	Australia
Lita	1		4		
Lois	22	27	2	2	8
Lola	2		2		
Lora	3				
Loraine		2	9	14	
Loreen	1	2		1	
Loren	5	2			
Loretta	8	20		1	
Lori	11	4			
Lorie	1	2			
Lorna	7	25	21	63	5
Lorraine	18	22	43	97	56
Lory	1				
Louisa	2	3		3	
Louise	18	36	15	32	38
Lu	1				
LuAnn	2				
Luanne	2				
Lucile	1	2			
Lucinda	6			2	
Lucy	10	7	2	3	6
Lydia	7	6		4	9
Lyn	3			2	2
Lynda	13	33	62	23	31
Lynette	5		9	2	144
Lynn	54	25	64	51	38
Lynne	19	15	66	36	44
Lynnette				2	12
Mabel	1			2	
Mable	1				
Madeleine	3	1	2		
Madeline	6		8	2	3
Mae	1	2		1	
Magdalene				2	
Mairi				15	
Maisie	1			1	
Mandy				4	4
Marcella	2	3			
Marcia	45	13	4	1	
Marcie	2				
Marcy	3				
Maree					25
Margaret	129	178	223	545	338
Margarita	2		2	1	
Margery	5	2			
Margo	8			6	5
Margot	3			2	
Marguerite	6	2		1	7
Mari	2				
Maria	20	56	23	32	75
Marian	9	27	14	6	25

	U.S.A.	Canada	England and Wales	Scotland	Australia
Marianne	14		2	4	8
Marie	19	60	29	59	44
Marilee	1				
Marilyn	63	78	40	6	94
Marina			6		12
Marion	12		40	90	44
Marisa		1		2	8
Marjorie	25	22	16	11	
Marjory	1	4		10	10
Marla	8				
Marlene	16	29	8	5	
Marlin	3				
Marlyn				3	
Marsha	27	11			
Marta	6			1	
Martha	66	7		13	4
Martina		6	2		8
Mary	397	254	98	347	144
Maryann	5				1
Maryellen	2				
Marylin		2			9
Matilda		3	2	2	
Mattie	1				
Maura	4				
Maureen	32	45	44	126	68
Mavis		2	4		
Maxine	5	1	13	2	1
May		11	4	13	
Melanie	14	4	14	2	1
Melinda	12		2		10
Melissa	18				
Melody	8	1	2		
Meredith	6				6
Merle	3	2			
Merry	1				
Mhairi				4	
Michele	31	7	6	6	50
Michelle	22	14	8	2	12
Mildred	5		2	1	
Mindy	5				
Miranda			4		
Miriam	6	15		2	8
Mitzi	1				
Moira		1	4	76	18
Molly	5	6		1	
Mona	6	20		1	
Monica	12	1	4	5	5
Morag				48	3
Moyra				5	
Muriel	2	6	4	11	2
Myra	4		2	10	
Nada	1	1			1
Nadine	3		2		
Nan	1	2		2	
Nanci	3				
Nancy	233	129	4	11	10
Nanette	2				3
Naomi	4	6	2		
Narelle					31
Natalie	4	1	2		25
Nellie	2			1	1
Nerida					4
Nicki	1				
Nicola			36	5	
Nicole		12	2		
Nina	8	4	8		
Noelene					18
Nora	6	7	2	3	
Norah		2	4	3	
Noreen		12		6	
Norma	9	24	10	29	6
Olga	1	12		1	14
Olive	1	2	2	4	
Olivia	4	1			
Olwen		1	4	1	
Oonagh				1	
Opal	1				
Otis	1				
Pamela	120	45	143	43	150
Patrice	4	1			
Patricia	251	193	257	162	225
Patsy	5				4
Patti	9	1			
Paula	53	20	34	5	4
Paulette	6	14	2		
Pauline	4	24	147	50	44
Pearl	4	2	8	6	
Peggy	31	13		2	
Penelope	3	9	51	3	56
Penny	6	3	4		
Peta					18
Philippa			4	1	37
Philomena				5	4
Phyllis	23	20	8	15	
Polly	7				
Priscilla	6	2	2	1	
Rachel	7	11	6	10	4
Rae	2	1	2	2	9
Ramona	6	2			
Randi	5				
Raquel	1				
Rebecca	73	18	11	5	10

	U.S.A.	Canada	England and Wales	Scotland	Australia		U.S.A.	Canada	England and Wales	Scotland	Australia
Regina	9	1		1		Shelley	17	45	4		
Rena				2		Shelly	3	4			
Renee	12	21				Sheona				2	
Rhoda	1		2	4		Sheree			4	2	4
Rhona			8	23		Sheri	5				
Rhonda	17	34	2	3	31	Sherri	5	26			
Rita	20	13	15	4	25	Sherrie	5				
Robbin	1					Sherry	19	10	2		
Roberta	26	27	4	8	6	Sherryl	4	4			
Robina			2	7		Sheryl	11	9	6		9
Robyn	5	6	2		150	Shiona				2	
Rochelle	6					Shirley	28	55	109	51	25
Roma		1		1		Shona		1		28	
Rona		2		10		Silvia	1				
Ronna	2					Sondra	1				
Rosa	2	12				Sonia		1	4	3	12
Rosaleen				3		Sophia		8		1	
Rosalie	4		2		3	Stacy	2				1
Rosalind		3	19	6	12	Stella	3	6	13	5	
Rosaline				1	1	Stephanie	17	26	15	2	31
Rosalyn		1	6	1		Sue	28	4			30
Rosanna	1	2		1		Susan	337	238	736	198	400
Rosanne	1	2		1		Susannah				2	
Rose	10	15	13	29	6	Susanne	4	4	6	4	4
Roseann	2	2		5		Suzanna	2				
Roseleen				1		Suzanne	44	20	23	8	125
Roselyn		4		2		Sybil	1			1	
Rosemarie	6	9	8	2		Sylvia	15	42	53	25	8
Rosemary	17	7	57	55	63	Tamara	3				4
Rosina				3		Tanya	2	2	2	1	1
Roslyn		3	6	4	68	Tara	1	1			
Rosslyn				2		Teresa	35	13	49	23	14
Rowena			6		6	Teresita	1				
Roxanna	1					Teri	4				
Roxanne	6					Terrell	2				
Ruby	5	4	2	3		Terri	13	4	2		
Ruth	40	47	19	34	31	Thelma	2	1	9	3	
Sadie				4		Theodora	1				
Sallie	1					Theresa	21	9	19	39	6
Sally	38	13	38	12	37	Therese	4			2	25
Sandra	107	93	160	124	138	Thomasina				2	
Sara	29	2	11	2	1	Tina	3	32			
Sarah	28	22	19	51	19	Toni	6	2			4
Senga				7		Tracey	2			1	
Seonaid				2		Tracy	2	2		1	1
Sharon	82	104	64	23	38	Trudi				5	
Shauna	3			2		Trudy	2	15	11		
Sheelagh				1		Twila	1				
Sheena		1	4	33	8	Una	1		2	4	
Sheila	19	55	70	78		Ursula	1				3
Shelagh		2	4	3		Val	2				

	U.S.A.	Canada	England and Wales	Scotland	Australia
Valeria	2				
Valerie	25	47	134	55	6
Vanda			2	1	
Vanessa	3		15	1	12
Vera	2	4	2	4	10
Verna	2				
Vernetta	1				
Veronica	5	16	21	16	11
Vicki	33	22	4	2	
Vickie	13				
Vicky	5	4	9		
Victoria	22	12	21	5	38
Violet		4		9	
Virginia	52	16		2	63
Vivien		6	11	4	24
Vivienne			21	5	12
Wanda	9	4	2	2	
Wendy	27	51	74	25	94
Wilhelmina		2		5	
Williamina				15	
Wilma	4	4		35	
Winifred	2	9	4	10	2
Yolanda	4	2		1	
Yvette	2			1	
Yvonne	10	16	74	71	38
Zelda		2	2		
Zena		4			
Zita					2
Zoe				1	

Boys

	U.S.A.	Canada	England and Wales	Scotland	Australia
Aaron	3		1		
Abraham	2	1	1		
Adam	1		5	13	
Adrian	2	4	53	6	41
Alan	66	66	238	226	118
Alasdair		1		14	
Alastair			4	46	
Albert	18	28	13	16	8
Alec	1	4	4	1	
Alex	4				2
Alexander	7	19	11	271	35
Alfred	15	16	17	9	10
Alistair		1	6	65	
Alister		1	2	6	
Allan	14	60	34	96	18
Allen	21		6	3	3
Alvin	8	10			
Andrew	39	42	291	218	147
Angus		1		32	12
Anthony	40	34	257	56	188
Antony		3	17	2	4
Archibald				35	1
Arnold	9	4	2	1	
Arthur	37	40	19	25	53
Austin	2	1		1	
Barrie	1	3	6	1	4
Barry	31	75	96	9	53
Bartholomew			2	1	
Ben	3	2	4		
Benedict	1				
Benjamin	12	4		4	3
Bernard	11	16	30	20	41
Bert	2				
Bill	5	1			
Blair		16		2	
Blake	1	12			
Bob	3	1			
Boris					10
Brad	5				5
Bradford	7	8			
Bradley	17	14		1	4
Brendan			9	4	4
Brent	14	13			6
Bret					1
Brett	3		4		17
Brian	44	204	162	251	65
Bruce	93	99	2	26	112
Bryan	7	12	21	14	4
Bryce				2	
Burton	2				
Byron	6	1	2		
Callum				6	
Calum				7	
Calvin	6	7		4	
Cameron		7		8	6
Campbell		1		8	6
Carl	34	24	15	1	
Carlos	7				

	U.S.A.	Canada	England and Wales	Scotland	Australia		U.S.A.	Canada	England and Wales	Scotland	Australia
Cecil	2	4				Earle	1				
Charles	186	85	60	117	29	Eddie	4				
Christian	2	1	2	1	1	Eddy	1				
Christopher	50	70	230	55	223	Edgar	2	3			
Clarence	8	12			2	Edmond	1	1			
Clark		7		2	1	Edmund	4	1	2	4	
Clifford	14	21	21	4	4	Edward	87	72	63	81	46
Clive	1	12	62	5	2	Edwin	14	6	15	3	11
Clyde	6	4			2	Eldon	2				
Colin	2	18	170	164	124	Eli	1				
Conrad	1				1	Elliot	3			1	
Cornelius				3		Ellis	1	1			
Craig	53	21	2	15	10	Elmer	3	1			
Crawford				2		Elroy	1	1			
Curt	1					Elvin			2		
Curtis	16					Emerson	1				
Cyril		1	2		2	Eric	35	55	30	32	17
Dale	35	28	4	3	3	Erick	1				
Damian	1		2			Erik	3				
Damien					4	Ernest	12	13	9	5	11
Dan	19	12				Ernie	1		1		
Daniel	122	70	17	54	29	Errol	1	1			
Danny			9		2	Euan				4	
Darrel	1	4				Eugene	26	16	2	2	
Darrell	10	9	2			Evan	2			2	
Darren	1					Everett	3				
Darryl	4	4			8	Ewan				12	
Daryl	7	12	2			Ewen				4	
David	410	387	679	558	471	Felix	1			1	
Dean	20	11		3		Fergus		1		4	
Delbert	2	1				Fernando	2				
Denis	1	4	6	9	18	Finlay				5	
Dennis	99	69	28	8	41	Floyd	5	1			
Derek	1	9	81	108	12	Forrest	5	1			
Derrick		1		3		Francis	21	33	21	72	41
Desmond			2		2	Francisco	3				
Dexter	1		2		3	Frank	55	36	21	72	41
Dick	1					Franklin	9	4			
Dirk	1					Fraser		4	2	12	4
Dominic	1			2	4	Fred	17		8		
Dominick	2					Freddie	2				
Don	13	4	2		2	Frederic	2	3			
Donald	129	200	19	92	41	Frederick	38	34	21	17	18
Douglas	91	142	21	107	47	Fredric	1	1			
Duane	10	4				Fredrick	2	9			
Dudley	2	1			2	Gabriel	1				
Dugald				2		Gareth			6	2	
Duncan	2	12	13	41	18	Garry	5	15	21	19	47
Dwight	8	4				Garth	1	18			6
Eamonn				3		Gary	171	107	113	39	82
Earl	10	14				Gavin		1	2	22	

	U.S.A.	Canada	England and Wales	Scotland	Australia			U.S.A.	Canada	England and Wales	Scotland	Australia
Gene	11						Jesse	5	1	2		
Geoffrey	9	4	100	8	118		Jim	4		2	2	
George	103	112	38	232	106		Jimmie	2				
Gerald	47	88	47	38	6		Jimmy	6				
Gerard	7	16	23	46	24		Joe	14	1			
Gilbert	7	9		6			Joel	18				
Glen	9	25	10	4			John	501	445	459	903	694
Glenn	27	31	23	4	19		Johnny	6				
Glyn			8				Jon	20	4		1	12
Gordon	16	122	47	173	24		Jonathan	23	10	45	7	29
Graeme		6	6	49	59		Jose	12				
Graham	2	13	213	100	88		Joseph	135	88	30	101	53
Grant	6	22		14	12		Joshua	2				
Greg	7				4		Juan	5				
Gregg	7						Judson	2				
Gregor				4			Julian		1	11	1	
Gregory	89	46	15	2	194		Julio	1				
Guy	10	1	13	1	4		Karl	14	16	2	1	3
Hamish				7			Keith	33	36	115	53	87
Harlan	1						Kelvin		12	13	1	
Harold	29		11	6			Ken	2	1			
Harris	1						Kenneth	112	161	106	180	50
Harry	22	21	21	14	6		Kent	16	8			
Harvey	9	14					Kenton	1	1			
Hector	1	1		4			Kevan			9	3	
Henry	27	21	13	42	10		Kevin	42	33	196	39	24
Herbert	9	15	4	1			Kirk	9	6	2		
Herman	3						Kurt	11	4		1	3
Homer	2						Lachlan				4	
Howard	37	21	28	4	29		Lance	4	4			10
Hubert	2						Larry	77	48	2		12
Hugh	7	24	2	83	8		Laurance	1				
Iain		1	2	83			Laurence	7	18	15	8	24
Ian	2	58	206	248	205		Lawrence	63	49	2	10	
Ira	7	1					Lee	34	1	7	1	31
Irvin	1	1					Leland	3				
Irwin	1	1					Leo	5	13		1	1
Isaac	1						Leon	3	6	2		4
Ivan	2	12	9	1	8		Leonard	17	21	36	1	18
Ivor			4	4			Leroy	3				
Jack	30	21	2	9	3		Lester	6				6
Jacob	3	10					Lewis	7		2	3	2
James	445	276	149	790	153		Lex	1	1			
Jeff	3	1					Liam			2	2	
Jeffery	8	6	4				Lionel		6			
Jeffrey	120	25	45	7	65		Lloyd	13	22	2	2	
Jerald	2	1					Lon	3				
Jeremy			40	3	12		Lonnie	5				
Jerome	16	10					Lou	3				
Jerrold	2						Louis	22	4	2	3	
Jerry	37	4	2				Lowell	2				

	U.S.A.	Canada	England and Wales	Scotland	Australia
Loyd	1				
Luis	4				
Lyle	3	8			
Magnus				1	
Malcolm	4	15	104	50	41
Manuel	6	1			
Marc	16	7			
Marcel	1				
Marcus	4		2		
Mario	3	1		1	4
Mark	204	75	104	38	159
Marshall	7	4		1	
Martin	27	16	189	59	24
Martyn			36	1	4
Marvin	11	14			
Matthew	13	12	8	31	12
Maurice	6	19	16	7	14
Max	3				
Maxwell			29	3	
Melville				1	
Melvin	8	1	14	1	
Melvyn			16		
Mervyn		7	6	2	16
Michael	420	284	468	214	488
Micheal	2				
Michel	1				
Mickey	2				
Mike	4	1			
Milton	5	1			2
Mitchell	9		2	2	
Monte	2				
Morgan	1				
Morris	3		4	2	2
Murdo		1		6	
Murdoch				2	
Murray	1	39	2	7	
Myles			2	2	
Myron	6	1			
Nathan	2				
Nathaniel	2		2	1	
Neal	9	1		1	2
Neil	10	37	45	80	47
Neill				2	14
Nelson	4			1	
Nevil		1	2		
Neville		1	15	1	2
Niall				4	
Nicholas	13	26	70	13	12
Nick		6			6
Nigel		4	121	10	4
Noel	4		8	1	12

	U.S.A.	Canada	England and Wales	Scotland	Australia
Nolan	1				
Norbert	2	12			
Norman	18	31	36	42	6
Oliver	2	1		2	
Orson	1				
Orval	1				
Oscar	3				
Owen	2	12	2	7	
Patrick	49	42	19	67	70
Paul	147	131	432	84	229
Pedro	2				
Perry	4	8			
Peter	80	185	436	183	641
Phil	2				
Philip	51	36	183	32	94
Phillip	19	6	10	2	135
Pierre	1	12			
Quentin	1	1	4		4
Quintin				1	
Raleigh	2				
Ralph	32	24	11	9	24
Ramsay				1	
Ramon	2				
Randal	6	16			
Randall	36	18		1	
Randolph	10	4			
Randy	28	8			
Raul	2				
Raymond	41	60	74	57	59
Reed	3				
Reginald	3	6	11	1	20
Reid	2				
Rex	5	4			6
Ricardo	2				
Richard	335	213	179	80	194
Rick	8				
Rickey	3				
Ricky	8	1			
Riley	1				
Robb	1				
Robert	492	472	366	486	371
Roberto	4				
Rocco	1				
Roderick	3	15	21	30	24
Rodney	17	21	19	2	29
Roger	51	18	66	7	29
Roland	6	4	6	1	26
Roman	2			1	
Ronald	125	145	70	103	88
Rory		1		2	
Ross	8	19	4	19	53

	U.S.A.	Canada	England and Wales	Scotland	Australia
Rowland			6		
Roy	22	13	72	21	24
Royston			8		6
Ruben	3				
Rudy	2	1			
Russ	2				
Russell	28	25	11	19	35
Ryan	1			1	
Salvatore	2				
Sam	5	1	2		2
Samuel	22	10	17	33	6
Sandy				1	
Sanford	2				
Scott	52	14		19	12
Sean	2		6	5	
Sergio	2				
Shane		1	2	1	
Shaun		1	10	3	
Shawn	3	4			
Sheldon	3	1			
Sidney	4		6	1	
Simon	2	14	49	9	24
Sinclair				3	
Spencer	1				
Stan	1				
Stanley	28	28	8	11	2
Stephan	4			1	
Stephen	168	97	604	153	247
Steve	15	8		3	
Steven	184	31	140	64	59
Stewart	4	6	8	45	29
Stuart	19	13	30	78	41
Sydney		12	6	3	5
Ted	6	4			
Terence	3		113	18	53
Terrance	4				
Terrence	7		2	1	29
Thaddeus	2				
Theodore	19	18			6
Thomas	289	110	68	320	82
Tim	3	4			
Timothy	84	39	64	8	59
Toby	3	1			
Todd	10				
Tom	3	1		2	2
Tommy	6				
Tony	3	4	34	1	
Trevor		12	132	7	47
Troy	1				
Tyrone	1				
Van	3	1			
Vernon	4	16	4		4
Victor	13	28	6	7	10
Vincent	14	16	15	9	
Virgil	3				
Wade	4	1	2		
Wallace	3	4		4	
Walter	37	34	6	21	6
Warren	15	19	4		29
Warwick					29
Wayne	32	48	17	2	34
Wendell	3				4
Wesley	10	6	2		3
Wilbur	1				
Wilfred	3	4		2	
Willard	3	1			
William	355	322	149	578	188
Willie	3		2		
Wilson				2	3
Winston				2	
Wolfgang	1	1			

Names used for girls and boys

	U.S.A.	Canada	England and Wales	Scotland	Australia
Billie	4				
Billy	8		2		
Bobbie	3		2		
Bobby	4				
Chris	14				
Dana	17				
Gale	6		2	1	
Jackie	7			2	
Jamie	8	1		1	4
Jan	25	12		5	29
Jay	17	1			
Jess	2				
Laurie	34	12		2	
Leslie	50	25	83	38	38
Lindsay	2		9	19	12
Ray	9			3	
Robin	48	11	36	15	38
Shannon	4		2		
Terry	57	19	13	3	12
Vaughan	3		4		
Vivian	9	4	6	3	25

19 Names in their Infancy

First names of the 1970s

The previous chapter showed which names were being given by parents, and to what extent, in the 1950s. I provide below notes about the names which have been most used in English-speaking countries since 1970. These are names in their infancy.

That does not mean, as will quickly become apparent, that the first names borne by today's children are necessarily new in themselves. Many have been used as first names for centuries by English-speaking people, but for one reason or another have made a special appeal to young parents in recent years. Some of the names are new as first names, but have long been with us as surnames or place names. Other names have perhaps enjoyed a local usage, somewhere in the English-speaking world, but have now spread to other countries.

Adults should check to see whether their name appears in this chapter. If they bear one of the names listed here they are fortunate in one sense: their names have either been rejuvenated recently or have managed to survive while retaining a youthful image. As for parents who have named a child in the last few years, they will be interested to see whether they caught the mood of the times. Finally, those who are searching for a name on behalf of a baby-to-be will find here the up-to-date information they need. To them I say: good hunting.

Aaron Brother of Moses. Formerly a Jewish name; now in American, Canadian and Australian top fifties. Increasing in use in Britain.

Adam Very popular everywhere. Seems destined to become one of the top five names in the English-speaking world.

Adrian Much used recently in Britain and Australia but now past its peak. Does not seem to have appealed to American or Canadian parents.

Alan (Allan, Allen) Still amongst the top names in England and Wales, but rapidly following the downward path that it has taken elsewhere.

Alexander This name has spread from Scotland to all the other English-speaking countries, where its use is increasing.

Alistair (Alastair, etc.) A Scottish form of Alexander which is also spreading to other countries, though not yet to the U.S.A.

Alison (Allison, Alyson, Allyson) The preferred modern form of Alice. Intensively used for twenty years in England and Australia and now fading. Still very popular in the U.S.A. and Canada.

Amanda Invented by Sir John Vanbrugh (1664–1726) but not generally used until 1950. Very popular everywhere, but beginning to fall away.

Amy A popular Victorian name now rapidly being restored to favour everywhere, especially in the U.S.A. and Canada.

Andrea The popularity of this feminine form of Andrew rose when Andrew itself came into fashion. Much used for the moment, but past its peak.

Andrew One of the most popular names in the English-speaking world in recent years. The inevitable reaction to such popularity has just begun to show itself.

Angela Currently a favourite everywhere, but beginning to fall away.

Ann(e) Now more popular as a middle name than as a first name. **Anna** seems likely to replace it in that role.

Anthony (Antony) A very popular name everywhere in recent years, but now fast fading.

Ashley Its recent popularity has been confined to Australia.

Barry Most used in recent years in England and Wales.

Belinda Especially popular at the moment in Australia, but fading. A flurry of interest in the name was shown in Britain in the early 1960s.

Bradley Well used by Americans and Canadians and still rising in Australia. Almost unknown in Britain. Presumably began as a tribute to the American general, Omar Bradley.

Brendan Currently in the Australian top fifty; usage in Britain increasing.

Brett Popular recently in Australia but now falling away.

Brian (Bryan) At its peak in England and Wales in 1950 and has since faded. The name reached the U.S.A. and Canada much later and is a current favourite.

Cameron A recent Scottish, Australian and Canadian favourite, borrowed from the Scottish surname.

Carl (Karl) This Germanic form of Charles is rapidly becoming more popular in England and Wales. In the U.S.A., Canada and Australia it is fading away.

Carly (Karlie, etc.) A girl's name in the Australian top fifty for 1975. Also used in Canada. **Carla** is becoming more popular in England and Wales, but Carly is as yet unknown there.

Caroline   An eighteenth-century name recently restored in Britain. This form is preferred there to **Carolyn**.

Catherine   (Katharine, Katherine, Kathryn, etc.) A steady favourite in its various guises throughout the English-speaking world.

Chad   A name currently being given to many American boys. Some usage in Canada and Australia, none to speak of in Britain.

Charles   Surviving well in the U.S.A. and Canada. Rapidly being replaced in England and Wales by Carl/Karl. Almost unused in Australia.

Charlotte   Restored to favour in England and Wales recently and rapidly becoming more popular.

Christian   Already in the Australian top fifty, and rapidly becoming more popular there as well as in England and Wales. It has been helped along by the popularity of Christopher.

Christine   The preferred feminine form of Christian since the 1960s, though **Christina** has also been much used in the U.S.A. and Canada.

Christopher   Currently immensely popular in all English-speaking countries and likely to remain so into the 1980s.

Christy   (Kristy) A feminine pet form of Christine or Christina popular in the U.S.A., Canada and Australia. Formerly a boy's name, from Christopher or Christian.

Clair   (Clare, Claire) At its peak in England and Wales in the late 1970s. Well used in Australia. American and Canadian parents not yet attracted to it to the same extent.

Colin   Fading away after ten years of intensive usage in England and Wales. Steadily used elsewhere.

Craig   Another Scottish surname used as a first name in Australia, Canada and England as well as Scotland itself. Becoming more popular in England.

Dale   Originally used for both girls and boys, but taken over by the boys since 1950. Now in the Australian top fifty. Usage increasing in Britain and the U.S.A.

Damian   (Damien) Better known in the U.S.A. and Canada as **Damon**, but little used there. Damian is coming in with a rush in Britain and Australia.

Daniel   In the top ten in most English-speaking countries and still improving its position. One of the better known biblical names which has recently found favour on all sides.

Danielle   This French feminine form of Daniel is increasing in popularity along with the male name.

Darren   (Daren) Recently much used in England and Wales as well as Australia. Now past its peak.

David Still an outstandingly popular name in every English-speaking country, though the number of young Davids around is beginning to make some parents-to-be think again.

Dawn Very popular at the moment in the U.S.A., Canada and England and Wales. Has not yet reached Australia in any numbers.

Dean Well used in the last decade in all English-speaking countries.

Deborah (Debra) Now well past its peak everywhere, English and Welsh parents being the last to relinquish it.

Denis (Dennis) This name has had far more impact in the U.S.A. and Canada this century than anywhere else in the English-speaking world. Now fading away from the American top fifty.

Donald Another North American favourite in recent times, though the Scots have long been faithful to this Celtic name. Now fading in the U.S.A. and Canada.

Donna The Italian 'lady'. Increasing in use in England and Wales and Australia.

Douglas After a spell of great popularity in Britain, this Gaelic name reached the U.S.A. via Canada. It is now falling away in America, having almost disappeared from view in England and Wales.

Edward Fighting for survival as one of the more popular names in the U.S.A. and Britain. The fight has already been lost in Australia and Canada.

Elizabeth (Elisabeth) Remains popular in its full form in the U.S.A., Canada and Scotland; fading somewhat in England and Wales and Australia. Usually at least one pet form of the name is fashionable (e.g. Lisa).

Emily A fine old name already clearly back in favour in the U.S.A. and gaining ground everywhere else.

Emma Very successfully revived in the 1970s in England and Wales and Australia, but not yet in the U.S.A. or Canada.

Eric (Erik) Those of Scandinavian descent are presumably responsible for the present popularity of this name in the U.S.A. and Canada. Elsewhere it has been out of fashion since 1935.

Erin An old Irish word for Ireland which has recently made a great appeal to American and Canadian parents. Used in Australia, but as yet no signs of frequent use in Britain.

Fiona Very popular in Scotland, but also in Australia, where it was in the top twenty for 1975.

Gary (Garry) Recently very popular for boys born in England and Wales. Now rapidly falling away.

Gavin A form of **Gawain** popular in Australia and becoming more so. Well used in the U.S.A. and Canada, but its bid for great popularity in England and Wales seems to have failed.

George   A survivor from the past, still in the American top fifty and well used in Canada and Scotland. Elsewhere it has been abandoned.

Glenn   (Glen) An Australian preference at the moment, though the Canadian pianist Glenn Gould helps the name along in Canada.

Graham   (Graeme) This Scottish name has been very popular in England and Wales since 1955, but it is now fading away.

Gregory   Now on the wane in the U.S.A., Canada and Australia. Belatedly shows signs of coming into fashion in Britain.

Hayley   The actress Hayley Mills seems to have been solely responsible for its use in Britain in recent years. The name is spreading rapidly.

Heather   A 1950–1960 name in England and Wales, but very much of the 1970s in the U.S.A. and Canada. In Australia Heather has gone out of fashion but **Heath**, as a male name, is gaining ground.

Heidi   Already in the American top fifty and rising fast in England and Wales. Johanna Spyri's children's classic, *Heidi*, perhaps influenced the use of this name. It is a pet form of the German **Adalheid**, or **Adelaide** as it is in its English form.

Helen   The name that has replaced **Ellen** in recent years in England and Wales but now beginning to fade away. A long-time favourite in Scotland, and formerly much used in the U.S.A.

Ian   (Iain) This Scottish form of John was taken up strongly in England and Wales and Australia. Canadians also used it, but it has never conquered the U.S.A. Now fading away except in Scotland.

Jacqueline   The name has enjoyed twenty years of great popularity in England and Wales, but it is now disappearing. Long out of fashion in the U.S.A. and Canada.

James   Amongst the top thirty names in all English-speaking countries, and enjoying something of a revival in England and Wales.

Jamie   An increasingly popular name for boys in Britain; used by both sexes in the U.S.A. and Canada.

Jane   Still a survivor in the top fifties of England and Wales and Australia, but clearly on the way out. Frequently used as a middle name.

Jason   The television character Jason King seems to have started the name on its way. It has had an enormous impact in the English-speaking world, but a reaction has now set in, especially in Britain.

Jennifer   Originally the Cornish form of **Guinevere**. The name has done amazingly well since 1945, sweeping through Britain and Australia and currently taking the U.S.A. and Canada by storm.

Jeffrey   (Geoffrey, Jeffery) Jeffrey is the preferred American spelling, Geoffrey the British. The name has been popular everywhere, most recently in the U.S.A. and Canada.

Jeremy   Most used in the mid-1970s in the U.S.A. and Canada, but **Jeremiah** (and **Jerry**) have long been popular in Ireland.

Less Frequently Used Girls' Names of the 1970s

Adelaide	Cilla	Jolie	Nerida
Ailsa	Cindy	Joy	Nerine
Aimee	Colleen	Justine	Nerissa
Ainslie	Coral	Karina	Nina
Amalia	Coralie	Karma	Nyree
Amaris	Coren	Katrina	Odette
Amber	Courtney	Kay	Odile
Aminta	Davinia	Keiranne	Olga
Andree	Delise	Kirby	Olivia
Andrienne	Delma	Kirrily	Pearl
Angelina	Dimity	Kyra	Pepita
Angelique	Dina	Lana	Petula
Angelita	Ebony	Lara	Polly
Anika	Elise	Larissa	Prue
Anissa	Elli	Leah	Raelene
Annabel	Eloise	Leandra	Raquel
Annalie	Elspeth	Leila	Rebel
Anouk	Esme	Lenice	Regan
Anthea	Estelle	Leonie	Richelle
Arabella	Felicia	Liana	Rochelle
Arden	Felicity	Linore	Romany
Arlette	Fleur	Lorena	Romy
Aurelia	Freya	Loretta	Ronelle
Becky	Gabrielle	Lorna	Salome
Benita	Gemelle	Lyndal	Selina
Berry	Gemma	Lynelle	Shannon
Bethany	Genevieve	Lynley	Shara
Bettine	Georgette	Manuella	Sharni
Bianca	Germaine	Mardi	Sharolyn
Bonnie	Gina	Maria	Sherryn
Brandy	Giselle	Marissa	Tabitha
Bridie	Greer	Marita	Tallulah
Briony	Helene	Marnie	Taryn
Bronwyn	Hollis	Martina	Tiffany
Brooke	Holly	Martine	Toni
Camilla	Honor	Maxine	Trilby
Candy	Ilona	Merinda	Trinity
Carina	Ingrid	Merryl	Trudi
Casey	Jacinta	Merryn	Vanda
Celeste	Jade	Mia	Venetta
Celestina	Janelle	Mimi	Venita
Cerise	Janine	Modesty	Vernetta
Cerys	Jasmine	Nadia	Zenda
Chantal	Jemima	Nadine	Zita
Chantelle	Joelene	Natalia	

Jessica　A name that is being increasingly used in the U.S.A. and Canada.

Jill　Currently popular in the U.S.A. **Gillian** was equally popular in England and Wales a few years ago, but has now gone out of fashion.

Joanne　The modern replacement of **Joan** in England and Wales. Australians also favour it. **Joanna** is much used, and may well rise as Anna takes over from Ann(e).

Jodie　(Jody, Jodi) Very popular Australian form of Judith which has spread to the U.S.A. and Canada, but not as yet to Britain.

John　Still in the top fifty of every English-speaking country, but there are very clear signs that its long reign is coming to an end.

Jonathan　Popular everywhere, and perhaps replacing John as the latter fades away.

Joseph　Staging a remarkable recovery on all sides. Back into the top fifty in the U.S.A. and England and Wales. Gaining ground in Canada and Australia. The Irish have always been loyal to it.

Joshua　Another form of **Jesus**, fast becoming very popular in the U.S.A., Canada and Australia.

Julie　Currently a favourite in all English-speaking countries but gradually going out of fashion.

Justin　This name has suddenly appeared in the top fifties of the U.S.A., Australia and England and Wales. Formerly used in Ireland.

Kane　A boy's name which is having great success in Australia but is as yet unknown elsewhere.

Kara　(Cara) Kara is the more usual form in the U.S.A., though this girl's name probably derives from Italian *cara*, 'dear'. Already in the American top fifty and rising elsewhere.

Karen　Brought to the U.S.A. by Danish immigrants, this name has been immensely successful throughout the English-speaking world since 1945. A form of Catherine, it is sometimes seen in its other Scandinavian guise of **Karin**. Now slowly going out of fashion.

Kate　In the Australian top fifty and becoming more popular in England and Wales.

Kathleen　Still frequently used, especially in the U.S.A. and Canada, but its recent run of popularity is coming to an end.

Keith　Most used at the moment in the U.S.A., but now out of fashion elsewhere.

Kelly　(Kellie) Converted from an Irish surname into a first name and given an enthusiastic welcome recently in all English-speaking countries.

Kenneth　A Scottish name popular in the U.S.A. and Canada, but now falling away there as it already has in England and Wales and Australia.

Kerry　(Kerrie) A fairly recent newcomer as a girl's name and highly successful.

Kevin　An Irish name recently very popular in the U.S.A. and Canada.

Also in the 1975 top fifty for England and Wales, but fading away. Already out of fashion in Australia.

Kimberly A girl's name which, as **Kim**, enjoyed a spell of intense usage in England and Wales in the 1960s. Kim is still very popular in Australia, but Kimberly is the preferred form in North America. At the turn of the century **Kimberley** was occasionally used in Britain as a male name. Rudyard Kipling's Kim was also male, his name being a short form of **Kimball**.

Kirsty A Scottish pet form of **Christiana**, currently popular in England and Wales and Australia.

Kristen A Scandinavian form of Christine much used in parts of the U.S.A. Also occurs frequently in Australia.

Kristy A variant of Kirsty, or a pet form of Kristen, now popular in Australia.

Kylie (Kyly) Used almost exclusively in Australia, where it is a very popular girl's name. It originated in Western Australia and means 'boomerang'.

Laura A long-time American favourite now rapidly taking hold in England and Wales. The Canadians use it a great deal, but it has not yet won over the Australians.

Leanne In the Australian top fifty and rising in Britain. A new 'blend' name for girls.

Lee (Leigh) There has been some confusion as to whether this is a boy's or girl's name, and whether it should be spelt Lee or Leigh. In Britain Lee is now usually male, and is becoming popular; Leigh is female. Both spellings are used for boys in Australia, where the name is also gaining ground.

Lisa Extremely popular in all English-speaking countries at the moment, its recent comeback having begun in the U.S.A.

Lori An American favourite. This form of Laura is currently in the U.S. top fifty.

Louise The English and Welsh have begun to use this name a great deal. Formerly a great favourite in the U.S.A. but now out of fashion.

Lucy Recently re-introduced in England and Wales and now well into the top fifty there. Little sign of its use elsewhere.

Luke A current favourite in Australia, together with **Lucas**. Making rapid headway in England and Wales as well.

Lynsey (Lyndsay, etc.) In its various forms has become one of the top girl's names in England and Wales. Also used in Scotland and Canada.

Mandy Falling away in England and Wales since the 1960s but very popular in Canada. A pet form of **Amanda** or **Miranda**.

Marie Replacing Mary in England and Wales. Often spelt **Maree** in Australia.

Less Frequently Used Boys' Names of the 1970s

Aidan	Clyde	Jordan	Rhys
Alaric	Corey	Keir	Richie
Alun	Curtis	Kelvin	Rodney
Ambrose	Dallas	Kent	Roland
Amos	Dane	Kes	Rory
Anton	Dermot	Kieran	Ross
Archie	Desmond	Kirk	Royston
Asa	Dion	Kurt	Rupert
Austin	Donovan	Lachlan	Russell
Barnaby	Drew	Lance	Sacha
Bart	Dudley	Leighton	Sandy
Bartholomew	Dustin	Lester	Sebastian
Basil	Dwayne	Lex	Sefton
Benedict	Dylan	Liam	Selwyn
Bernard	Elliott	Lincoln	Shannon
Blair	Elton	Lonnie	Sheridan
Blake	Elwyn	Lyle	Simeon
Boyd	Errol	Lyndon	Sonny
Brady	Evan	Magnus	Spencer
Brandon	Fabian	Marcel	Tarquin
Brent	Felix	Marlon	Theodore
Brock	Fergus	Marshall	Toby
Bruno	Fraser	Matthias	Trent
Bryce	Garrick	Maxwell	Trenton
Bryn	Garth	Melvin	Tristan
Burt	Gene	Micah	Ty
Byron	Giles	Milton	Tyrone
Cade	Grant	Mitchell	Tyson
Caleb	Guy	Montgomery	Vaughan
Callum	Harley	Moss	Vernon
Calvin	Haydn	Murray	Wade
Campbell	Hugh	Myles	Ward
Carlton	Israel	Noel	Warner
Cary	Jacob	Oliver	Warren
Casey	Jake	Oscar	Wesley
Chay	Jarrod	Owen	Winston
Clark	Jay	Perry	Yuri
Clay	Jesse	Quentin	Zane
Clayton	Jethro	Randall	
Clifton	Joel	Reid	
Clinton	Jolyon	Rhett	

Mark (Marc) One of the most frequently used names in the English-speaking world in the mid-1970s. The French -c spelling is becoming more widespread.

Martin (Martyn) Now fading away after a spell of great popularity, especially in England and Wales.

Mary The name has survived best in the U.S.A., but its use is declining in all English-speaking countries.

Matthew One of the top five names in the English-speaking world in 1975 and certain to be much used for a further ten years.

Megan This Welsh (or Irish) pet form of **Margaret** is much used in Australia, where it is in the top twenty. Becoming more popular in the U.S.A. and Canada.

Melanie From a Greek word meaning 'black', so suitable for dark-haired girls. Currently in the top fifty in the U.S.A., Canada, Australia and England and Wales.

Melinda (Malinda) In the Australian top fifty and well known in the U.S.A.

Melissa The Greek equivalent of Deborah, 'bee'. Well established in the U.S.A. and Canada; becoming stronger in Australia and England and Wales.

Meredith Originally a boy's name in Wales, now a girl's name and popular especially in Canada.

Michael A favourite name throughout the English-speaking world. The French form **Michel** is also used in Canada. **Michaela** has aroused interest recently as an alternative to Michelle.

Michelle (Michele) Top name in Australia in 1975, and very popular in other English-speaking countries. Borrowed from France around 1930.

Naomi An Old Testament name currently much used in Canada and Australia.

Narelle A favourite Australian name for girls, unknown in any other English-speaking country.

Natalie An especially appropriate name for a girl born on Christmas Day, since it comes from a Latin phrase meaning 'birth of the Lord'. Much used in England and Wales and Australia. The Russian form of the name, **Natasha,** and its pet form **Tasha,** are also making a great impact on all sides. A correspondent in New Zealand reports on the introduction there of Natasha following the showing of the B.B.C. series, *War and Peace.*

Nathan This name has burst upon the scene in all English-speaking countries since 1965. Already in all top fifties and rising fast.

Neil (Neal) A top name in England and Wales; very well used in the U.S.A. and Canada. Formerly a Scottish name.

Nicholas Well used throughout the English-speaking world since 1950.

Nicola (Nicole) The Nicolas are mostly British, the Nicoles American or

Australian. Canadians use both forms. Its great popularity has paralleled that of Nicholas.

Nigel   Coming to the end of a spell of great popularity in England and Wales.

Patrick   Usually thought of as an Irish name, but currently very popular in America and Canada.

Paul   Still very much in fashion in Britain, Canada and Australia, but on the wane in the U.S.A.

Paula   Most used in England and Wales and Canada. Its fortunes seem to be linked with those of Paul.

Peter   Has been very well used in all English-speaking countries this century, most recently in Australia and England and Wales. Now on the way out.

Philip   (Phillip) Still well used in all English-speaking countries, but clear signs that it is going out of fashion.

Rachel   (Rachael) Used extensively in all English-speaking countries recently, and seemingly still very strong.

Rebecca   (Rebekah) Very similar to Rachel in its use, perhaps even more popular. On its way to the very top.

Renée   Popular recently in Australia. It means 'born again' and is pronounced Renay. The French masculine form is **René**.

Richard   Still popular everywhere, increasingly so in England and Wales.

Robert   One of the most solidly-established names in the English-speaking world.

Robin   (Robyn) Popular as a girl's name in the U.S.A., where it is perhaps thought of in connection with the bird rather than as a pet name from Robert.

Ryan   An Irish surname turned first name that has already reached the top ranks in the U.S.A. and Canada. Rapidly coming into fashion elsewhere.

Sally   Still popular, especially in England and Wales and Australia.

Samantha   A great favourite in the late 1970s everywhere, except perhaps the U.S.A.

Sarah   One of the most successful name changes of all time. Originally the Hebrew **Sarai**, 'quarrelsome', but the change to Sarah made it 'princess'. In the latter form it has had tremendous success in all English-speaking countries in recent times.

Scott   Still 'arriving' in Britain and Canada, but probably already past its peak in Australia and the U.S.A.

Shane   Like **Shaun, Sean**, etc., a form of John. Shane's use is increasing, possibly because its spelling makes the pronunciation clearer than is the case with the Sean variations.

Sharon   A biblical place name that has been much used recently as a girl's first name, but now going out of fashion.

Simon Very popular in recent times, especially in England and Wales and Australia. The feminine form **Simone** has gained favour in Australia because of it.

Stacy (Stacey) A girl's name that is being taken up on all sides at the moment. Presumably a pet form of **Anastacia** or **Eustacia**.

Stephen (Steven) One of the most popular names of recent times if the two spelling forms are taken together. Now just past its peak. **Stephanie** has been drawn upwards with it and continues to rise, but presumably will now level out.

Stuart (Stewart) A Scottish name that has been taken up in England and Wales recently. Also much used in Australia.

Susan Slowly fading away in all the English-speaking countries after a lengthy spell at the very top. **Suzanne** is now the more fashionable form.

Tamara Always **Tamar** in the Bible, where it occurs as a female name meaning 'palm tree', a symbol of beauty. Tamara is a Russian form, from a famous poem by Lermontov, which is becoming popular everywhere. **Tammy** is even more frequently found, especially in the U.S.A., but this may derive from Thomas via **Tamsin** (a Cornish name for girls). **Tara** is also coming into fashion, and may be another form of this name.

Tanya (Tania) Another Russian pet form, from **Tatiana**, rapidly becoming fashionable. Shakespeare's **Titania** may have been a deliberate re-fashioning of Tatiana in order to amuse the groundlings.

Teresa (Theresa) Long a favourite in Ireland, and recently mildly popular in England and Wales, the U.S.A. and Canada.

Thomas Coming back into fashion in England and Wales, likewise in Australia. Surviving well in the U.S.A. and Canada.

Timothy Reasonably popular everywhere at the moment, but going out rather than coming in.

Tina A pet name from Christina which has independently reached the English and Welsh top fifty recently.

Todd A surname turned first name which has found favour in the U.S.A. and Canada. Some Australian boys are also now receiving the name.

Tonya (Tonia) Presumably from **Antonia**. A newcomer to the American top fifty.

Tracy (Tracey) Usually explained as a pet form of Teresa, but the surname must have greatly influenced its use. It has enjoyed a spell of intense usage, but is now on the decline.

Travis A boy's name, from a surname, much used in Australia at the moment.

Troy A long-familiar name in the U.S.A. and now being taken up strongly in Australia.

Vanessa Appealing in the mid-1970s to Australian, Canadian, English and Welsh parents.

Victoria Especially popular in England and Wales, but its use has levelled out prior to its decline. Used elsewhere, but not to the same extent.

Wayne Currently making ground in England and Wales. Also in the Australian top fifty. A surname that became a first name after the American Revolutionary War.

Wendy Well past its peak in England and Wales but a current favourite in the U.S.A.

William Seemingly abandoned a few years ago, but the name has started to make a come-back in England and Wales. Survives well in the U.S.A., retaining its place in the top fifty.

Zoe Difficulties with its pronunciation cause the occasional **Zoey** and even **Zowey** to be used. A greek translation of **Eve**, meaning 'life', and becoming very popular in England and Wales.

20 Nonce Names

Unusual first names

I have concentrated my attention in this book on the more common names of the English-speaking world. I know there is great interest, however, in the unusual first names that are bestowed from time to time. I seem to be asked about once a week, in fact, whether I have come across any 'really *odd* names'. The question is: how does one define 'oddity' in this context? Here are ten names which have been used as first names by English-speaking people. How many of them do you consider to be odd?

Boadicea	**Starling**	**Chelsea**	**Rufina**	**Nebuchadnezzar**
Mozart	**Milan**	**Dolphin**	**Anthonyina**	**Word**

Historical, legendary and fictional characters

Of these, Boadicea is in one sense a well-known name, that of an early English queen. Her statue is to be found in London, and most English children have heard of her. Nevertheless, not many modern parents would think of calling their daughter Boadicea.

The practice of borrowing a famous name, however, is by no means unusual. There have been many girls named **Cleopatra**; **Drusilla** was once a fairly common name, **Cassandra** even more so. I have also noted a **Cupid**, an **Archimedes** and an **Achilles**, all naming children in the nineteenth century.

> 'It is a curious name,' remarked Captain Levison. '*Joyce—Joyce*. I never heard such a name. Is it a Christian or surname?'
> Mrs Henry Wood, East Lynne (*1861*)

Amongst literary names I have noted a **Sherlock, Nemo, Cinderella, Hiawatha, Scarlett** and **Lemuel**, the latter name being more associated now with *Gulliver's Travels* than with the Old Testament. Sherlock Holmes and Scarlett O'Hara (of *Gone With The Wind*) are so famous that one might expect their names to be used more often.

Unusual surnames as first names

The next name in my preliminary list was **Mozart**. It is rare as a first name, but again I find it difficult to think of it as odd. The use of famous surnames, those of statesmen, generals, writers, musicians and the like, is a well-established custom. To stay with musicians for a moment, it is not difficult these days to find examples of **Haydn** used as a first name. I have also seen an **Elgar** and a **Rossini**. The latter blends in surprisingly well with our first name system, for anyone bearing it would be addressed as **Ross**, the Scottish name now established throughout the English-speaking world.

A great many rare first names are simply nonce conversions of surnames. The wife's maiden name may be kept in use by making it the child's first name instead of the more usual middle name. This practice can lead to some odd-looking names and might mislead a casual observer into thinking that new sources of names were being tapped. **Starling, Lamb, Lion** and **Basset,** for instance, do not indicate parents who have turned to the animal kingdom for inspiration. These are all normal surnames which have been pressed into use as first names.

I have also seen **Boozer** used as a first name, though the bearer of the surname must have known what kind of jokes it was likely to cause. The boy called **Feather** may also have had reason to reproach his parents later in life. In such cases, one would have thought that the women who gave up these names at marriage would be relieved to escape from tiresome jokes. It is a little difficult to understand why they choose to pass on to their children names that would immediately become far more noticeable as first names.

Most parents realize that even perfectly ordinary surnames can make not only uncommon, but decidedly odd, first names. There is all the difference in the world between the two. An *uncommon* name, in the statistical sense, might be an asset; an *odd* name is almost invariably a disadvantage to the person who bears it.

Duplicated names

Some parents follow the formerly aristocratic habit of duplicating their own surname to produce a first name. The child emerges with a name like **Smith** Smith. The reasoning is: Smith is a common surname and needs an uncommon first name to go with it. Smith is uncommon as a first name, so

The following names were all bestowed on children whose surname was Smith. The examples come from the Indexes of Births for England and Wales, 1838–1900.

Abbot	Bugless	Golden	Raper
Aberilda	Butler	Goliath	Reason
Abishag	Butter	Halcyon	Saint
Acey	Buz	Ham	Salmon
Aden	Carry	Herald	Salome
Admiral	Celtic	Hymen	Same
Aesop	Christmas	Indiana	Senora
Africaner	Cicero	Janus	Seville
Albany	Clapham	Jeberechiah	Siffy
Albino	Cockshott	Jolly	Silence
Albion	Columbus	July	Sippy
Alderman	Concordia	Kaiser	Smart
Almond	Costuma	Last	Squire
Amber	Cupid	Lear	Stranger
Ambler	Cyprus	Leoline	Strongitharm
Amorous	Dark	Lettuce	St. Valentine
Anchor	Despair	Liberty	Syren
Arena	Dixee	Little	Tarry
Ark	Dozer	Lucky	Tempest
Armour	Driver	Lustrous	Tenant
Arrow	Effecate	Marvelle	Thistle
Asia	Egypt	Minniehaha	Thursday
Atlantic	Elfin	Mystic	Trafalgar
Auburn	Elimelick	Newlove	Tram
Augustiania	Energetic	Novello	Unity
Baker	Esquire	Nurser	Uz
Banker	Euphrates	Omar	Venicc
Barker	Fairly	Only	Virtue
Barman	Farewell	Oxford	Wales
Baron	Feaster	Patient	Water
Beacon	Fiancé	Perpugilliam	Welcome
Berry	Flow	Perseverance	Wiltshire
Bibby	Fortune	Philadelphia	Windsor
Blossom	Friar	Pickles	Wisdom
Bold	Gent	Plato	Wonderful
Bonus	Gentle	President	Xenophon
Boy	German	Providence	Zezia
Brained	Gipsy	Queenation	Zuba
Britannia	Glass	Rap	Zylpha

let the child be Smith Smith. A check made by Mr C. V. Appleton on first names used by the Smiths in England and Wales before 1900 revealed twenty-two examples of Smith Smith in sixty-two years. That does not make it as common as the Robert Roberts, William Williams, etc., who are to be found in Wales, but neither is it as uncommon as the parents concerned probably believed.

Another idea that has occurred to parents in search of a novel first name is to use part of their surname. Had my wife and I thought along these lines our eldest son might have become Dunk Dunkling. (**Dunk** is listed as a slave name in *Black Names In America*). As it happens, **Dunks** is his school nickname, which he readily accepts. I doubt whether he would have thanked us, however, had we given him that name officially.

Some nicknames, incidentally, become as famous as an individual's first name or surname. I was not especially surprised to come across an American named **Stonewall**, though **Jackson** is the more usual choice of parents who wish to honour this man.

Place names as unusual first names

I asked at the beginning of the chapter whether **Milan** and **Chelsea** were unusual first names. Your answer will have depended on where you live, for both names are fairly common in different parts of the English-speaking world. Milan is to be found amongst immigrants from parts of Central Europe who now live in North America, while Chelsea is an up-and-coming girl's name in Australia.

Milan does not necessarily belong in a discussion of place names used as first names. Its original is explained in a book of Hungarian names, *Keresztneveink, Védöszentjeink*, by Dr Fekete Antal. Dr Antal gives it as a common pet name from **Aemilianus,** which became French **Emile**, German **Emil** and Welsh **Emlyn**. Emlyn has an alternative origin from a Welsh place name, and for that matter, one can never rule out the possibility of English-speaking parents naming a child Milan because they were living there at the time of the birth. There were too many Milans amongst American university students in 1975, however, for this to be always the case.

Why Chelsea should suddenly have been picked upon by Australian parents is difficult to say. There is an Australian place of that name which probably owes its origin to the London Chelsea. The name is significant to English people in another context, for it is roared out every week by thousands of football fans. Even the ardent supporters of the Chelsea Football Club, however, would probably be surprised at the idea of naming their daughter after the team.

Yet Chelsea fits in perfectly well with other first names. It is as easy to say

CERTIFIED COPY OF AN ENTRY OF BIRTH

REGISTRATION DISTRICT *St. G*

1878. BIRTH in the Sub-district of *Belgrave*

Columns:— 1	2	3	4	5	6
No.	When and where born	Name, if any	Sex	Name and surname of father	Name, surname and maiden surname of mother	Occupat of fath
116	Twenty eighth March 1878, 5 Passmore Street	Murder John	Son	Murder Smith	Patricia Smith formerly Edwards	Priva Solde 2ⁿᵈ Batta Scot Guar

CERTIFIED to be a true copy of an entry in the certified copy of a Register of Births in the Di

Given at the GENERAL REGISTER OFFICE, LONDON, under the Seal of the said Office, the

BXA 250795

This certificate is issued in pursuance of the Births and Deaths Registration Act sealed or stamped with the seal of the General Register Office shall be received a proof of the entry, and no certified copy purporting to have been given in the said

CAUTION:—Any person who (1) falsifies any of the particulars on this certifi to prosecution.

Form A502M (S.355267) Dd.323476 110M 12/75 H/w.

'The birth certificate of Murder John Smith, named after his father, Private Murder Smith.'

as **Elsie** or **Kelsie**—the latter name being borne by Kelsie Harder, Secretary of the American Name Society. His twin sister was named Elsie and he became Kelsie. The name has given him a few problems I should think, for I see that the authors of *What To Name Your Baby*, acknowledging help received, refer consistently to Mrs Kelsie B. Harder.

Names at sea

The next name amongst the examples I gave was **Dolphin**. It was the subject of a letter I received recently from Mrs Dorothy Cox, who lives in Western Australia. Mrs Cox wrote:

> My mother was born at sea in the year 1860, on board a ship named the *Dolphin*. Her father was an English soldier named Isaac Smith who was sent here to watch over the convicts. It was a stormy rough trip out from England, and so the baby born at sea was named Dolphin Mercy. Could you tell me if my mother is the only person to have been christened Dolphin?

That is the kind of letter I very much like to receive, for it gives as well as asks for information. I was able to tell Mrs Cox that a Dolphin Smith was named in England in 1838, and that others were named in 1843, 1868 and 1879. Her mother was therefore by no means unique, though she bore a name very rarely used as a first name.

Dr David Aitken has made a special study of children named at sea, and transferred ship names occur regularly. A child called **Berengaria** perhaps makes the source of the name obvious, but **Exeter** is misleading. The child given that name was born on the ship called the *Exeter*, so as with Milan we have an apparently simple place name transfer which is nothing of the sort. In the same way, **Pilgrim** and **Tremendous** as first names do not reflect religious fervour or the parents' reaction on seeing their child. Both were used to commemorate births at sea in ships of those names.

Sea-births can bring other names into being. In Shakespeare's *Pericles* there is a princess called '**Marina** for I was born at sea'. Dr Aitken has also discovered people who were named **Oceanus, Seaborne, Seamercy, Neptune, Atlantic** and **Sou'wester**. Marina has in modern times been used for many children born on dry land, but the other names remain unusual. Nevertheless, they are a common kind of incident name.

Incident names

Another kind of incident name records the time of birth rather than the place. This is very common outside the English-speaking world. In most of West Africa, for instance, every child receives a 'day name' as well as other given names. The Ghanaian day names are as follows:

	Boys	Girls
Sunday	**Kwashie**	**Awushie**
Monday	**Kedjo**	**Adojoa**
Tuesday	**Kobla**	**Abla**
Wednesday	**Kwaku**	**Aku**
Thursday	**Kwao**	**Awo**
Friday	**Kofi**	**Afua**
Saturday	**Kwame**	**Ama**

Kofi is thought to have been taken to America by slaves and to have become the common name **Cuffee, Cuffy** or **Coffee**.

We have no such regular system of day-naming, but it occurs to many parents to remember the time of birth in the name. Common names of this type, as we have seen, are **April** (or **Avril**), **May** and **June**. When **August** occurs as a male name it is usually meant to indicate someone who is august, or venerable, rather than a boy born in that month. Other month names do occur, however, and I have a record of children named **March, July** and **September**. Further examples of seasonal first names include **Easter** (which is sometimes a form of **Esther**), and **Christmas**. More specifically, a child born in 1898 was named **Mayday**, and one born in 1873 was given the names **Midsummer Maurice**.

The names of the days are occasionally used as first names by English-speaking parents, and I once came across a **Thor** who was born on Thursday (Thor's day). Perhaps **Woden** would be a logical name for a boy born on Wednesday, **Freya** for a girl born on Friday.

I have seen one example of **Night**—a name which presumably indicated time of birth. **Dawn** is now so common, as I have mentioned before, that it probably no longer has that kind of significance. **Evening** would actually make a satisfactory name, bearing in mind that it would have the pet form **Eve**.

Russian first names

Let us move on to **Rufina**, which was another of the names I asked about at the beginning of this chapter. In this case the parents have simply borrowed a name from another language, something the English-speaking peoples have been doing for centuries. The names we think of as our own come from such languages as Hebrew, Greek, Latin, French, German, Italian and Spanish. Recently we have begun to borrow names from Russian—**Natasha** and **Olga** being obvious examples. Rufina belongs with them, a recommended name for Russian girls in a calendar published in 1973. It could as easily be taken into English as other foreign names have been in the past.

It is surprising that those parents who prefer unusual names do not turn more often to the first names used in other countries. Many of our favourite names are international, of course, and simply take on a different form elsewhere. Other names are common in certain countries but almost unknown to us. The same Russian calendar that mentioned Rufina, for instance, also gave as girls' names **Ulyana, Serafima, Nonna, Maya, Kira, Larisa, Kaleria, Inna, Zoya, Darya** and **Alla**. As it happens, Marina was also officially recommended to Russian parents in 1973; so too was **Tamara**. Boys' names in the list included **Yury, Roman, Oleg, Nikita, Ilya** and **Vadim**.

Swiss first names

As a fuller indication of the resources available when one turns to foreign names, I give below some examples from Switzerland. The Swiss name stock is a particularly interesting one, mainly mixing names from France,

First Names–Languages of Origin

The examples below show some of the main languages from which the first names of the English-speaking world have been borrowed.

Hebrew

Abel	Deborah	Hannah	Judith	Miriam	Samuel
Abigail	Delilah	Jacob	Leah	Nathan	Sarah
Abraham	Dinah	Jeremy	Magdalen	Rachel	Solomon
Adam	Edna	Johanna	Mary	Raphael	Susan
Anna	Elizabeth	John	Martha	Rebecca	Thaddeus
Benjamin	Eve	Jonah	Matthew	Ruth	Thomas
Daniel	Gabriel	Jonathan	Melchior	Salome	Tobias
David	Gideon	Joseph	Michael	Samson	Zacharias

Greek

Agatha	Andrew	Cynthia	Helen	Monica	Sophia
Agnes	Angela	Daphne	Irene	Nicholas	Stephen
Alexander	Barbara	Dorothy	Iris	Peter	Theodore
Alexis	Basil	Eugene	Katharine	Philip	Theophila
Anastasia	Christopher	George	Lydia	Sebastian	Timothy
Andrea	Christian	Gregory	Melanie	Sibyl	Zoe

Latin

Adrian	Candida	Felix	Laura	Natalie	Urban
Alma	Cecil	Flora	Laurence	Octavia	Ursula
Amanda	Cecilia	Florence	Leo	Paul	Valentine
Antony	Clara	Gloria	Lucia	Prudence	Victor
Aurelia	Cornelia	Julia	Marcus	Regina	Victoria
Beatrice	Diana	Julian	Martin	Silvester	Vincent
Benedict	Fabian	Justin	Miranda	Stella	Viola

French

Adele	Blanche	Denise	Jacqueline	Louise	Nicole
Alison	Charlotte	Fleur	Jeanne	Madeleine	Rene
Annette	Claire	Genevieve	Jeannette	Marion	Roger
Antoinette	Claudette	Georgette	Jeannine	Michelle	Yvette
Arlette	Danielle	Henriette	Louis	Nanette	Yvonne

Spanish

Anita	Carmen	Dolores	Elvira	Esmeralda	Ramona

Nordic

Astrid	Dagmar	Freya	Hedda	Inga	Karen
Axel	Eric	Greta	Helga	Ingrid	Karin

Celtic

Aidan	Alan	Bridget	Donald	Douglas	Leslie

Slavic

Ivan	Natasha	Olga	Sonja	Vera	Yury

German

Adelaide	Albert	Gertrude	Karl	Leopold	Rupert

Germany and Italy but readily accepting names from other sources. In my brief selection I have omitted names which are already in common use in English-speaking countries:

Girls: **Ambra, Annina, Astrid, Babetta, Clarisse, Cyrilla, Dania, Donata, Emerita, Fabia, Fabiana, Fabiola, Flavia, Florina, Giona, Helga, Imelda, Karine, Katja, Ladina, Liana, Lisia, Lona, Lorella, Marilena, Melania, Menica, Mirella, Monette, Odile, Orsina, Orsola, Ottavia, Ottilia, Pia, Purissimma, Ramona, Renata, Sabine, Silva, Sira, Uschi, Verena.**

Boys: **Anselm, Anton, Blaise, Clement, Donato, Egon, Elvin, Etienne, Flavian, Heinz, Klaus, Linus, Manfred, Marcel, Marius, Marlo, Nino, Olivier, Pablo, Paulo, Reno, Timo, Vitus, Zelimir, Zoltan.**

It would be easy to find far more exotic names by looking still further afield, but like most English-speaking people I would see little point in using a name like **Tsholofelo**, for instance, even though I am told that it is a common name for a girl in Botswana, meaning 'hope'. By our conventions the name would be odd, not just unusual, and that is what one wishes to avoid. For different reasons the Hausa girl's name **Binta** would be unsuitable for a child surrounded by Jennifers and Amys. It would be interpreted as an extension of the slang word 'bint', a derogatory term for a girl. Names which would be acceptable, however, include some given to Moslem boys, such as **Zaki, Amal** and **Salim**, and others given to Asian girls, such as **Vanna, Kuma** and **Amara**.

Unusual spellings

Some unusual looking names are simply spelling variants of names commonly in use. When I first saw **Alley** as a first name I forgot for the moment about pet forms of **Alice** and wondered whether other 'street' names had been used. Was there someone walking around called **Crescent**, perhaps? I was in good company, for Dickens indulged in a similar flight of fancy over **Abbey**. Miss Abigail Potterson, proprietress of The Six Jolly Fellowship Porters in *Our Mutual Friend*, was thus known to her customers. Dickens remarks that 'some of them thought that she was named after or in some way related to the Abbey of Westminster'.

I have seen the name **Alfer** only once, and feel sure that Dickens would have enjoyed it. The Greek letter **Alpha** was presumably meant, for this occurs from time to time as a first name. **Beta** has also been used, probably in a family that was prepared to work its way through to **Omega**, which likewise is to be found as a first name. What is so pleasant about Alfer is the way it brings a rather learned name down to earth. Heard by those who were more familiar with **Alfred** than with Greek letters it is easy to understand how Alpha was interpreted as an upper-class version of **Alf**.

Other pet forms of familiar names which, like Alley and Abbey, have been given a new look, include **Wash, Elm** and **Herb**. Wash was once regularly used in the U.S.A. as a pet form of **Washington**, while Elm and Herb were not botanical but short forms of **Elmer** and **Herbert** used as first names in their own right. I have seen a genuine tree name, **Willow**, used for a girl, and there in my view is an unusual name at its best. Perhaps it is the occurrence of **Cherry**, from **Charity** or the French *cherie*, that has led to the occasional fruit names used as first names, such as **Orange** and **Almond**.

Anthonyina, which was in my preliminary list, is an unusual name, but probably not odd. The process that led to it is totally familiar: it is the simplest kind of link name using a common suffix. The resulting name is extremely clumsy and is unlikely to be imitated, especially when far more pleasant forms such as **Antonia** are available.

Unusual biblical names

Nebuchadnezzar, also in my preliminary list, must be classed with names like **Mephibosheth, Jezebel** and **Cain**, all biblical names that are little used. The first two are clearly less common because of their length and difficulty, the others because of the reputations of the biblical personages. All do occasionally occur as first names, however, I have seen references to at least six children who were named Cain, for instance.

My general point here is that unusual names can derive from perfectly normal first name sources. Even **Word**, the last example I gave as a test case, is not especially odd from this point of view. At one time it was a custom for parents to open their Bibles at random and use the first word on the page as a name for their child. It was a way of demonstrating trust in God's guidance. As with the odd-looking Puritan names of former times, the motivation for such naming was good, even though the results sometimes made a mockery of the good intentions.

Cruelty to children

Sometimes a helpless child will have a name imposed upon it which is wrong in every way. The naming process becomes a form of cruelty to the child, thanks to the ignorance or vindictiveness of the namers. As a result, we get those absurd names beloved by journalists, who usually report on the names as if they are jokes to be shared. I am afraid I cannot think of these irresponsible parents as funny in any way, and I detest the thought that yet

> '*There was a boy called* **Eustace Clarence Scrubb**, *and he almost deserved it.*' (C. S. *Lewis*, The Voyage of the Dawn Treader.)

another article about odd names may encourage someone else to be 'clever' at his child's expense.

It is, of course, the naming of a child in a really *odd* way that I object to, not the bestowal of an *unusual* name. A rarely used name can individualize the person who bears it while causing no adverse comment. An odd name, I seriously believe, can disfigure a child for life, doing a great deal of psychological damage. Most parents are well aware of the risks, and they play safe with the well-tried names. In my view they are quite right to do so.

21 Assessing a Name

Evaluating one's own name and choosing a baby's name

It is now time for me to begin my summing up, so let me return to the thesis presented at the beginning of this book. Our first names are not merely names: frequently they act as our ambassadors, representing us to the outside world. They are a part of our personality as others see it—often as we ourselves see it. Our names play an important role in our lives, and it is right that we should ask ourselves objectively whether they are doing a good job on our behalf.

I have called this chapter 'Assessing A Name', implying that a name has a value than can be measured. But first names do not have an absolute value that holds good in all circumstances. One name is not in itself worth more than another. The value of a particular first name to the person who bears it depends not only on the name itself, but on such factors as the surname, age, profession and nationality of the name-bearer. A name assessment can only be made on a purely individual basis.

Surname influence

As we have seen, a surname influences a first name in several ways. In extreme cases it converts an inoffensive name like **Ann** into a joke (e.g., Ann Teak, Ann Noyes). There are undoubtedly parents who have deliberately tried for such an effect, but the place for name games of that sort is a humorous column in a newspaper, not on a child's birth certificate. Some women have been unlucky enough to acquire a surname by marriage that 'kills' their first name. I heard recently of a lady who had just become Heather Feather.

Most people would consider such a name to be a minor disaster, but in certain circumstances the name-bearer could consider it an asset. Imagine, for example, someone whose job it is to sell a product or a service by making telephone calls to potential customers. That person is constantly having to begin conversations with strangers. The unusual name combination might serve very well as an ice-breaker, allowing the hard sell to be made after an initial joke or two.

Not everyone acquires a rhyming name at marriage, of course. What may well happen, however, is that a first name that formed part of a pleasant-sounding unit in front of the maiden name suddenly seems like an unpleasant jangle because of the new surname. One way of avoiding such a problem is for the bride to change her first name as well as her surname at the time of marriage, thus acquiring a completely new name personality. Another way is to question whether the custom of automatically assuming the surname of the husband is the one to follow. There is no legal reason why the *bride*'s surname should not be the one adopted by the couple. They could also continue to use their separate surnames, hyphenate their surnames, or adopt a name that is new to both of them.

Initials

Surnames also contribute to a name-bearer's initials, and I discussed earlier the question of those which form words such as M.A.D. A friend of mine who was a P.O.P. made a slight adjustment and became O.P.P. People now assume that he has dropped his first name in favour of his middle name. He is in fact avoiding the tiresome repetition of a comment he does not find funny.

In spite of superstitious beliefs about initial words being lucky, parents should obviously avoid forming words that are unpleasant. Anything that could conceivably lead to jokes about a child's name is unfair to the child. If his name is ridiculed he will come to feel that he himself is an object of ridicule. As for adults who find themselves with a set of initials that form a word—perhaps once again because of marriage—changing the order of the names might be the solution. Alternatively, the middle initial can be dropped completely or an extra one can be added.

Common names

It might be thought that parents with a common surname, such as Smith, Brown, Johnson, etc., would want to balance the surname with an uncommon first name. This may be true of some parents, but not of the majority. It can very easily be shown, for instance, that when **John** was at the height of its popularity, the Smiths consistently made it their first choice.

Logically it seems a good idea for a first name to balance a surname from the point of view of frequency, but the decision to use a popular name as

> '*Whether it is marvellous coincidence, or whether it is that the name itself has an imperceptible effect upon the character, I have never yet been able to ascertain; but the fact is unquestionable, that there never yet was any person named* **Charles** *who was not an open, manly, honest, good-natured and frank-hearted fellow, with a rich, clear voice that did you good to hear it, and an eye that looked you straight in the face, as much to say:* "*I have a clear conscience myself, am afraid of no man, and am altogether above doing a mean action.*"'
>
> *Edgar Allan Poe*, Thou Art The Man
> (*In Poe's story, Charles Goodefellow is later revealed as the murderer.*)

opposed to an uncommon first name seems to be made on other grounds. Parents who are naming a first child are in any case often unaware of which names *are* popular at that time and which are being used less frequently. It is only when they have a child in a playgroup or nursery that the names of the other children begin to register. That at least need not be the case with readers of this book, who have only to turn back to 'Names In Their Infancy' to see which names are popular now.

There is no simple advice that can be given as to whether a common name is preferable to an unusual one, or vice-versa. Parents cannot know whether their child will ultimately become a public figure whose unusual name adds something positive to his public personality, or whether his working life will be spent in an environment where unusualness of any kind will be looked upon with suspicion or ridicule. Perhaps the only answer to this parental problem is to give a child one or two popular names *and* a less common one.

Number of names

This brings up the general question of how many names a child should be

> '*A young gentlemen marries Mabel Ethel Beatrice Evangeline Planta-genet Toedmag Saxon. If he permit his imagination to take only moderate exercise he can easily persuade himself that he has married not one, but a whole bevy of girls; that he has emptied a young ladies' boarding-school by wedding every female in it, governesses included; that he is, in fact, the possessor of a harem, for the equal of which a Moslem emir might pine in vain. He has a tiff with Mabel? He can leave her and spend an hour in soft dalliance with Ethel. . .*'
>
> *W. Stewart Ross*, Janet Smith

Remembering people's names is an age-old problem. In ancient Rome candidates for public positions considered it essential to greet their fellow citizens in the street by name. Many of them employed special servants called 'nomenclators'. These men had the job of walking ahead of them and reminding them of the names of people who were approaching. Appius Claudius used to boast that he had no need of a nomenclator because of his own excellent memory. The emperor Hadrian used to amuse himself by correcting his nomenclator's mistakes.

Teddy Roosevelt was apparently not quite as successful at remembering names. One story about him concerns a haberdasher named Kaskel who shook his hand and began to say: 'Mr President, I made your shirts . . .' Mr Roosevelt immediately interrupted to say: 'Oh, yes, Major Shurtz, I remember you well.'

With a new acquaintance one can legitimately begin a conversation by exchanging names. In *The Tempest* Ferdinand demonstrates how to ask for someone's name with exquisite delicacy:

> I do beseech you,
> Chiefly that I might set it in my prayers,
> What is your name?

When the name has been given, repeating it several times is said to help fix it in the mind. I usually ask people to spell their names to me as well. In fact, many of the conversations I have with new acquaintances begin with fairly extensive discussions about their names. I do not necessarily recommend this as a way of remembering names, for I invariably forget them.

Actors and actresses have long had the habit of addressing one another as 'darling' until they can learn by some means who it is they are speaking to. One actor known to me usually asks someone to name the other people in the room, explaining that he has a terrible memory. When the informant gives his own name, knowing that it, too, has been forgotten, the actor invariably says: 'Oh, no. I remembered you. It was everyone else I'd forgotten.'

We use such tortuous devices because we know how flattered we are to have our own names remembered, and we would like to please others by remembering theirs. Scipio Africanus, however, was one Roman who refused to become involved in this social game. He made no attempt to remember the names of others or to conceal that fact. He explained that he was too busy trying to make his own name known to others to worry about learning theirs. Perhaps, after all, honesty is the best policy.

given at birth. G. B. Stern, in *A Name To Conjure With*, tells an anecdote about one of her friends who had nine names. It came about entirely by accident, for the parents had been arguing until the last moment about what the first name was to be. They handed the rector a piece of paper a few minutes before the baptismal ceremony with their final choice written on it. Before anyone could stop him, however, he had read out the nine names which were on the other side of the paper—the whole of the parental short list.

From time to time parents have the 'original' idea of giving their child twenty-six names, beginning with each letter of the alphabet. There is no law which can prevent such silliness. Mr and Mrs Average give their children a first name and one middle name, but there seems a lot to be said for giving a child at least two, possibly three, middle names. It is difficult to see how the additional names could in themselves cause any embarrassment. On the other hand, they might well provide some kind of insurance against unforeseen future events that cause the first name to become unsatisfactory. The name-bearer will have a wider choice of reserve names.

Extra middle names can also be used for family purposes, keeping names alive in the family which would otherwise disappear. As far as the name-bearer is concerned, such names will normally remain in the background, appearing only as initials. Personally, I see only advantages to be gained from the bestowal of an extra middle name or two, and they certainly come at a bargain price. They cost the parents only a little time and thought.

Old names or new

As to what the names should be, I have already suggested a mixture of the popular and the less common. The next question is: should one use old-established first names that have only recently, or perhaps never before, been used as first names?

I know from the letters I receive from parents that many people think of 'newness' as a desirable quality. There are, it is true, many social pressures upon us which encourage us to think of new things as good things. But names are not consumer goods, and we should use different criteria in selecting them.

The older-established first names have usually acquired an agreed spelling form that most people know, an agreed pronunciation, and a definite association with one of the sexes. By contrast, new first names, whether newly created or newly transferred into the first name system, can run into difficulties on all these counts.

The old-established names also have a high status value for many people because of their age. They are like antique pieces of furniture which still function in a practical way in modern times, but speak of a long heritage. For those who must have novelty, many names used by English-speaking people in the seventeenth century or before have remained in the background for a long time. Some of them could certainly be brought back into use. Such names would have a 'new' look about them, but they would be carrying on linguistic and social traditions that are worth preserving. Many examples of the names I have in mind can be found in earlier chapters.

Dated names

The age of a name has nothing to do with its being 'dated', of course. As we have seen, this is entirely due to intensive usage of a name at a particular period, followed by its virtual disappearance as it goes out of fashion.

As a general rule it can be assumed that any name which is intensively used for a period will ultimately become dated. The dating, however, can easily spread over twenty years or more. Someone who is given a name that is coming into fashion may therefore be quite safe. If the name hits its peak five or ten years later, then levels out for a few years before beginning to fall away, the date on the name will be well on the right side of the name-bearer's real age. It is when someone is given a name that is rapidly going out of fashion that problems are caused.

Any name that has been in a country's top fifty since 1950 presents no dating problem for the moment. Similarly, with a name that has never been in any top fifty, no problem exists. It is a name which was being much used before 1950 but not afterwards which may require attention. It becomes an embarrassment if it suggests an age which is considerably older than the name-bearer's real age.

For those who do bear embarrassing names, reference to the top fifties quoted in earlier chapters may well be a formality. They will have been given many indications in their social and professional life that their name is 'wrong' in some way. Facts and figures are likely to confirm what they already know or what they have not wanted to admit. Once it *is* admitted that one's name is projecting the wrong kind of image, then a decision must be made. The inconvenience can be accepted, or the name can be changed.

Dr Paul Plattner, a psychiatrist working in Berne, was visited by a patient who wanted his approval to have an abortion. He asked her what name she would have given the baby had she kept it. The patient thought about it for a moment, then announced that she had changed her mind. Dr Plattner, who watched the patient as she thought about the question of a name, said later: 'I had the feeling that I was witnessing the birth of the person of her child.' The story is related by Paul Tournier in What's In A Name?

Parents searching for a name for a baby will be interested to know that each day of the year has the names of certain Christian saints associated with it (though there is no universally-accepted calendar of name days). The list that follows gives a selection of name days. Further information about those named is to be found in such publications as *Names and Name Days* and *A Dictionary of Saints*, both by Donald Attwater. The Roman Martyrology should also be consulted. It will be noticed that many of the names are linked to more than one day because several saints bore them.

January

1. Basil; Martina
2. Caspar; Stephanie
3. Daniel; Genevieve
4. Gregory; Christiana
5. Edward, Simon; Emily (Amelia)
6. Andrew
7. Felix, Lucian
8. Laurence
9. Adrian, Julian, Peter
10. Dermot, Gregory
11. Honorata (Honora)
12. Benedict; Tatiana (Tania)
13. Mungo; Veronica, Yvette
14. Felix, Hilary
15. Paul
16. Mark; Priscilla
17. Antony; Rosaline
18. Peter; Christine, Margaret
19. Henry, Marius; Martha
20. Fabian, Sebastian
21. Alban; Agnes
22. Dominic, Vincent
23. John, Raymond; Gladys
24. Timothy; Vera
25. Paul
26. Aubrey, Conan; Paula
27. John; Angela
28. Cyril, Peter
29. Francis
30. Sebastian; Hyacinth, Martina
31. Aidan, John, Mark; Louisa, Marcella

February

1. Henry, Ignatius; Brigid
2. Laurence; Catherine, Joan, Mary
3. Blaise, Oscar
4. Andrew, Gilbert, Joseph; Joan
5. Paul; Agatha
6. Titus; Dorothy
7. Richard, Theodore; Juliana
8. John, Stephen
9. Cyril; Apollonia
10. William
11. Benedict, Lucius; Mary
12. Antony; Eulalia, Marina
13. Stephen; Beatrice, Katherine
14. Cyril, Valentine
15. Claud; Georgia
16. Gilbert; Juliana
17. Finan, Fintan, Julian, Reginald
18. Flavian
19. Conrad
20. Peter; Amy, Mildred
21. Noel, Robert
22. Peter; Margaret
23. Peter
24. Matthias (Matthew)
25. Claud, Ethelbert
26. Leo, Victor; Isabel
27. Augustus, Gabriel, Leander; Ann
28. Oswald; Antonia
29. Hilarus, Roman

March

1. Christopher, David; Antonia
2. Chad, Henry; Agnes
3. Aelred
4. Casimir, Christopher
5. Kieran, Theophilus
6. Cyril; Colette, Felicity, Perpetua
7. Jermyn, Thomas
8. Felix, John, Julian
9. Dominic, Gregory; Catherine, Frances
10. John
11. Angus, John; Teresa
12. Gregory, Maximilian, Paul, Simon Seraphina
13. Gerald, Roderick; Euphrasia, Sanchia
14. Arnold; Matilda
15. Clement, William; Louisa
16. Gabriel, Herbert, Isaac, Julian, Paul; Eusebia
17. Joseph, Patrick; Gertrude
18. Christian, Cyril, Edward
19. Andrew, Joseph
20. Baptist, Cuthbert, Herbert, Martin; Alexandra
21. Benedict, Nicholas; Cornelia
22. Basil, Nicholas, Zachary; Catherine, Leah
23. Joseph; Sibyl
24. Gabriel; Bertha, Katherine
25. James; Lucy, Mary
26. Basil, Felix, William
27. John, Rupert; Augusta, Lydia
28. John; Gwendolen
29. Jonah, Mark; Jane
30. John, Peter
31. Benjamin, Guy; Jane

A First Name Calendar

April

1. Gilbert, Hugh; Catherine
2. Francis, John; Margaret, Mary, Theodosia
3. Pancras, Richard
4. Ambrose, Benedict, Isidore, Tierney
5. Gerald, Vincent; Gillian
6. William; Catherine, Marcia
7. Alexander, Ashley, Herman, Ralph; Ursula
8. Walter; Julia
9. Hugh; Mary, Monica
10. Mark, Terence
11. Leo, Philip; Gemma
12. Angelo, Zeno
13. Edmund, John; Ida
14. Caradoc, Justin; Lydwina
15. Anastasia
16. Benedict, Magnus; Bernadette
17. Robert, Stephen; Clare
18. Mary
19. James, Leo
20. Robert, Simon; Agnes
21. Anselm, Conrad, Theodore
22. Bartholomew
23. George, Giles; Helen
24. Egbert; Euphrasia
25. Mark, Robert, William
26. Clarence, Peter, Stephen
27. Antony, Peter; Zita
28. Louis, Paul; Theodora
29. Hugh, Joseph, Peter
30. Benedict, James, Miles; Catherine, Marian, Rosamund

May

1. James, Peregrine, Philip; Isidora, Patience
2. Zoe
3. Alexander, Aylwin; Maura, Viola
4. Walter; Antonia, Monica
5. Hilary; Judith
6. Antony; Benedicta, Prudence
7. John; Flavia
8. Michael, Peter, Victor
9. Gregory, Nicholas
10. Isidore; Beatrice
11. Francis, Walter
12. Ignatius, John; Flavia, Jane
13. Andrew, Robert; Imelda
14. Giles, Michael; Petronilla
15. Nicholas; Magdalen
16. Brendan, Simon; Maxima
17. Bruno, Pascal
18. Eric, Felix; Claudia, Julitta
19. Dunstan, Ivor; Celestine
20. Bernardine
21. Andrew; Daphne
22. John, Peter; Julia, Rita
23. William
24. David, Philip, Simeon, Vincent; Susan
25. Gregory; Madeleine, Mary, Sophie
26. Augustine, Philip; Eve, Mariana
27. Bede, Julius
28. Bernard; Margaret
29. Richard; Mary Theodosia
30. Ferdinand, Laurence; Joan
31. Angela, Camilla, Petronilla

June

1. Conrad, John; Angela
2. Nicholas, Stephen; Blandina
3. Cecil, Charles, Claudius, Kevin; Clotilda, Olive
4. Francis
5. Boniface, Ferdinand, Niall; Marcia
6. Bertrand, Norbert; Pauline, Valeria
7. Robert; Ann
8. John, William; Calliope
9. Columba, Vincent; Ann, Diana
10. John; Margaret, Olive
11. Barnabas, Peter; Flora, Paula
12. John, Stephen; Antonia
13. Antony; Aquilina
14. Basil, Valerius
15. Vitus; Germaine
16. John; Justina
17. Adolph, Harvey; Teresa
18. Elizabeth, Marina
19. Gervase, Humphrey; Gillian (Juliana)
20. Francis, Thomas; Michelina (Michelle)
21. Aloysius; Demetria
22. Alban, Innocent, John
23. Thomas; Audrey
24. John
25. Guy, William; Febronia, Lucy
26. John, Paul
27. Samson
28. John; Irene
29. Paul, Peter; Emma, Judith
30. Bertram, Godwin, Paul

July

1. Derek, Theobald
2. Otto; Mary
3. Aaron, Anatole, Julius, Leo; Bernardine
4. Andrew, Henry, Martin; Bertha
5. Antony, Michael; Edna, Philomena
6. Romulus; Dominica
7. Cyril, Peter, Prosper, Ralph; Hedda
8. Eugene; Isabel (Elizabeth), Veronica
9. Adrian, Godfrey, Thomas; Jane
10. Amelia, Rufina
11. Oliver; Amabel, Olga
12. David, John; Veronica
13. James, Silas, Thomas
14. Bonaventure, Humbert
15. Donald, Henry, Swithin; Angelina, Edith
16. Mary
17. Alexis, Kenelm
18. Emlyn, Frederick
19. Ambrose, Vincent; Justa, Rufina
20. Elias, Jerome; Margaret, Paula
21. Laurence, Victor; Julia
22. Mary
23. John; Joan, Romola
24. Boris, Francis; Antoinette, Charlotte, Christine
25. Christopher, James, Rudolph; Valentina
26. William; Ann
27. Joyce, Lucy
28. Antony, Samson
29. Olaf; Martha
30. Everard
31. Ignatius; Helen

August

1. Peter; Charity, Faith, Hope
2. Basil, Stephen; Alfreda
3. Augustine, Peter, Stephen; Lydia
4. Dominic
5. Thomas; Mary
6. Peter
7. Albert; Claudia
8. John; Joan
9. Oswald
10. Laurence; Asteria
11. Alexander, Peter; Philomena, Susan
12. Clare
13. William; Gertrude
14. Antony; Athanasia
15. Stephen; Mary
16. Joachim; Serena
17. Clare, Hyacinth
18. Beatrice, Helen
19. John, Louis; Emily, Sarah
20. Bernard, Oswin
21. Abraham, Bernard; Jane
22. John, William
23. Eugene, Philip
24. Bartholomew, Nathaniel, Owen; Emily
25. Gregory, Louis; Joan, Patricia
26. Adrian, Thomas; Elizabeth
27. Amyas, David, Joseph; Margaret
28. Augustine, Julian, Moses
29. John, Richard; Candida, Sabina
30. Felix; Rose
31. Aidan, Raymond

September

1. Giles, Michael; Joan, Verena
2. Stephen, William; Adeline, Margaret
3. Antony; Phoebe
4. Boniface; Hermione, Rebecca, Rose
5. Laurence, Urban
6. Bertrand; Beata
7. Ralph; Regina
8. Adrian; Mary
9. Isaac, Kieran, Peter; Wilfrida
10. Ambrose, Charles, Nicholas; Dominica
11. Daniel, John
12. Guy; Mary
13. Philip, Roland
14. John, Louis
15. John; Catherine, Mary
16. Cornelius, Cyprian; Edith, Euphemia, Ludmilla, Ninian
17. Francis, Lambert; Hildegard
18. Joseph; Richarda
19. Theodore; Emily, Mary
20. Eustace, Vincent; Philippa
21. Laurence, Matthew; Agatha, Maura
22. Felix, Maurice, Thomas
23. Adam, Linus; Helen
24. Gerard, Robert; Mary
25. Finbar, Vincent; Aurelia
26. Cornelius, Noel
27. Cosmo, Damian; Delphine
28. Laurence, Wenceslas; Bernardine
29. Michael, René
30. Francis, Gregory, Jerome, Otto; Sophia

October

1. Christopher; Julia
2. Angela
3. Thomas; Josepha, Teresa
4. Francis
5. Placid; Felicia
6. Bruno; Faith, Mary
7. Matthew; Justina, Mary
8. Bridget, Laurentia, Margaret
9. Denis, John, Louis
10. Daniel, Francis
11. Alexander, John, Kenneth; Mary
12. Edwin, Maximilian, Wilfrid
13. Edward, Gerald; Magdalen
14. Dominic
15. Leonard; Aurelia, Teresa
16. Bertrand, Gerard
17. Richard; Margaret
18. Luke; Gwen
19. Peter, Philip
20. Andrew, John; Irene
21. Peter; Celine, Ursula
22. Philip; Mary
23. Ignatius, John; Josephine
24. Martin, Raphael
25. Crispin, Isidore, Thaddeus
26. Lucian
27. Caleb, Vincent; Sabina
28. Jude, Simon; Anastasia, Eunice
29. Maximilian, Valentine; Eusebia
30. Jermyn, John; Dorothy
31. Quentin

November

1. Julian; Mary
2. Ambrose, John
3. Hubert; Ida, Silvia, Winifred
4. Charles, Emery; Frances
5. Martin, Zachary; Bertilla, Elizabeth
6. Leonard; Helen, Margaret
7. Engelbert, Ernest, Peter; Carina
8. Geoffrey
9. George, Theodore
10. Andrew; Florence
11. Bartholomew, Joseph, Martin, Theodore
12. Gabriel, Martin
13. Nicholas
14. John, Laurence
15. Albert, Leopold, Roger
16. Edmund, Lewis; Agnes, Gertrude, Margaret
17. Denis, Gregory, Hugh; Hilda, Theodora
18. Paul, Peter
19. Crispin; Elizabeth
20. Edmund, Felix
21. Albert; Mary
22. Cecily
23. Clement, Gregory; Felicity, Lucretia, Margaret
24. Flora, Mary
25. Catherine, Elizabeth, Joyce
26. Conrad, John, Leonard, Silvester
27. Fergus, Leonard, Virgil; Bernadine
28. James, Stephen
29. Cuthbert, Frederick
30. Andrew; Justina, Maura

December

1. Alexander, Edmund, Hugh; Natalie
2. Adam; Vivienne
3. Edward, Francis
4. Osmund, Peter; Ada, Barbara
5. John, Nicholas; Crispina
6. Nicholas; Denise
7. Ambrose, Martin, Urban
8. Lucina, Mary
9. Cyprian, Julian; Delphine, Valeria
10. Brian, Sidney; Eulalia
11. Daniel, Jerome
12. Antony; Denise
13. John; Jane, Lucy, Odile, Ottilie
14. Conrad, John
15. Paul; Christiana
16. Sebastian; Adelaide, Mary
17. Ignatius, John
18. Rufus
19. Timothy, Urban; Fausta
20. Dominic, Ignatius
21. Peter, Thomas; Esther
22. Judith
23. Nicholas; Victoria
24. Gregory; Adele, Irmina
25. Emmanuel, Noel; Anastasia, Eugenia
26. Denis, Stephen
27. John; Fabiola
28. Antony, Francis
29. David, Thomas, William
30. Eugene, Rayner; Margaret
31. Silvester; Catherine, Melania

Name-changing is nothing new, and there is nothing extraordinary about it. Many biblical characters, we are told, changed their names. There are many cultures where the adoption of a new name in adulthood is a standard practice. Even in our own society, half the population undergoes a change of name at the time of marriage—one's surname being as much a personal name as one's first name. Actors, entertainers, writers and many others often change their names, yet in spite of this, the idea of changing one's own name can be very difficult to accept. People also dislike the idea of having a tooth out, but there comes a point when relief from constant discomfort and irritation cannot be obtained in any other way.

That is not to say that changing one's name is in any way a painful operation. One way of proving the point is to organize a 'fancy name' party. For this kind of function, everyone is told to adopt a new name for the evening and is addressed by it. The whole thing can be treated as a joke, but anyone who is thinking seriously about a change of name will see how refreshing it can be to take on a new identity.

Adapting a name

Sometimes a name does not need to be changed, merely adapted. This is true of standard names that happen to have been given in weird spelling forms. **Peatah** keeps his name, but becomes a more normal **Peter**. Often a slight adaptation, especially to a female name, will change its character. The out-moded **Liz** can become **Liza** or **Lisa**; **Betty** becomes younger as a **Bettina**. This last example also suggests translation of a name as a way of changing it. I mentioned in a previous chapter that **Gladys** became **Claudia** by this means, removing the date-tag and other unfortunate associations from the name at a stroke.

The example of Liz becoming Lisa also reminds us of pet names as a topic. In the chapter that dealt with the emergence of pet names as first names in their own right, I argued strongly in favour of giving a child a 'full'

'What's little missy's name?' said Tom at last, when he thought matters were ripe to push such an enquiry.

'Evangeline St. Clare,' said the little one, 'though Papa and everybody else call me Eva. Now, what's your name?'

'My name's Tom; the little chil'en used to call me Uncle Tom way back thar in Kentuck.'

'Then I mean to call you Uncle Tom, because, you see, I like you,' said Eva.

Harriet Beecher Stowe, Uncle Tom's Cabin

name. The pet name can be used in the way it was originally used, as a kind of nickname, but the formal name will be there in the background. There is likely to come a time in the life of Liz, or Betty, or Lisa, when the dignity of Elizabeth will be appreciated. Pet names, after all, are like informal clothes, worn for everyday comfort when relaxing amongst family and friends. They are not necessarily appropriate for all occasions.

Adults who were given pet names as first names have almost a right, in my view, to re-interpret their parents' wishes in the way that clergymen were prone to do before the eighteenth century. Parents then might indicate their intention to call their daughter **Maggie**, but the vicar would have registered the child as **Margaret**. The full form of the name, of course, also has another advantage in that it allows a choice of pet forms. A Margaret of today might feel younger as a **Madge**, but a future change of name fashions could make **Meg, Peggy, Greta** or **Rita** more fitting.

Verbal associations

A topic I have not specifically commented on elsewhere in the book concerns a name's verbal associations. 'John', for example, is defined by Webster's as 'toilet', which is not a meaning one would choose to have linked to one's name. In this case the word derives from the name, but some names derive from words. In such cases embarrassment can be caused when a word changes its meaning. This has happened recently with 'gay'.

Many first names have dictionary meanings as words, and parents would be well advised to make a check before finally deciding on a name. An example that usually amazes English people is the name **Randy**, a pet form of **Randall** or **Randolph** that is fairly often given as an independent name in the U.S.A. Girls also emerge as **Randi**, deriving the name from **Miranda**. The modern meaning of 'randy' is 'lecherous' or 'lustful', deriving from the word 'rant' as used in the phrase 'rant and rave'. The word is not and never has been very fortunate in its associations. Anyone bearing the name no doubt has to put up with countless jokes about being 'Randy by name and randy by nature', which may be acceptable when one is at school or college. More seriously, one wonders how the name would affect the prospects of a budding politician or candidate for high office.

A name can have other associations as well as verbal. It might suggest a particular racial group, in the way that **Clyde**, for instance, suggests a West Indian to most Englishmen. It might suggest a religious denomination, in the way that **Wesley** links with the Methodists. Many other names carry strong national overtones, especially Scottish, Irish and Welsh names. Such associations are neither good nor bad in themselves, but parents who are choosing names, and for that matter, adults who bear the names, should be aware of them.

	One's own name	Naming the baby
A Dated Name?	Does your name hint that you are older than you want to be? (*Adjust or change it as suggested in this chapter.*)	Do you want to avoid names that will 'date' your child? (*Do not use names that are very popular now, especially those beginning to go out of fashion.*)
New or old?	Is your name an established first name? If not, how do people react to it? (*If they consistently say: 'That's an odd name,' adjust or change it.*)	Is the name you have in mind established as a first name? (*Old-established names avoid many of the inconveniences that go with 'new' or newly converted first names.*)
Pet name?	Is your name a pet name rather than a full name? (*Feel free to restore and use the full name as necessary.*)	Is the name you have in mind a pet name? (*It would be better to give the name in its full form even if you use the pet form.*)
	Do you always use one pet form of your name? (*Consider the effect of changing to another, or reverting to the name in its full form.*)	Are the pet forms of the name you have in mind acceptable? (*List them. You may not use them, but others will.*)
Spelling	Is your name spelt oddly, or mis-spelt? (*Correct to the standard form or one that complies with normal spelling conventions.*)	Are you using the most usual spelling for the name you have in mind? (*Deliberately mis-spelling a name will cause the child endless inconvenience.*)
Sexual confusion?	Is your name sexually ambiguous? (*If it is, and you don't want to change it, using the middle name in full as part of your signature may help.*)	Does the name that you have in mind apply to both sexes? (*Such names are better avoided.*)

	One's own name	Naming the baby
Pronunciation?	Is your name consistently mispronounced by those who see and hear it? (*If so, would a change of spelling or pronunciation help?*)	Is the pronunciation of the name you have in mind in any doubt? (*Check with friends and relations to see whether it gives them problems.*)
Initials?	Do your initials form a word that causes comment? (*Change the order of your names, drop an initial or add one.*)	Have you checked to see whether the name you have in mind creates an unfortunate set of initials? (*Avoid forming initial words or meaningful groups such as W.C.*)
Euphony?	Does your first name sound ugly when followed by your surname (e.g., your married name)? (*Change the first name or surname.*)	Have you checked the overall sound of first name and surname? (*Don't play the Holly Day kind of joke on your child.*)
Verbal associations?	Does your name have an unfortunate meaning as a word? (*Amend or change the name.*)	Have you checked a good dictionary to see whether the name you have in mind has any unsuspected meanings? (*Do so.*)
Number of names?	Have you only one middle name, or perhaps no middle name at all? (*There is no reason why you should not give yourself an extra name.*)	Are you planning to give your child a first name and one middle name? (*An extra name or two would do no harm and might do some good.*)
Etymology?	Have you ever checked the original meaning of your name? (*It might suggest an alternative name to you, different, but closely linked to your original name.*)	Have you chosen a name because of the 'meaning' it had hundreds of years ago? (*That meaning is irrelevant in modern times.*)
Selfishness?	Did your parents choose your name to please themselves or you? (*Be selfish about your own name, amending it or changing it as you wish.*)	Are you choosing a name because *you* like it? (*That is not a good enough reason. For the child's sake the name must be checked objectively from all angles.*)

I offer a check list of these various points on pages 268–69, together with a brief summary of what I hope is practical advice. My object here, and throughout the book, has been to convince you that your own name is worth thinking about objectively, that the names of other people can be fascinating, and that the names of your children must be chosen with the greatest possible care.

22 Further Information

Of the many books that deal with first names I have found the following to be most useful. I recommend them for further study.

Winthrop Ames, *What Shall We Name The Baby?*
Christopher Bice, *Names For The Cornish*
Rev. Reuben S. Brookes and Blanche Brookes, *A Guide To Jewish Names*
Sue Browder, *The New Age Baby Name Book*
Alfonso Burgio, *Dizionario dei Nomi Propri di Persona*
William Camden, *Remains Concerning Britain*
Albert Dauzat, *Dictionnaire des Noms de Famille et Prenoms de France*
Trefor Rendell Davies, *A Book of Welsh Names*
Günther Drosdowski, *Lexikon der Vornamen*
Charles Johnson and Linwood Sleigh, *The Harrap Book of Boys' and Girls' Names*
J. J. Kneen, *The Personal Names of the Isle of Man*
Stephen Langton, *By What Sweet Name?*
Sophy Moody, *What Is Your Name?*
Maxwell Nurnberg and Morris Rosenblum, *What To Name Your Baby*
Roger Price and Leonard Stern, *What Not To Name The Baby*
Lareina Rule, *Name Your Baby*
Elsdon C. Smith, *Naming Your Baby*
Elsdon C. Smith, *Treasury of Name Lore*
Ruth Stephens, *Welsh Names For Children*
Helena Swan, *Girls' Christian Names*
Christine C. Thomson, *Boy or Girl: Names For Every Child*
Ernest Weekley, *Jack and Jill*
E. G. Withycombe, *The Oxford Dictionary of English Christian Names*
Patrick Woulfe, *Irish Names For Children*

Additional information about first names can often be found in general etymological dictionaries, as well as dictionaries of place names and surnames. Amongst the latter I have especially made use, while writing this book, of:

P. H. Reaney, *A Dictionary of British Surnames*
George F. Black, *The Surnames of Scotland*
George R. Stewart, *American Place Names*
Various publications of The English Place Name Society

The Names Society

Research into the aspects of first names discussed in this book continues all the time, and has fortunately been increasing in recent years. The investigation of first name usage in different parts of the English-speaking world, now and in the past, is mainly being carried out by members of The Names Society, based in Thames Ditton, England. Members are currently studying name usage in the U.S.A., Canada, England and Wales, Scotland, Australia and New Zealand. The Society maintains a library of specialized reference books and is prepared to answer queries about first names and other personal names (e.g., the original meanings of surnames) on payment of a search fee.

The Society is particularly glad to receive letters from parents explaining why first names were chosen, or giving information of any kind about first names, nicknames or surnames. Those interested in carrying out name research projects, large or small, should contact the Hon. Secretary. There is a special need for studies in particular countries, such as Ireland and South Africa, and for historical studies in the U.S.A., Canada, Australia and New Zealand. Studies of religious and racial groups, and of the names used in literature, are also needed.

The address to write to is: The Hon. Secretary, The Names Society, 7 Aragon Avenue, Thames Ditton, Surrey, KT7 0PY, England.

Further information about The Names Society can also be obtained from the following:

Kathleen Sinclair, 128 Girton Boulevard, Winnipeg R3P OA5, Canada.

Cecily Dynes, 74 Wyong Road, Cremorne 2090, N.S.W., Australia.

Cleveland Kent Evans, 1707 Broadview Lane 116, Ann Arbor, Michigan 48105, U.S.A.

The answers to the photo-quiz on p. 19 are **Catherine and Keith.**

Index